Changing O

Changing Organizational Culture
The Change Agent's Guidebook

Marc J. Schabracq
University of Amsterdam, The Netherlands

BICENTENNIAL
1807
WILEY
2007
BICENTENNIAL

John Wiley & Sons, Ltd

Copyright © 2007   John Wiley & Sons Ltd. The Atrium, Southern Gate, Chichester,
West Sussex PO19 8SQ, England

Telephone   (+44) 1243 779777

Email (for orders and customer service enquiries): cs-books@wiley.co.uk
Visit our Home Page on www.wiley.com

Other Wiley Editorial Offices

John Wiley & Sons Inc., 111 River Street, Hoboken, NJ 07030, USA

Jossey-Bass, 989 Market Street, San Francisco, CA 94103-1741, USA

Wiley-VCH Verlag GmbH, Boschstr. 12, D-69469 Weinheim, Germany

John Wiley & Sons Australia Ltd, 42 McDougall Street, Milton, Queensland 4064, Australia

John Wiley & Sons (Asia) Pte Ltd, 2 Clementi Loop #02-01, Jin Xing Distripark, Singapore 129809

John Wiley & Sons Canada Ltd, 6045 Freemont Blvd, Mississauga, ONT, L5R 4J3, Canada

Wiley also publishes its books in a variety of electronic formats. Some content that appears
in print may not be available in electronic books.

Anniversary Logo Design: Richard J. Pacifico

Library of Congress Cataloguing-in-Publication Data

Schabracq, Marc.
   Changing organizational culture : the change agent's guidebook / Marc J. Schabracq.
      p.   cm.
   Includes bibliographical references and index.
   ISBN 978-0-470-01482-0 (cloth : alk. paper) – ISBN 978-0-470-01483-7 (pbk. : alk. paper)
   1. Organizational change.   2. Corporate culture.   3. Leadership.   I. Title.
   HD58.8.S295   2007
   658.4′063–dc22   2007019142

British Library Cataloguing in Publication Data

A catalogue record for this book is available from the British Library

ISBN 978-0-470-01482-0 (hbk)   978-0-470-01483-7 (pbk)

Typeset in 10/12pt Times by Aptara, New Delhi, India
Printed and bound in Great Britain by Antony Rowe Ltd, Chippenham, Wiltshire
This book is printed on acid-free paper responsibly manufactured from sustainable forestry
in which at least two trees are planted for each one used for paper production.

Contents

About the Author

Dr Marc J. Schabracq (1949, Amsterdam, The Netherlands; schabracq@humanfactor.nl) is a work and health psychologist. As an independent organizational consultant, Marc Schabracq has acquired much experience with the human aspect of organizations (organizational culture change, leadership, personal transitions, stress management and personal integrity) in a great number of profit and non-profit organizations. In addition, he has worked at the University van Amsterdam since 1973, and subsequently in clinical psychology, social psychology and – since 1987 – work and organizational psychology. He has produced more than 20 scholarly and professional books about psychology, as well as more than 100 articles and book chapters. In addition, he has written three novels and a bundle of short stories.

Introduction

This book is about changing organizational cultures, and is written for professionals and leaders who are, or want to be, the agents of that change. However, the book is not written for people who want to do the job in separation from reality by applying rigid models and methods. Neither is it written for people who want to hold on at any expense to targets that create their own, mostly unproductive realities. This book is meant for change agents who dare to accept the challenge to think for themselves, and want to be their own instrument in changing culture. Therefore, the book gives techniques, pointers and exercises for developing your own thinking, feelings, intuition, fantasy and perception: all of that for the sheer reason of becoming a well-tuned, effective change instrument.

The book focuses on the hardcore element of changing culture, namely changing the people involved. As it is, cultural change implies that the people involved change their assumptions and goals, and behave accordingly. Getting people that far demands considerable care, skill and effort from the change agents. However, that's not all. Though the objective of cultural change is to bring about improvements for all concerned, changing assumptions, goals and behavior implies for the individual members of that culture significant personal transitions, which are typically accompanied by all kinds of mostly unpleasant emotions. The change agents must be able to guide the people involved through these emotions, in order to prevent needless damage that would be harmful for the organizational members, the change agent and the organization as a whole.

The main objective of a good change agent, and of a good leader too for that matter, is the joint optimization of the outcomes for the organization as a whole, as well as for its individual members and other stakeholders. This joint optimization demands the application of all kinds of virtues. Justice may spring to mind here first, but courage, moderation, prudence, honesty, humility and many more virtues play a role too. Why this enumeration of lofty concepts? Essentially to make clear that being a change agent has a heavy ethical load – a fact that is ignored all too easily, both in practice and in theory.

When you are a change agent, really changing a culture and the people involved implies deploying yourself as the catalyst of that change. Being a catalyst does not leave you unaffected. Going through the process of being a catalyst is taxing, and demands thorough self-management. Still, the outcomes of the process are essentially positive: you refine yourself in the process, also in the field of ethical awareness. Being a change agent thus implies a continuous process of personal growth, and this book wants to contribute to such growth. To that end, the book also examines a number of personal items – such as the influence of unfinished business in your life, your mortality, your background, your leitmotifs and your transitions – which influence your role as a change agent and can evoke resistance to change. Insight into these personal items also helps you to assist the other parties involved to deal with the same issues.

No models, no ready-made methods, no holding on to targets at any expense. Does that mean that the approach described in this book misses all structure? Not at all: the approach is highly outcome-oriented, applies a step-by-step method, uses a painstaking diagnosis and pays attention to evaluation. Its main concern, however, is to prevent premature formalization of targets and spreadsheets. By such premature formalization all relevant information disappears in a black box, where it is no longer open to our scrutiny, nor to feedback from external reality. In this way, these prematurely formalized targets then can start to lead a life of their own and influence the environment by evoking and rewarding all kinds of undesirable adaptations. In short: spreadsheet fundamentalism in progress.

No models, but still a goal-oriented approach. Could it perhaps be that the approach is a-theoretical? Far from it. I subscribe to Kurt Lewin's device that 'nothing is as practical as a good theory' (Lewin, 1952, p. 169) and this book *is* based on a new way of thinking about organizational cultures, an approach that combines the functional and structural features of cultures. Everyday reality is the alpha and the omega of this approach. The central theme within everyday reality is attitude, which is a three-faceted concept here: it has a mental, a behavioral and a cultural side. Moreover, an attitude has its goals and is assumed; that is, an attitude is based on its own assumption. Furthermore, attitude serves as an easily transferable unit of culture and personality, a *meme* in Dawkins' terms. As such, attitude can be considered to be a central concept in the embodied mind approach as well.

Culture is the result of a historical, self-organizing development. By taking certain forms other forms are excluded, and so are the possible developments that would have taken these other forms as their points of departure. This coming about of certain forms and the exclusion of other forms imply, among other things, that only certain cultural changes are possible, while other changes are no longer an option. Put differently, successful changes cannot transgress the limits of a notional field of potential development, even though the specific location of these limits is far from clear. The important questions here are what *can* be done with respect to cultural change, and *how* that can be done in an appropriate way.

To bring about cultural change, the book offers the following three approaches, which can be most successfully implemented when they are combined:

- A leader, or a team of leaders, can initiate and actualize changes in the goals of the organization to make the organization more effective and pleasurable.
- From the same point of departure – that is, to make the organization more effective and pleasurable – the members of the organization can solve many of their own problems by themselves. The book contains a number of checklists to map such problems.
- Lastly, a more fundamental approach is discussed. This involves extending and enriching the assumptions underlying the culture, especially by synthesizing them with other assumptions. This more fundamental approach can be realized in dialogue-based group sessions.

The application of these three interventions presupposes a good assessment of the organization and its environment. In this book, such an assessment encompasses the status quo, the causal network of this status quo, the preferred solutions and the forces for and against each of these solutions. To this end, the book formulates a great number of questions, and also contains three scales to map the culture's effectiveness seen through the eyes of the organizational members. In the approach described in this book, building relations with the organizational members and – based on that – building support for the interventions are important functions of the assessment. Lastly, attention is paid to evaluation of the interventions.

Supplementary Website

The scales, checklists and exercises are available free online to purchasers of the book. Visit www.wiley.com/go/culture to access and download these flexible resources.

PART I

Changing Organizational Culture

CHAPTER 1

Organizational Culture

This book is about changing organizational cultures. The concept of organizational culture, which for reasons of brevity from now on is simply called 'culture', is hard to define. This difficulty partly stems from the wide and diverse use of the term culture, partly also from the fact that most of culture is hidden from the eye of the beholder, like the proverbial iceberg of which only one tenth sticks out of the water. That is why in this book I follow the logic of the biblical saying that one knows a tree by its fruits. To fit with this metaphor, one can say that culture produces the everyday reality of an organization. This everyday reality is, at least in principle, open for inspection to anybody who is interested. Everyday reality is also a central concept of the book. Though this may recall the story of looking for a lost object under a lamppost – not because we have lost it there, but because there is at least some light – everyday reality is also central to my conception of culture.

What does the everyday reality of an organization consist of? Everyday reality involves what happens in the organization and what its stakeholders do and experience. By stakeholders I mean not only the members of the organization – i.e. the employees, managers, owners and shareholders – but also the clients, suppliers, the government and other involved parties. The everyday reality not only entails members' recurring activities, their routines, but also matters such as the premises and layout of the organization and the common reality stemming from those, with the blueprints they offer for behavior, perception, thought and feeling.

Though the actual forms of such an everyday reality have come about in somewhat coincidental ways, the result is a highly predictable way of doing things in a familiar setting. Everyday reality proves to be a solid and relatively stable shared reality, in which the organization's members can firmly believe, without any need to question that belief. All in all, everyday reality boils down to people doing normal things in normal surroundings. Other possible approaches have never developed, simply because the original approaches were good enough: they apparently worked, and something can take only one form at a time. The organization's members just keep on enacting the everyday reality's forms, as if their routines represent the only possible way to do things, making the everyday reality even more solid in the process. By acting in this way, the organization's members actually make these routines the only possible way to do things: a typical case of a self-fulfilling prophecy.

This coming into being of an everyday reality, and of the culture as a whole, can be compared to how a river evolves. By running in a certain direction, determined by the law of gravity, the water makes its own bed, determined by the interaction of the height and hardness of the soil and the forces of gravity acting on the water. Once a river bed has come into being, it determines in its turn the flow of the water, in this way preventing other river trajectories from coming into being. The river's coming into being does not mean that the flow of the river cannot be changed any more, but it does mean that the actual form the river has taken is a more or less independent factor in its further development. Elsewhere (Maturana & Varela, 1980) this is called 'autopoiesis', a state resulting from a self-organizing system (de Bono, 1990). This parable shows us that culture cannot be changed without taking into account the culture's development up to now: a culture can further evolve, but cannot at will be replaced by another culture.

Culture can be studied from the perspective of the functions it performs, as well as from the perspective of how it is structured. In this book the functional and structural approaches are integrated into a single, innovative model.

The first approach – that is, the functional approach – studies what a culture wants to attain and how it goes about accomplishing this. Essentially, such an approach sees culture as the ways in which the organization survives and flourishes by solving its recurrent problems. As is to be expected from a functional approach, these problems stem from the organization's reason for being there or, put differently, its goals. The functional approach to be used in this book is the RACE model, RACE being an acronym for Reason for being there, Adaptation, Coordination and Everyday reality. The RACE model actually came about by accident. I developed it unknowingly, mistakenly thinking I was describing Parsons' Adaptation–Goals–Integration–Latency (AGIL) model (Parsons, 1960), as it had been – completely correctly – described by Iva Embley Smit (Schabracq, 2006; Smit, 1997). However, my mistaken model suited me fine, especially as it proved to be very applicable in a practical context, and after some deliberation I decided to change some terms and stick to it.

The second, or structural approach, not surprisingly, studies how a culture is structured, its architecture so to speak. For the structural side of culture, I turn to an adapted version of Schein's model. Schein (1985) distinguishes four 'layers' of organizational culture, namely forms, mythology, rules and norms, and assumptions. Each of the successive layers is further removed from awareness than the previous one.

My approach here is that Schein's layer of forms – that is, the surface layer of actual behavior and artefacts – is incorporated into the 'everyday reality' of the functional approach, which also involves the experiential sides of the forms. The integration of the functional and structural approach is then based on the fact that both approaches share the 'everyday reality' level. All seven concepts are described – and adapted – in the following sections.

REASON FOR BEING THERE

An organization must have a sound *raison d'être*, a purpose, a legitimate reason for being there. The reason must have importance and meaning inside as well as outside the organization. A valid reason for being there integrates the goals of the organizational members with the needs that exist in its environment in a non-zero-sum way; that is, in a way that benefits all parties involved (Wright, 2001). It gives meaning to the organization and the work of its members. Such a reason, or mission as it has been called, can be explained in a mission statement. In addition, an organization can develop a vision, a representation of the future that the organization sets out to realize within a certain time span, for example a period of five years.

Handy (1994), writing about the search for meaning in organizations, came up with what he called the three senses: the sense of continuity, the sense of connection and the sense of direction. Each of these senses adds to the organization's meaningfulness, as well as to the importance of being part of the organization. The sense of continuity is the idea that the organization contributes to something that goes beyond our life, something that is also valuable to those who will live after us. A beautiful example here is contributing to building a cathedral, which takes several centuries to finish. The sense of connection concerns belonging to the organization, the options it offers to its employees to be a real member of it, being at home at their work and being part of the community of the organization. The sense of direction, lastly, refers to a cause, a purpose beyond ourselves, making the world a better place. All three add meaning to working in an organization; only that is, of course, to the degree that they can be realized there.

When one thinks about improving an organization, it is always interesting to ask oneself what part these three senses play in that organization. Of course, for many organizations the full realization of these senses may be highly utopian, unrealistic and even an occasion for a good laugh. Still, these senses show us directions for potential improvement. Besides, aren't utopias the carthorses of reality?

A valid reason for being there provides the organization and its members with a clear direction and definite goals or objectives. Without such direction and goals, the organization and its members are in big trouble. In practice, almost all organizations do have goals, though they could be clearer and stronger. An organization without goals does nothing, or does something that nobody notices or finds important. Such an organization will not be able to get sufficient support from its environment, while such an organization will also have a hard time motivating its members. As a result, it cannot continue to exist. This does not only apply to organizations, but to individuals as well.

At the individual level, losing goals affects vitality, just as it does in organizations. As such, goals are a crucial condition for staying alive. According to Frankl (1978), setting goals and sticking to them is a matter of taking responsibility. However, put in Frankl's own words, goals are not only a matter of what we expect from life, but also of what life expects from us. Absence of clear goals implies sterility, its essence being uselessness, described by May (1969) as living in the land of the dead. Frankl's and May's statements also apply to organizations.

The reason for being there is essentially laid out and shaped by the founding fathers, or mothers, of organizations, to whom a mythical status has gradually been ascribed. The leaders who devise and implement important changes in the reason for being there are also made to be quite special. It is as if laying out or changing the reason for being there is something heroic, the outcome of a hero's journey: a hero who goes out there, has all kinds of adventures and slays a few dragons, to return with a treasure that will change the fate of the organization (Campbell, 1988). However, not all leaders are heroes. Put more strongly, hero-leaders are relatively rare. Most reasons for being there are handed down by previous leaders and many, if not most, organizations have only a vague idea of why they exist, and what they want to accomplish.

In the case of a new organization, its reason for being there may be still under development, but in most cases the reason for being there is treated as a datum, something that already exists and does not require special attention. However, this reason does need to be articulated and possibly even adapted. This articulation involves questions that the leader and the top of the organization have to ask themselves and each other: What are we actually doing and for what reason?

Another issue is that, when the reason for being there is valid and well established, it still must be shared by all the other members of the organization as well. This sharing is far from self-evident, particularly when those at the top of the organization want to adapt the reason for being there. If the sharing is not realized effectively, meetings at all levels are required. In these meetings, what exactly the reason for being there implies for that level and that specific department can be determined. This customizing of the reason for being there to all levels and departments implies that everyone involved can influence its final form. The idea behind this way of customizing is that this kind of influence generates commitment to the reason for being there.

On the one hand, the reason for being there involves what the organization wants to accomplish for the outside world, such as manufacturing certain products or rendering certain services; that is, providing something that the environment needs. These needs must be so essential that their fulfillment justifies the organization's existence.

On the other hand, the reason for being there is also concerned with the inner world of the organization; that is, with the organization's individual members. The reason for being there must make sense of and give meaning to what the employees are doing. To that end, their work must be sufficiently attuned to what they are best at and want to do. Ideally, the reason for being there also helps them to develop themselves, leading them into a promising future, on a journey of adventure and discovery, without jeopardizing their safety and well-being, giving their work a self-evident and logical line of action.

As long as the organizational goals are aligned with the goals of its employees in the ways implied above, organizations can concentrate on what they are good at, resulting in products and services that clients want and need. If they succeed in that, the way in which they do it is usually difficult for the competition to copy. Prahalad and Hamel (1990) speak of core competencies in this respect.

All in all, an organization's reason for being there is a matter of the degree to which the organization succeeds in doing something that is attractive and self-evident to all parties involved. This also implies, of course, that the goals in question have to be in line with the law and the prevailing ethical norms. The discussion so far leaves change agents who want to optimize the organization's reason for being there with the following 'reason for being there' rules of thumb:

- Try to define core competencies together and let the members of the organization devise the best possible products and services stemming from these competencies. Let them try to innovate, create and develop (Prahalad & Hamel, 1990).
- Learn about the needs of clients and potential clients that the organization's products can fulfill. See the world through their eyes and make this the guideline for forming new alliances. Find out how you can improve the added value of these products for them in terms of quality, delivery time, price and service (Hammer, 2001).
- Think about the longer term (Handy, 1994).
- Think also about the greater good the organization can realize in this way, the cause it can serve (Handy, 1994).
- Learn about the needs and goals of employees, and determine how all of the above contributes to the fulfillment of these needs and goals. Examine as well how employees' satisfaction can be improved.
- Encourage the development of employees, not only by formal education and training, but especially by learning from experimenting and taking risks.
- Point out the necessity of errors and transform these errors into learning experiences.

To the degree that we identify with the organizational goals, these goals provide a focus for what we do. The goals then more or less automatically gear our skills, creativity and effort to achieving the future state that they imply. In the old French literature of suggestion, this mechanism is described as the 'law of unconscious intentionality': once a goal is accepted, finding and adapting appropriate means happen in subconscious ways (Baudouin, 1924). Because most work does not consist of reinventing the wheel, identifying with such a goal induces us to go automatically through a string of familiar situations, each with its own well-known outcomes. These situations can then be conceived as sub-goals on the road to full goal attainment. In this way, these goals help to organize our life in the organization. Outcomes of this way of organizing our life are that we know exactly where we are in the course to goal attainment and can feel at home in these situations. Such a string of familiar situations can then evolve into a pleasurable comfort zone.

This means that a change of goals implies finding and selecting new strings of situations and activities, as well as leaving behind the old sequences. Since we have invested a great deal in appropriating the old way of working, we often are not overly eager to switch over to a new one. Moreover, our assumptions – which will be discussed in more detail in Chapter 3 – limit the range of our possible goals. Some goals are simply not compatible with our assumptions. Goals that are incompatible with our assumptions cannot be part of our everyday reality, and cannot be easily achieved. Accomplishing such goals in any case then demands that we adjust our assumptions. However, we are not overly eager to adjust these assumptions either, even when we are conscious of them, which usually is not the case. In addition, adjusting assumptions has its limits. We can develop our assumptions, we can extend and enrich them, but it is very hard to eradicate them fully or to change them at will. Consequently, goals that go clearly against our assumptions are not likely to be attained.

Nevertheless, changing or adapting goals is the royal road to a change of culture. First, goals that lie outside the scope of our assumptions are an important way to surface our – mostly tacit – assumptions. Becoming aware of our assumptions is a necessary initial step in adjusting these assumptions and, in that way, our reality. Goals can have this change agent function because they are much more explicit and accessible to our awareness than the more structural characteristics of culture, such as our assumptions (see later in this chapter).

Moreover, as goals point by their nature to the future, they refer by definition to something that has not yet got a form. This means that goals are actually much less fixed than assumptions. In principle, goals can take the form we want to give them. Another point is that envisioning a good future can be very motivating for attaining goals. Envisioning a good future is an effective technique for bypassing the initial resistance to change that is often triggered by having to occupy yourself with a problem. Envisioning a good future is also one of the critical components for success in solution-oriented coaching (see Chapter 6).

In developing an appropriate organizational mission, promising personal visions may actually provide a good point of departure. The next step then is aligning these personal visions into a shared organizational vision (Senge *et al.*, 1994) within the context of a real dialogue or work conference (see Chapter 5). This can be a very effective approach. Lastly, in Chapter 6 a number of criteria and tests are described, which we can apply to make a goal more realistic, worthwhile, effective and efficient.

This does not mean at all that such a form of cultural change is easy. In fact, it usually is not easy at all. However, it does mean that, at least in principle, cultural change is possible, and that goals can serve as a pull factor here.

ADAPTATION

Logically speaking, every organization has an environment. Adaptation refers to the success of with which an organization interlocks with that environment. Most of the time, the environment is not so much a matter of physical surroundings as of the relevant people and institutions. Adaptation then entails effectively attuning the organization to the different stakeholders outside it, to achieve the organization's reason for being there by setting and attaining mutual goals with them. The attuning involves clients, but also suppliers, shareholders, fellow organizations in the trade including competitors, the government and its rules, neighbors and the surrounding community at large. Such interlocking should be a non-zero-sum game (Wright, 2001) for all parties involved.

If everything turns out fine, adaptation is a two-way street of giving and receiving. The environment provides the organization with all it needs to survive and flourish. This involves an appropriate location, sufficient safety from outside threats and the right quantities of resources in general. Moreover, if everything works well, the environment also provides the money to pay expenses, make a profit and grow.

To survive, flourish and grow, an organization must make itself an attractive, easily accessible, affordable and self-evident interaction partner to all stakeholders. Becoming such an interaction partner means earning and guarding trust, respect and prestige. To this end, one needs to know all the stakeholders well. What do they need? What do they want to know from the organization? Relations with suppliers, for example, can focus on quality, price, work flow and delivery time. Partnership means building stable relationships with each of these parties, resulting in mutual trust and loyalty (Reichheld, 1996). Consciously managing contacts with these partners and making employees thoroughly aware of the relevance of doing this then become important tasks.

As organizational environments have become more turbulent and variable (Schabracq & Cooper, 2000), adaptation has more and more become adaptation to change. This kind of adaptation requires creating an early warning system for change, involving all employees and especially the ones on the front line. The interview techniques described in Chapter 6 can be used for this task. The idea is to make employees into detectives or journalists. Let them develop a deep insight into all stakeholders, especially the 'end clients', as they are the ones who pay for everything. Let them dig up information about what the clients and the competition find new, interesting and exciting, about the changes they want and foresee, as well as what they think the organization can do best in this respect. Specify to the employees what you want to know. The next step then consists of bringing the information together, as well as categorizing, analyzing and interpreting it so it can be acted on. The last step is making sure that the insight gained is actually used in the intended way. Monitoring and operating this system should be a well-managed process (Hammer, 2001; Sun Tzu, 1993). In some cases, using the insight gained can mean that the organization has to change itself in a radical way.

Adaptation can also consist of narrow cooperation with clients and other stakeholders. An example is making accounting a joint operation with customers, such as banks do with their cash machines. Though many people don't realize this, we are actually doing the bank's accounting when we operate their cash machines to take out our money in the rain. The same applies to banking by internet. Another example is sharing distribution channels, shops and storage facilities with other companies in different trades. In this way, all parties can move products in relatively small quantities at a low price, which usually is exclusively reserved for bigger quantities. Still another form is involving the organization in the product development and production processes of its suppliers, distributors and clients, for instance by temporarily seconding its employees to other companies, or having employees of other companies seconded to it in their turn (Hammer, 2001; Schabracq, 2003c).

Adaptation can also be a matter of joining forces in one production chain with other organizations. Each organization then can take care of that part of the production chain at which it is best. Joining forces in one production chain enable each organization to serve the end customer in the best, cheapest and quickest possible way. Of course this joining of forces must be well managed, so that it is not overly liable to coincidences and is independent from improvisation and unusual performance, a process from which all double work, for instance in accounting, is removed (Hammer, 2001).

Another issue in adaptation is how to deal with competition. In addition to competing with other companies, you can use them as a source of information. For example, ask customers about the strong and weak points of the competition: one can always learn from one's competitors (Hammer, 2001). When there are mutual interests, cooperation and alliances, temporary or permanent, are definite possibilities. Often realizing these possibilities demands that assumptions on both sides are adjusted. Examples are the possibility of complementing each other and sharing facilities, increasing market share in this way, as well as preventing a third party from becoming too powerful. Sometimes it may just be a matter of disrupting or preventing another alliance that threatens the organization's survival (McNeilly, 2001). And last but not least, the competition is always an incitement to do better.

All of this leads to the following 'adaptation' rules of thumb:

- Know the organization's stakeholders well.
- Make the organization a self-evident, respected and reliable partner for all stakeholders. Make it pleasurable, easy, affordable and lucrative to do business with the organization. Determine what the organization can do for its stakeholders, as well as what the stakeholders can do for the organization in this respect.
- Determine how the organization can better attune its information system and production process to the needs of its stakeholders, and make this the guideline for forming new alliances.
- Try to broaden the organization's scope: there are many more possible stakeholders out there.
- Monitor relevant change and respond to it appropriately.

COORDINATION

Coordination refers to organizing all the activities of departments and individual employees within the organization in such a way that the reason for being there and an appropriate adaptation to the environment can be realized. The need for coordination stems from the trend toward specialization, which results in role differentiation. Such a trend is inherent in the development of organizations. Coordination is then about staying aware and taking care of the interconnectedness of all contributions, to optimally serve all stakeholders, especially customers. For the employees good coordination means that they can work effectively and pleasantly, and changes can be implemented smoothly.

Coordination ideally leads to integrity; that is, to acting as a whole, as one organism, focused on bringing about the organizational reason for being there. Coordination is creating the conditions for synergy, the generative principle underlying cooperation, which gives the outcomes of that cooperation a surplus value that goes beyond the sum of the separate contributions of all the individual participating parties. In short, synergy is the outcome of a non-zero-sum game (Wright, 2001), this time within the organization. To bring about synergy, everybody involved must understand the reason for being there and the necessary adaptation, as well as how one's own work relates to that. Essentially, it is a leader's task to coordinate all the related processes and to safeguard the resulting coordination. This can be done by systematically asking questions such as:

- What are the effects of what you're doing for your colleagues in different departments?
- And what are the effects for the client?
- And for the organization as a whole?
- What improvements can you bring about in these respects?

As emphasized elsewhere in this book, asking the right questions and using appropriate interviewing and listening techniques are crucial leadership skills. In Chapter 6 this subject is discussed in more detail, while Chapter 8 provides accompanying exercises.

Apart from the overall synergy, outcomes of coordination are a smooth work flow and the prevention of needless divisions and fruitless conflicts stemming from pursuing departmental and individual interests. Of course, the other side of integrity – the ethical part – is an issue here as well. Not letting one's own interests prevail over the common good is after all a clear ethical consideration. However, ethics plays an important role in every aspect of culture. In practice, coordination can be helped by clarifying and adjusting the mutual expectations of departments, as well as of individuals, aiming at a smooth work flow and a pleasurable work climate, in which all involved will help and support each other when needed.

In order to achieve coordination, the following 'coordination' rules of thumb are important:

- Pay sufficient attention to what goes on in the organization and avoid being focused exclusively on the outside world. Make sure that you get all the information you need. Ask everybody involved questions, explain the necessity of that information, make people responsible for sharing relevant information with you and make it a two-way process.
- If possible, establish co-management (Schabracq, 2005a) or team leadership; that is, divide the leadership role between two people or over a whole team. In this way each issue can be dealt with by a specialist within the team. In co-management coordination tasks are typically given to one of the two leaders. Such an approach demands a kind of 'constitution' for collective decision making to be followed, focusing on the interests of the whole organization and all of its stakeholders (Schabracq, 2005b). This presupposes that everybody knows what they can expect from all relevant others.
- See to it that people find out how to collaborate and communicate, and emphasize the greater good of the reason for being there. Offer them training programs on these issues (see Part II). Reward good collaboration and communication.
- Help to create a climate that fulfills the organizational members' need to belong. Create possibilities for mutual social support; that is, a climate in which there are possibilities for emotionally supporting each other, actual help, information exchange and building relationships.
- Improve coordination between departments and organize based on end-to-end processes. For example, improve coordination between independent strategic business units. Try to

provide the external client with one interface, as well as with shared service centers and standardized approaches (Hammer, 2001).
- Don't let work be needlessly dumped on other departments. Take care that departments and individuals communicate properly about expected work flow effectively and habitually. Solve inter-group communication problems and address stereotypes and prejudices.
- Solve constraints in the end-to-end process and focus each time on the main constraint (Goldratt, 1990), such as bottlenecks in equipment, information or human resources.

EVERYDAY REALITY

The joint realization of the previous three functions (reason for being there, adaptation and coordination) results in a self-evident everyday reality. This everyday reality more or less coincides with Schein's layer of forms; that is, the physical layout and design of the organization, as well as the personal appearance and behavior of its members, with its standard routines and approaches. The forms that make out everyday reality are, at least in principle, open to inspection, though usually nobody inspects them. As long as these forms are properly displayed and do not deviate too much from the norm, the members of the organization do not pay much conscious attention to them. When the members are fully socialized, the forms are just experienced as self-evident parts of reality. This is also why I incorporate Schein's layer of forms in 'everyday reality'. The main difference between Schein's forms and everyday reality is one of degree: everyday reality encompasses the experiences of members and onlookers, while Schein's layer of forms does not. We are talking about a difference of degree here, as the forms essentially presuppose a perceiver as well.

The self-evident forms or everyday reality provide the members with a multitude of cues signaling what is happening (the play), the ongoing activities and their integration (the roles in the play and their interaction) and where they are in the play (the scene and the lines). These cues enable others to display the appropriate behavior, which in its turn provides cues for the next step. So one's posture and movements give proposals to enact a certain situation and relationship, as well as directions for how to proceed from there (Schabracq, 1991). Though these cues are in principle completely open to inspection, they are hardly perceived as proposals and directives. They are just automatically being acted on.

This everyday reality essentially consists of non-problematic routines, habitual ways to respond to the permanent or recurrent demands resulting from fulfilling the three above-mentioned functions. This is a characteristic of all cultures: providing recurrent solutions for recurrent problems. People continuously re-enact, re-construct, re-cognize, re-present and re-cite the forms and meanings of culture (Moscovici, 1984) and abstain from other possibilities. People even re-create themselves. Much of the repetitious character of all this activity stays out of awareness. Though essentially a never-ending form of hard labor – a real Sisyphean task – we just do it, do not pay attention to other possibilities and ignore the fact that we do not pay attention to these other possibilities. So we create a reality that provides stability and continuity, as well as normality and perceived safety. To the degree that this is effective, we can lose ourselves in our work without being needlessly distracted and disturbed, blissfully ignoring all the trouble involved, while everybody knows what they have to do, what they have to attend to and whom they must involve in it. A more extensive discussion of this phenomenon is to be found in Chapter 3.

If this self-evident everyday reality is not realized, the functionality of the organization and the effectiveness of its members diminish accordingly, and stress and alienation ensue. Of course, stress and alienation are undesirable, but they also serve an important signalling function. They clearly indicate that something is wrong (Schabracq & Cooper, 2001): the culture apparently does not provide a proper solution here.

Everyday reality can be divided in five domains:

- the work itself
- the physical environment of the work
- the social embedding of the work
- the fit between the values and goals of individual employees and those of the organization
- the perceived safety of the work and its environment

In each of these domains disturbances can arise, which can be described as 'too much' or 'too little' of something that in itself is a good thing. These disturbances result in a situation in which the individual must do something that they cannot or don't want to do, which results in a loss of control and effectiveness, as well as in stress and alienation (Schabracq, 2003a). This subject is further elaborated in Chapter 4.

Safeguarding the everyday reality in an organization is usually a full-time job. Nevertheless, many managers are more focused on the external world than on internal organizational affairs. As it is, managers are not really selected or rewarded for minding what goes on within the organization, and their own ambitions usually are also focused elsewhere. Appointing a co-manager, as discussed in the previous section, who is responsible for internal affairs, can be a solution for safeguarding the everyday reality as well (Schabracq, 2005a).

In order to realize a functional everyday reality, the following rules of thumb can be followed:

- See to it that jobs are challenging but workable.
- Make sure that the physical layout of workplaces enables employees to work effectively and efficiently.
- Create a climate of trust and pleasant contacts, which allows employees to belong, prove themselves and establish rewarding relationships, without being disturbing or too overwhelming. This is a matter of setting the example yourself and of correcting clear deviations.
- Take care that the organization's values and goals do not deviate too much from the personal ones of the employees. Take care that the employees are in a position to guard their own limits.
- Create a good level of perceived safety in the work and its environment.
- Periodically assess the situation by observation and questioning, as well as by surveying variables such as work satisfaction, work stress, alienation and commitment with the help of (online) questionnaires, such as ASSET (Faragher, Cooper & Cartwright, 2004). Recognize stress risks as early as possible. Use stress reactions and alienation (apathy, indifference) as signals. Be alert to phenomena such as harassment, scapegoating and stereotyping. Break the taboo on talking about these phenomena and discuss them with your employees at an early stage. Know when to refer to or call in a specialist.
- Ask about problems, their causes and their possible solutions. See to it that people take responsibility for reporting problems and thinking about solutions, even when this does not seem to be their primary responsibility.

- Gather enough knowledge about a department's or team's past (from different sources!) and the problems that occurred in it. Find out who the opinion leaders are.
- Engage in sessions to gain improvements. Put problems consistently on the agenda and discuss these in a constructive way in work progress meetings, and in individual talks with the people with whom difficulties are occurring.
- Inform employees as early as possible in face-to-face interactions about any radical changes that are going to happen. Let them have an active say in the ultimate design of the change. Be alert for emotions triggered by change. Give bad news in such a way that you are there to deal with the emotions it may evoke.
- Know what to do in case of crisis and traumatic events (hold-ups, accidents, layoffs and so on). Give extra time and attention to employees who have experienced traumatic events, particularly to let them talk about these events.
- Keep in touch with ill employees, prepare their return to the department or team, and invest extra time and attention in them after their return.
- In times of reorganization and merger, discuss matters periodically during work progress meetings. Ask explicitly about rumors during meetings, and comment on these as openly as possible to prevent needless worrying.
- Assist and protect your employees and offer emotional support, if needed.
- Serve as a coach, who gives employees the room they need to function properly and really listens to them, even when their concerns are a criticism of you. Apart from creating the proper conditions, this implies a stimulation of self-steering and giving advice if necessary.
- Regularly interview employees about their individual activities and career and, if necessary, offer training, coaching or mentoring.
- Show approval for good performances and taking responsibility.

THE STRUCTURAL SIDE OF CULTURE

Mythology

As the layer of forms has been discussed already in the previous section, we start here with the layer of mythology. Every organization has a body of tales, notions and images, which Schein (1985) calls its mythology. The mythology gives the organization's members some principles regarding good and bad actions and characters in that culture. In this way it portrays the relevant virtues and vices of the culture. By setting examples, the mythology serves as a frame of reference. As such, it provides standards and guidelines for what to do and for what is normal, which consequently influences actual behavior. Moreover, mythology helps to give meaning to the behavioral forms and integrates them in a more or less historical context. The stories and images inherent in the mythology are of course open to inspection, but cannot be exchanged for other ones just like that. They are felt to be data from the past and the past cannot be changed. In this way, mythology has a stabilizing effect on the culture. Nevertheless, mythology can be doctored. New myths can be introduced, which seem to follow logically from the old ones, using intentionally the old forms and language, but which introduce in reality a new set of dos and don'ts.

Rules and Norms

Rules and norms shape organizational functioning more or less directly. The roles to be enacted or the plays to be played follow certain standardized formats, which are subject to sets of tacit rules and norms. These rules and norms make up the next layer of organizational culture, which most of the time operates outside awareness, though rules and norms are in principle accessible to reflection. Usually rules and norms only enter our awareness when they are openly transgressed. Harold Garfinkel (1967) has made purposeful transgression of rules into a part of sociological methodology, called 'garfinkeling'. Rules and norms take the form of 'if . . ., then. . .' As such, they link the cues inherent in the forms to well-specified responses. They are the result of a long history of modeling and self-conditioning (Schabracq, 1991) and shape both mythology and the everyday reality. Mythology then can be seen as a set of stories that exemplify the rules and norms and the consequences of their transgression. By shaping and tending our environment and by automatically adhering to the proper behavioral forms – that is, by enacting everyday reality – we ourselves install these cues.

Assumptions

The deepest layer is that of 'assumptions'. These assumptions involve notions about what must and must not be attended to. Thus, they determine what is and is not perceived as real, and what should and should not be perceived as real, as well as what we should and should not occupy ourselves with. Assumptions steer our attention, focusing it on what is meant to be and ignoring what is not meant to be. So these assumptions lay the groundwork and set the limits for the rule system. According to Schein (1985), assumptions are not open to conscious reflection and are hard to put into words. As such, they are considered to be the most important factor in the culture's resistance to change.

The nature of Schein's assumptions remains somewhat unclear. How do we acquire these assumptions? Are they abstractions of the rule structure that develop later in life? I think not. In Chapter 3 this matter is discussed more extensively.

STABILITY

Both the functional and the structural approaches to culture indicate a number of factors that make culture a relatively stable and unchanging phenomenon.

First, there is the huge shared investment of effort and skill by all concerned in jointly enacting the everyday reality each time afresh. This makes one think of the punishments of Sisyphus and the Danaids in Tartaros, the Greek lower underworld.

> As a punishment from the gods for his trickery, Sisyphus was compelled to roll a huge rock up a steep hill, but before he reached the top of the hill, the rock always escaped him and he had to begin again (Odyssey, xi. 593). The Image personifies Vain labor. (http://en.wikipedia.org/wiki/Sisyphus)
>
> . . . the Danaids were punished in Tartarus by being forced to carry water through a jug to fill a bath and wash off their sins, but the jugs were actually sieves, so the water always leaked out. (http://en.wikipedia.org/wiki/Danaids)

Though both the hellish punishments and keeping up everyday are highly repetitive jobs, there is one important difference: enacting reality is not in vain at all, it works just fine; that is, as long as we are healthy. Executing these routines time after time has become part of us, and a self-evident part at that: these routines have become a part of our identity, which we don't want to give up just like that. Jointly enacting this reality each time afresh also implies a shared investment of a great deal of effort by everyone concerned.

We protect our investment. Why? Because this investment provides us with a valuable yield. By enacting everyday reality, we are able to be in the situations we have selected and do the things we want to do. As these routines are enacted without much awareness, we can keep their minds free for what we deem important. The fact that until now these automatic actions have done the job most of the time implies a powerful reinforcement for them. As this reinforcement is partial as well as random, the resulting responses are hard to extinguish (see for example Deese, 1952). In this way, we have created for ourselves a comfort zone, which provides control over our own functioning, some sense of quiet, avoidance of needless risks and acceptance by relevant others. Moreover, the comfort zone enables us to keep our mind free for what we find important, as these routines are enacted without much awareness. This mix of yields turns out to be a powerful and even addictive reinforcement for us doggedly repeating the forms of culture (McGraw, 1999; see also Chapters 3 and 7).

The tacit nature of the way in which we enact everyday reality in itself contributes to its stability as well. To summarize the different levels of culture, there is the tacit nature of the assumptions, rules, norms and the cue qualities of the forms, and there is the matter-of-factness or self-evidence of the mythology and the forms of everyday reality. All of these imply that we don't question what we are doing: we just do it, over and over.

As a result, we experience pressure to change our everyday reality as a violation of our identity, certainly when the changes are forced on us from outside. This may evoke stress reactions in us, involving all kinds of unpleasant emotions. Generally speaking, we prefer to prevent and avoid such a state of mind. At the level of the content of the change, we cannot know how things will turn out. This response to having to give up our familiar ways of doing things resembles the reactions of animals when their territory is invaded. Moreover, we are not alone in these feelings. We share them with many of our colleagues. It feels only logical to support each other on this point, which can make our resistance surprisingly effective and well coordinated.

Holding on to the status quo when we are confronted with forced change has been termed 'resistance to change'. This term entails a disqualification, intended to discredit this holding on activity. The term resistance is derived from psychoanalysis, where it refers to a more or less unconscious and certainly irrational form of resistance against the salutary influence of the analyst. Resistance to change has thus become a pseudo-clinical term for unconscious and irrational resistance against a change for the good. It is only logical that the term mostly comes from the mouth of change agents.

Thus many factors make organizational culture a very stable datum, which is hard to change at will. As a repertory of standard solutions to standard problems, it is only logical that a culture aims at stability and continuity. This is, after all, why an organizational culture is such an excellent provider of reality and normality for its members.

The effectiveness of resistance to change has led to the idea that culture cannot be changed at all in a preferred direction. References to organizational culture have even become a habitual excuse for avoiding the responsibility to intervene: it is just culture.

Support for this stance especially stems from structure-oriented ways of theorizing about organizational culture. Though the structure-oriented approaches have given rise to useful and pertinent warnings that cultural change is far from easy, these approaches have also led to an obviously counterproductive paralysis of all attempts to change culture.

In this book, I defend the notion that culture can be changed, though the change process will be far from easy. I will also demonstrate that the unconscious nature of much of culture can even be used to bring about intended change. Changing culture is best done when direct and indirect approaches are combined. Of the two, the latter is the more decisive. Essentially, this approach rests on principles described by Sun Tzu's *The Art of War*, a Chinese treatise probably from the fifth century BC (as elucidated by McNeilly, 2001), which teaches us how to win a war without fighting.

The matter of changing culture becomes urgent when there are obvious – that is, at least to external observers – flaws and lacunas in the culture. The same applies when the environment changes in a radical way, so that adaptive changes become a necessity for organizational survival.

FLAWS AND LACUNAS

The effectiveness of culture as a problem-solving device can be diminished by all kinds of flaws and lacunas. This can be a matter of goals that are irrelevant or counterproductive, insufficient adaptation to the environment or bad coordination. It also can result from a bad rapport between structure and functions. All these flaws and lacunas can interfere with an effective everyday reality. This can have negative consequences for the overall organization, as well as for individual employees who cannot work effectively any more. We will examine some of these flaws and lacunas a little more closely in the following paragraphs.

One flaw of organizational culture may stem from an incompatibility between what actually happens and what is said about what happens, a contradiction between the so-called 'theory in use' and the 'espoused theory' (Schon, 1983). The espoused theory usually heralds all kinds of morally and ethically correct views and approaches, while the 'theory in use', which actually determines everyday conduct, is much more down to earth and usually less ethically correct. As a result, the organizational culture creates difficulties for employees who take the espoused theory literally. An example is a hospital that advertises that it exists to give its patients the best possible care and treatment, but actually keeps its beds filled at the highest possible profit per bed. Such an inconsistency can cause problems for employees who came to work there because of their attraction to the espoused theory. This may seriously affect their effectiveness, and may even cause severe stress and burnout problems. This, of course, particularly happens in organizations that attract highly ethically driven personnel, such as schools, hospitals and churches (Cherniss, 1995; Maslach & Leiter, 1997).

Though solving problems more or less automatically is a basic characteristic of all cultures and has great positive outcomes, it also has a less desirable side. Once we have devised a feasible solution, we make it part of our repertory and do not question it any more. It is buried in a 'black box' (Usher, 2006). In this way, we often settle for 'just good enough' solutions. These solutions do the trick, though they are not optimal. However, they do not create a major constraint in the organization (Goldratt, 1990); that is, as long as other factors are more critical in this respect. The same principle also plays a role in biological evolution. Calvin (1989) gives the following example of such a 'just good enough' solution. Ducks eat duckweed and because of that they have to be in the water for a relatively long time. To stay afloat they have fat glands under their wings, which allow them to make their wings fatty and water repellent with their bills. Cormorants, being very proficient fishers, are much more efficient in collecting sufficient food in a very short period. Thus there is no need for them to grow fat glands under their wings to prevent them from sinking, but then they have to sit for hours with their wings spread out to dry them. They keep at their just-good-enough solution until they get hungry, then dive into the water again. Turning again to organizational culture, good enough solutions can become a source of trouble in times when improvement and change become necessary.

Other flaws stem from the fact that each organizational culture, as a treasury of standard solutions for standard problems, also has its unproductive standard explanations ('It's a cultural thing'), solutions ('Just a matter of budget') and blind spots ('There is nothing wrong with that') (Argyris, 1983). These have their own rhetoric, which makes them sound as if we are talking about the effects of a law of nature that are 'really' too simple to explain. The blind spots involve certain problems, as well as certain options and solutions, which go against prevailing rules or assumptions. These unproductive standard explanations, solutions and blind spots especially come to the fore when something for which the organizational culture does not have an adaptive approach goes wrong. These standard solutions then are used to deny that things are going wrong at all. Their general logic is something like: 'There is no problem because there cannot be a problem. No, it is only a matter of . . ., and we just should . . .' As these reactions prevent 'real solutions' from being achieved, they can actually aggravate the problems of individual employees, who are bothered by such problems. As such, these reactions may lead to ineffectiveness, and they also put employees in a problematic situation without acknowledging its problematic character and therefore no insight into a solution. Unproductive standard explanations, solutions and blind spots are also used when the organizational culture is threatened by an imposed change.

Another flaw in the effectiveness of culture stems from the fact that the culture determines what we *don't* do in our organization, and also what we should not say, think and feel about it (Ryan & Oestreich, 1988). As a result, the culture determines – at least to a degree – what is impossible, unthinkable and unspeakable within the organization (Schabracq *et al.*, 2001). Consequently, certain solutions, approaches and policies are out of the question. This may even be the case when these are clearly the best option, not only to 'objective' outsiders but also to members of the organization who honestly are of the opinion that 'It is a pity that this is just impossible here'. Some options are even considered to be unthinkable. We are not supposed to put these into words – unless as a joke in bad taste – because they are incompatible with the organizational frame of reference. Lastly, there are the 'unspeakables': options we can talk about but only with reliable and familiar colleagues, and certainly not with those who can make a difference on this issue. As we are talking about the consequences of deeply rooted assumptions, doing something effective about impossibilities, unthinkables or unspeakables implies a serious change in the culture, which of course is difficult.

Usually, these mechanisms only become manifest or are felt if there is a serious problem in a particular area. However, even then they prevent us from dealing effectively with that problem. As such, these mechanisms can keep certain problems alive. Moreover, they also undermine the everyday reality.

Chapter 4 gives a more systematic overview of the different flaws and lacunas in an organizational culture, which there are taken as sources of ineffectiveness. It also provides a general approach for dealing with these sources of ineffectiveness.

CHANGE

Though by their nature cultures fight change, this can be a deadly course. The point is that fighting change may disturb the organization's adaptation to the environment, even though the occurrence of change in that same environment has increased explosively and still is increasing at an ever-accelerating pace. This is obviously related to the globalization of the economy and technology, and the enormously accelerated development of the latter in various areas. The other factors that usually determine the organizational environment – such as socio-cultural and political-juridical developments – can only follow and add to the turbulence (Schabracq & Cooper, 2000).

Many companies have only one option, namely adapting, as fast as they can. This means using the latest technological developments and attuning to the demands that such developments generate. It also implies other ways of working, producing and organizing. To employees, it means different contracts, permanent education and new ways of training and learning. Moreover, they are confronted with all kinds of reorganizations, mergers, management buyouts, outsourcing and so on. Though this of course does not apply equally to all organizations to the same degree, it has become clear that employees everywhere are confronted more and more with changes they did not ask for.

Albeit inevitable, these changes upset the effectiveness of the everyday reality, and its way of solving recurring problems in recurring ways. Moreover, the problems themselves change rapidly and need new solutions. The new solutions then have to be integrated in a new everyday reality. Though it is unclear whether this integration is possible at all, change has become the normal state of affairs in many organizations. We might say that this is an anomaly or even a perversion of our culture, but such a statement is not very helpful when it comes to adapting to this continuous stream of changes.

And here, we have arrived at the central theme of the book: how can we ever effectively change culture without jeopardizing the functionality of the organization and the well-being of its individual members? We have a few certainties here, though. First, effectively changing culture will never be easy. Secondly, there is no ready-made, one-size-fits-all approach. Thirdly, effectively changing culture without jeopardizing the organizational functionality and the individual organizational members' well-being can only be done by people of good will, who are willing to be very open to each other. And fourthly, and certainly not the least important, changing organizational culture always involves changing individual identities.

CHAPTER 2

Assessing the Organization and Cultural Change

To understand the organization and its culture, the change agent questions the different organizational stakeholders about the organization and its culture. By answering these questions, the different stakeholders share their information about the organization and its culture. Both the sharing and the information are important here. Though these two aspects are in practice impossible to separate, it is still important to be aware of both of them. The reason for this is that the sharing part is often overlooked in favor of the information gathering. As the sharing of information is an important opportunity to build the relationships that form the basis for the culture change, neglecting this sharing part can be quite devastating for the intervention. Moreover, making the distinction between sharing the information and the information itself also accentuates that getting information is not a matter of a clear-cut diagnostic stage; that is, the first stage of the intervention. Information sharing actually goes on during the whole intervention and it has to be a two-way process as well. For example, it plays a major part during the dialogue sessions (see Chapter 5) and towards the end when we are evaluating the approach (see later in this chapter). Moreover, many of the exercises described in Chapter 8 have a primarily diagnostic purpose as well. Both sharing and information gathering are discussed separately in this chapter.

To come to an understanding of the organization and the culture, the change agent needs the cooperation of the most important stakeholders, primarily the relevant members of the organization. They are the experts here and they already possess most of the knowledge that the change agent is trying to gain. Moreover, they do not only have knowledge about their organization, they also have the greatest interest in what will happen to the organization, which is another important reason to consult them.

To make the intended change a success, the best approach is to establish a relationship with the relevant members of the organization as full and equal partners in change. We can make the relevant members equal partners by granting them their expertise, as well as full responsibility for making the change a success. In that way learning about the organization and its culture also becomes a way to gain support and to build the platform on which the change can be realized. Together the members of the organization and the change agent then determine what they want to be changed and how. This sharing of information is not concerned with solid facts, let alone the utmost truth, but with the opinions, interests and even prejudices of the organization's members, and also with their relationships and preferences. As a change agent we should take this information very seriously, as it represents the building blocks of the organization's reality, as well as of the change in that reality that we intend to bring about.

The gist of this discussion of sharing is: remember that gathering information does not only involve finding out about things. We are also there to establish relationships with the members of the organization. So attend as fully as possible to all interaction partners, not only by listening to their words but also by observing their non-verbal behavior and attitudes (see Chapter 8), really being with them and 'seeing' them (see Chapter 6): feel what they feel, think what they think and let them be aware that you are doing this. Gathering information also means being alert, keeping sufficient eye contact and active listening, displaying all the verbal and non-verbal behavioral elements involved (see Chapter 8). In short, gathering information means that we practice the art of 'inquiry' (see Chapter 7). In addition, gathering information also implies being clear about our own position and intentions, and – if possible and necessary – the assumptions and goals underlying our approach, which boils down to practicing the art of 'advocacy' (see Chapter 5).

Besides establishing support and a platform for implementing change, having an understanding of the culture must of course yield the information the change agent needs for helping to bring about the intended cultural change.

SOME GENERAL PRINCIPLES

Before going into the different measures that can be taken, we discuss some general principles.

Methods

The change agent should as quickly as possible gain some understanding of the organization, its place in its environment and the determining factors there. All the available methods to gather relevant information should be used. In the words of William James, the consultant should be a 'radical empiricist' (James, 1890/1950). Besides consulting the available experts, working through the accessible documentation and applying checklists and questionnaires, this is also a matter of making the most of the first visits to the organization: sniff the atmosphere, observe how people relate to each other, assess their mood and map what can be noted about their possible alienation and stress. And most importantly, interview key players to find out about their points of view and ask for relevant archive data.

Underlying Assumptions and Goals

When gathering information, we essentially must focus on surfacing the underlying assumptions and goals (see Chapters 1, 3 and 5). These assumptions and goals are the basis for the organization's *modus operandi*, while they also underlie the solutions that different people prefer and their 'political' disagreements. This approach also involves the arts of inquiry and advocacy, described in Chapter 5.

Evaluation

Part of the information – which part has to be decided in advance – can and, if possible, should be used as a pre-test for evaluating the intervention. That means that this measuring must be done twice, before the actual intervention starts as well as when the intervention has been completed. To examine the effects of the intervention, the pre-test and post-test results on the same variables can then be compared and statistically tested for significance.

Retrospective Pre-Test

When there is no real pre-test it is often possible to use a retrospective pre-test, by which the respondents indicate how, after the intervention, they would score the state of affairs before the intervention. An example of an item from such a retrospective pre-test could be: 'To what degree was it clear to you what was expected from you in the months before we reorganized things?' The scores on a scale composed of such items can then be compared with the scores on a real post-test; that is, a scale measuring the situation after the invention. Even when there actually is a real pre-test, a retrospective pre-test can be of benefit as well, as it can help to circumvent the effects of a change in perception caused by the intervention, a so-called response shift (Sprangers & Hoogstraten, 1989).

Prospective Post-Test

A different form of evaluation, intended to question the mindset of certain people and to do some reality testing, uses the opposite approach, namely a prospective post-test. This prospective post-test can be used, for example, to let a board of directors make estimations of how their people will score on certain questionnaires, before as well as after a cultural change intervention. The chances are that both sets of scores will turn out to be too optimistic. This outcome is then an appropriate occasion to address their overly optimistic view on personnel matters.

Control Group

Sometimes it is possible to apply the same pre-test and post-test measures in a different but comparable part of the organization, which will only later, or not at all, be subjected to the same intervention. This other part of the organization serves as a control group. The use of a control group helps to determine whether the possible effects found in the group that is subjected to the cultural change intervention can really be attributed to the intervention, because it enables one to exclude some other explanations. In the terms of Cook and Campbell, the use of such a control group gives the evaluation study the status of a quasi-experiment (Shadish, Cook & Campbell, 2001).

Anonymity

When using questionnaires, we must be very precise about confidentiality, which in practice often boils down to keeping things anonymous. Employees' concerns about anonymity can considerably lower response rates in organizations where employees do not dare to speak freely, because they are afraid of the consequences of openly ventilating their critique and worries. This is often the case in organizations with big problems, and it makes sense in such organizations to keep things strictly anonymous. Consequently, it is worth the effort to stress anonymity when distributing the questionnaires.

Disadvantages of Anonymity

However, anonymity also has disadvantages. By not treating employees as individuals but as representatives of their 'kind', we negatively affect their responsibility for what they say, and perhaps also their motivation to think seriously about solutions. Moreover, we may seduce them into exaggerating issues, because they see the chance of attaining improper goals (lower job demands, higher pay, causing problems for their manager and so on). Moreover, anonymity implies that we miss out on all kinds of interesting information, which we could have obtained by going back to the employees and asking them for elaboration and concrete examples. This information might involve further elaboration of solutions or further information from employees who see big problems where others do not. Lastly, anonymity makes it impossible to help employees who report problems.

Dealing with Anonymity

It is probably best to present respondents with a brief outline of the advantages and disadvantages of anonymity, then let them decide for themselves whether they want anonymous treatment or not, and honoring their wishes completely.

THE PROBLEM AND ITS SOLUTIONS

The first task of the change agent is to find out why they have been called in in the first place and what the differences of opinion are in this respect between the different stakeholders. Thus, who in the organization sees what as a problem? And why is that a problem? The idea is to find out about the underlying assumptions and goals of the different stakeholders. The same applies to the goals they want to reach and the solutions they envision. Other important questions here are whether the presented problem can be solved at all and whether the envisioned solutions are feasible. It is important to realize that the presented problem is often not the real problem or is only a part of it. Sometimes there is even a definite hidden agenda that we have to discover. This may consist of using the change agent to come up with information that implies very bad news for a certain party, if not using them for doing something the stakeholders in question do not want to take responsibility for. Though this may sound as an exercise in paranoia, it actually is quite common practice.

For example, imagine you are a change agent who is approached because of the high frequency of sick leave in a certain department. You know the literature teaches that frequency of sick leave is positively related to stress complaints and work dissatisfaction, but according to the people who want to hire you, this is all a matter of the culture of that department. You take their diagnosis as being compatible with your bit of knowledge, yet you also vaguely register it as a truism, and not a very enlightening one at that. However, they then propose that you help them with what they call a radical culture change: 'We have decided that something real has to be done here, something thorough. And that is why we thought of you, for we have heard some very good things about you.' Good will all around, friendly people and a proud change agent, who actually could use some ego boosting. Still, some probing – 'What in that culture makes these people report themselves sick so often? – teaches you that the employees' motivation in that department is very low. Put more strongly, they appear to be completely demoralized. Some more questioning brings up that a number of incidents have happened. 'What kind of incidents are we talking about?' you ask and it appears that the employees took some initiatives to improve the functioning of the department, which the department manager did not appreciate at all. A conflict resulted and two of the initiators were laid off. The manager in question is not present, you now suddenly notice. You point out the possible relationship between these events and the high frequency of sick leave and the atmosphere, which already has lost some of its merriness, is not pleasant at all any more. The people who a minute ago were such agreeable company check each other's faces and look somewhat nervous. Trouble? What do they want? Do they applaud the initiatives of these employees and do they want to get rid of the manager? After all, he is not present. Or do they just want the employees to be disciplined? Both options suddenly make the radical cultural change considerably less attractive. You suppress a sigh, you feel how tense you are and you hear yourself ask: 'What do you think about the performance of the department manager?'

All in all, we have to surface what our assignment really involves, and then we have to decide whether we want and are able to take it on. A good guideline for determining what the change should be about is limiting ourselves to the matters that allow for the greatest improvements.

Once we have a clear idea about what we are going to do, we can start gathering information. The clarity about what our assignment is enables us to be selective in this respect. Though this may seem obvious, it must be stressed that not all information that can be gathered is equally relevant. This relevance mostly depends on what the change is about. Once we have determined what the change involves, it is important to measure and map only what is relevant in this respect and to be quite reticent about information that is not. Asking questions that lead nowhere is downright counterproductive when we want to induce change. So in general, start with determining what variables are relevant. We'll return to this aspect later, when we examine the individual measures.

DIFFERENT KINDS OF INFORMATION

The information involved in understanding culture has several aspects:

- Discerning the most relevant weak and strong points of the existing everyday reality and their impact.
- Determining the underlying factors of the existing everyday reality.
- Mapping possible preliminary goals for the intervention – that is, improvements in both the weak and strong points – as well as ways to realize these improvements.
- Mapping points of agreement and differences of opinion among the different stakeholders concerning the weak and strong points, as well as what are possible goals and ways to accomplish these goals.
- Mapping possible undesirable side effects of the different solutions.

Existing Everyday Reality

First, there is information about how the organization operates. This involves information about the organization's environment, its performance, its culture in general, how well the culture achieves its functions, possible sources of ineffectiveness of its everyday reality and a number of variables measuring the employees' evaluation of their work and organization. Essentially, the information about how the organization operates concerns what goes well and what goes wrong, both according to the different informants and according to some index numbers. An additional point here is that knowledge must be collected about what has already been done before in relation to what is not going well now, and what the effects have been of those interventions.

Underlying Factors

The change agent also needs information about the factors underlying the present state of affairs: its causes. Experience tells us that the so-called Pareto principle is applicable here. The Pareto principle states that 80% of effects are usually caused by only 20% of causes. Consequently, not only must we know what factors play a part, we also want to know their relative importance. Put more simply: What are the most important underlying factors? The answer to this question enables the change agent to focus on the right causes in order to change the culture as effectively and efficiently as possible. Another interesting question here is: What underlying factor is the easiest to deal with? The reason for asking this question is that it is often advisable to start the intervention with a relatively simple action that results in a quick, appealing effect: a quick success to boost morale.

Goals and Solutions

In addition, the change agent wants to learn about what the stakeholders involved see as the possible outcomes of the intervention. It is important to realize that this information is probably even more divergent than the information about how the organization is doing: different members may come up with completely different goals and solutions.

Theoretically speaking, there are several kinds of solutions and all of them can be valuable. First, it is often possible to do something that is of direct influence on what we want to improve. For example, we can repair a machine that has broken down or we can tidy our cluttered desk. Likewise, we can strengthen a successful part of the business by providing it with more resources and by deploying more people. This direct influence can also consist of taking away or loosening up limiting conditions. For example, we can make communication in a bureaucracy more effective by eliminating rules that limit the possibilities of communication between certain departments or levels. Another example is provided by an organization that is more or less paralyzed as a result of a stalemate in a conflict between its two most important managers. It then makes sense to organize a dialogue or mediation session to solve the conflict (see Chapter 5), and this will then take care of the paralysis too. In addition, to improve matters we can focus on the factors underlying the present state of affairs. For example, we can get rid of many planning problems by improving communication between departments about when certain orders can be expected. The underlying factors that determine everyday reality can be approached in different ways: apart from taking the underlying factors away, we can change them, give them another meaning and shield ourselves from their effects.

Sometimes threatening underlying factors cannot be taken away, but they can be influenced in a way that renders their effects less threatening. Examples are a cash shortage that can be temporarily overcome by borrowing money, a low share price that is boosted by spreading rumors about being taken over by another company, or a more positive example: when well-trained personnel are hard to recruit, an organization can decide to educate its own employees.

Yet another approach consists of changing underlying factors by changing one's own mindset and perception of these underlying factors. Examples here are all organizations – and people – that are in a tough spot, have run into trouble and have got themselves into a state of 'learned helplessness' (Seligman, 1990). This learned helplessness implies that they don't undertake much action to improve things and do not see – or better, do not pay any attention to – opportunities to get out of their difficult situation. By changing this mindset of learned helplessness into one of self-efficacy – that is, into the conviction that we can influence our fate and that opportunities will present themselves – we can change our difficult situation into a field of opportunities. Essentially, overcoming learned helplessness involves looking for and seeing possibilities and acting to turn them into reality.

A final way to deal with underlying factors is to shield ourselves from their effects. This is sometimes the easiest, though not in itself the best, approach. An example is a waiter who regulates his task load by saying 'Coming' while he walks away. Other examples are changing the name of the company after a scandal has taken place, or letting employees use earplugs to prevent damage from noise. Problems with such approaches are that they often do not work completely and they usually have undesirable side effects. The waiter, for example, annoys his customers, while employees with earplugs cannot hear each other

The information of the status quo on the one hand and information about the goals and solutions on the other lead together to information about agreement and differences in opinions about these issues between different parties in the organization. This information can be used to make an *analysis of the forces for and against* certain goals and solutions. This analysis gives answers to questions such as the following:

- What is the importance of the problem as perceived by the different parties in the organization?
- What interests in the status quo do the different parties have?
- Who assumes responsibility for the problem?
- Why has nothing been done about it before?
- To what causes do the different stakeholders attribute the problem?
- Who wants to be involved in solving the problems?
- What do they want to do about it?
- To what degree do these interventions interfere with the normal ways of working?
- What reactions would the project evoke in other departments and how might they deal with that?
- What interests in the possible solutions do the different parties have?
- What role do they have in mind for the change agent?
- What do they consider to be the best possible solutions?

The answers to all these questions lead to a sketch of the organizational force field with respect to the problems and possible solutions, and give an initial indication of what support there is in the organization for the project. In general, it must be clear what parties, interests and differences of opinions are involved regarding the problems, causes and possible solutions.

Undesirable Side Effects

When solutions are proposed, it is advisable to ask what kinds of unwanted side effects each of the solutions might have. For example, when an organization wants to manage its performance by systematically reinforcing behavior that is measured by certain index numbers – such as volume of sales, time used for a customer contact or number of phone calls made – this often suppresses other behavior that is also needed in the organization, such as helping each other or the amount of money saved or earned per customer contact or phone call, but is not measured and not reinforced (Cohen, 2006; Klein, 2003).

COMPILING THE INFORMATION

When the information has been gathered, as far as it is available up to that time, the most relevant bits of information can be used as the building blocks of a vivid story about how things are looking now, and how they should become. Of course, creating such a story always involves a certain weighing of the information that has been gathered. Some issues get more attention and emphasis, others less. Such a story of bringing about a better reality should give us a pleasant feeling and evoke all kinds of images and pictures. This story begins with the sketch of a desirable future, as it may develop from the present situation, provided we put in sufficient effort. The leading idea here is that a lively vision of a desirable possible future can evoke a strong motivation to make this imaginary state true. Moreover, such a motivated approach circumvents the reluctance to do the hard work involved in doing something difficult without having a view of real improvement (see Chapter 6).

Moreover, by contrasting the undesired present situation with a desired future one, we evoke the tension that can serve as a motor for the change project (Ofman, 1995). This is essentially a special case of F. Scott Fitzgerald's (1945) saying that 'the test of a first-rate intelligence is the ability to hold two opposing ideas in mind at the same time, and still retain the ability to function'. This case is special because the ability to function here lies in being able to resist the temptation to think already beyond the goal and to keep one's eyes on the task at hand, a pragmatic form of intelligence indeed (that is, intelligence as 'the ability to apply knowledge to manipulate one's environment', Merriam-Webster OnLine, www.m-w.com). Giving in to the temptation would interfere with the tension that serves as the motor for the change project, and as a result goal accomplishment would become difficult, if not impossible.

Moreover, the imagined future state is a good point of departure for thinking 'backward' to outline our path to the goal. Realizing such a point of departure requires that we must have a vivid image of that future state and that we use it as a viewpoint from which we can ask the following questions:

- What did we do to get here?
- What was the first step?
- Who helped us?

- What were the greatest difficulties?
- How did we overcome these difficulties?
- How did we succeed in collaborating so effectively?

This technique of envisioning a desired future state and using it as a position from which to ask questions about how we got there is further elaborated in Chapter 6.

In the following sections we discuss different kinds of information. In essence, this involves a mixture of information about the status quo, possible changes and differences of opinion.

INFORMATION ABOUT THE ENVIRONMENT

The change agent must have some understanding of the position of the organization in its environment. The central question here is whether the environment is of such a nature that it allows the organization to survive and flourish:

- Does the organization stand a real chance?
- What does the organization have to do to attain its objectives?
- What opportunities does the environment provide?
- What can the organization learn from the developments in its environment?'
- What differences of opinion are there on this issue?

Seek information about the following issues to gain a picture of the turbulence and hostility of the environment:

- new technological developments relevant to the organization
- the economic environment and the position of the organization in market developments
- socio-cultural changes
- political and legal developments

Technological Developments

Technology is changing more quickly than ever. When I was a little kid, the only man who could program a computer in The Netherlands was a professor, who happened to be a world chess champion as well. Now toddlers are so familiar with their Game Boys that they develop RSI complaints. Thirty years ago, an IBM electronic typewriter, the one with the golf ball, was a mean piece of technology. Now we can buy one, for a considerable price, at an antiques auction. Think of all the developments in IT, telecommunications, genetics, biotechnology, nanotechnology, new materials, agriculture and construction. The development of the Internet and all kinds of expert systems, for example, has made it possible for western companies to take their call centers to countries such as India or Bulgaria, where the wages are a fraction of those in western countries, and people are quite willing to learn the languages of all the countries that the call centers serve.

So here too, some questions have to be answered:

- What are the decisive technological innovations in the organization's field of business?
- What are the consequences of these technological innovations for the organization and how can it cope with these consequences?

- What opportunities do these developments generate?
- How is the competition dealing with these innovations?
- What is the influence of the Internet in this line of business?
- What are the opportunities here?
- How can and should the organization make use of these opportunities?
- Again how do the opinions of organizational members differ here?

Economic Environment

The economic environment involves the organization's market, its competition and its suppliers. Markets are changing quickly today. Apart from the sheer increase in the number of people living on the planet, global communications, transport and trade have increased at an unprecedented rate. The economies of countries such as China and India are growing spectacularly. The number of member states of the European Union doubled in recent years, resulting in greater availability of relatively cheap labor from the accession countries. The separate national economies of the world, stemming from completely different cultures, are becoming more and more interdependent. In many lines of business competition has become a global affair, making the fight for sufficient market share much more fierce and complex.

The grueling competition has forced organizations to adapt by reorganizing themselves. Some of these reorganizations have proved to be quite successful for the moment. Consequently, there is the possibility that competitors may have gone through one or more such transformations, which may have made them much stronger while making the approach of other players completely obsolete.

A number of different principles have given rise to all kinds of transformations. However, many of these transformations are only successful in financial terms, and often only in the short term as well. When we look at the development, motivation, pleasure and health of the employees involved, a different image arises. The main objectives of these transformations are higher production speed, lower production costs, better product quality and/or being more oriented to the (end) customer (Hammer, 2001). Here follows a – far from exhaustive – list of principles underlying these transformations:

- Minimizing labor costs, by automation or by taking production to countries with lower wages.
- Making more efficient use of the means of production, for instance by using them 24 hours a day, seven days a week, 365 days a year.
- Deploying employees to do (more) different tasks.
- Deploying employees only when, and as long as, needed.
- Introducing a kind of 'neo-Taylorization' in jobs; that is, simplifying and standardizing work by hooking employees up with highly computerized robots – for example on production lines – or expert systems, as in call centers.
- Introducing production lines that can manufacture different products, in huge or small quantities on demand.
- Accomplishing better coordination between marketing, production and research and development.

- Reducing the number of hierarchical levels and pushing responsibility down to the lowest level possible, for example by forming autonomous task groups or quality circles, to improve product quality and reduce errors.
- Just-in-time management and other logistically driven forms of organizing, to prevent needless investment of money in materials, half-products and products that do not generate an immediate return on investment and take up too much storage space.
- Outsourcing all kinds of staff and service departments, in order to be able to focus on one's own core competencies.
- Integrating one's company in a product chain with other specialized companies, in which each company does what it does best, aiming at bringing products to the end client at maximum speed, for a minimum price and at optimal quality.
- Strategic alliances with other companies, in order to be able to influence all kinds of developments.
- New forms of organizing, such as in matrix, project and network organizations.
- Mergers or acquisitions, to accomplish advantages of scale or vertical integration, at a national or international level.
- Trying to become a learning organization, resulting in the development of core competencies that cannot easily be copied.

It is important to realize that none of these approaches is *the* cure. In fact most of them have serious undesirable side effects, many of them can fail and some of them are mutually exclusive. Still, it is crucial to know whether, and how, the competition is using these ideas and which – if any – of them is appropriate for the organization that is the subject of the change. Studying the economic environment therefore has to encompass studying how the competition has adapted to its economic environment and keeping oneself informed of the latest developments. It might turn out that the company has much to learn. This implies that, as a change agent, we should have – and maintain – some general knowledge about the different approaches and their advantages and disadvantages. It is also recommended to have some specialists in that discipline in our own organization or professional network.

All in all, studying the economic environment of the organization implies finding answers to the following questions:

- Is the market in which the organization operates growing, shrinking or stable?
- Are there big changes in the market?
- Can the organization deliver in such a way that it keeps up with the competition?
- What does the competition look like?
- What kinds of adaptations have the competitors made to changes in the market?
- How successful were these adaptations?
- What can be learned from that?
- Is the organization reaching the right customer population?
- What is the situation with suppliers?
- What can and should the organization do in all these respects?
- How do the organizational members differ in opinion here?

These questions are essentially similar to or the same as those in the section about adaptation (see Chapter 1).

Socio-cultural Changes

Almost all organizations are confronted with the challenge of feeling at home in a rapidly changing, multicultural environment, where they have to cope with the influences of vaguely known powers from all over the world. Some of these developments open windows of vast opportunity, other options are far from friendly. A shortlist of socio-cultural developments would involve the following phenomena:

- the increase in worldwide transport and telecommunications and the resulting globalization of our whole life
- the increasing control over our life by computers and databanks
- the increasing role of the Internet
- the greater role of television
- global streams of migration
- the increasingly multicultural nature of our societies and workforces
- the ageing of the working population in the West and in Japan
- changing relations between the sexes in different cultures (division of roles; increase in divorce rate; the declining incidence and importance of the 'classic' family)
- the shift from agriculture to industry to services
- the shift from manual work to knowledge work
- fundamentalist opposition to all this and the reactions to this opposition, resulting in still wider gaps, terrorism and wars

Many of the above-mentioned phenomena imply that change has become a part of our culture. Though this may seem a simple conclusion, it is also a highly paradoxical one, because a culture, as we saw in Chapter 1, is supposed to be a set of standard solutions to standard problems. In some tribal societies, people still consult their parents when they need advice. If they don't get a suitable answer they go to their grandparents, and if their grandparents don't know the answer either they can still turn to the spirits of their ancestors. That is what culture is all about. It is telling that in western society when we do not know whether to use control-alt or alt-delete we're unlikely to ask our grandmother.

All in all, it is becoming more and more important to be able to adapt to big changes in the nature of work and organizations. This is a matter of learning and acquainting ourselves with the right knowledge, time after time, because knowledge and skills tend to become obsolete at an increasing rate. Consequently, it is no longer sufficient to be only well educated when we enter the labor market. We should be, of course, but on its own it is not enough. In order to adapt to ongoing changes, we must learn and educate ourselves again and again during our whole working life: life-long learning has become a necessity.

Though continuous adaptation to change and life-long learning are necessary, it has proven to be far from easy, especially when the changes are forced on us. When these demands are felt to be infringements and intrusions on the way we want to live, they will induce stress and threaten our well-being and health in a major way (see for example Benson, 2001). These problematic consequences imply that the change agent – and all other stakeholders for that matter – must be very alert to stress reactions, try to implement changes so that these changes evoke the least stress responses and abstain from needless changes. Being able to bring about changes without inducing needless stress may well become the most critical bottleneck for the survival and flourishing of our organizations (Schabracq *et al.*, 2000; Schabracq, Cooper & Winnubst, 2003).

For a change agent who aims at cultural change, the story about change described above implies that they must examine whether the above-mentioned forms of change and development are relevant to the organization in question:

- What socio-cultural changes in the organization's environment are relevant here?
- How do they affect the organization?
- What possible implications are there for the workforce?
- What opportunities do these changes and developments carry with them?
- What can and should the organization do with these opportunities?
- What differences in opinion play a part here?

Political and Legal Developments

Though political and legal developments have their own dynamics, they often are a response to the other changes in our societies as well. After all, politics and law are supposed to be ways to regulate our societies as well as possible; that is, so that everything more or less runs well, preferably in a way that is not morally offensive. As a result, there are a lot of political decisions and laws that are specially focused on mitigating or preventing the negative effects of the developments in the previous sections. Though these laws and rules have very understandable and even laudable objectives, they often do interfere with the easiest ways of arranging things in organizations. Examples of legislation focusing on mitigating the effects of some of these developments can be found in the fields of working conditions and working in general. Other examples are environmental and antitrust laws and changes to them.

For legal and political developments the same applies as for the previously discussed developments: some can interfere with organizational interests, while others may provide all kinds of opportunities by opening up lucrative niches. Political decisions and laws do not have to be limiting and restrictive per se. As it is, sometimes governments intentionally open up spaces of opportunity by providing infrastructure and subsidies. Because a change agent specializing in cultural change is less likely to be specialized in such subjects, it may be advisable to consult experts in these fields. Examples are a specialized lawyer, an expert in subsidies and a knowledgeable civil servant.

All in all, the change agent can get some idea of the relevant legal and political developments by answering questions such as the following:

- Have there been changes in the political environment, for example because of recent elections, that are of influence to the organization?
- Have there been changes in taxation?
- Has legislation changed recently in a way that affects the functioning of the organization?
- Is it possible to structure the project in such a way that it takes advantage of any subsidies or tax advantages?
- How has the competition handled these changes?
- What can and should the organization do in these respects?
- And what about differences of opinion on these issues?

ORGANIZATIONAL PERFORMANCE

Organizational performance can be measured – that is, to a certain degree – with the help of all kinds of indicators, each of which says something about a different aspect of performance. On the one hand there are financial and economic indicators, on the other hand indicators that give some information about the social climate and the well-being of personnel.

The financial and economic numbers give indications about the profitability and the financial health of the organization. Examples are figures for net profit, return on investment, volume of business, production, cash flow, share capital, property values, number of employees, all kinds of costs (for example personnel, housing, supplies and energy) and so on.

In addition, there are indicators that tell us something about the 'climate' within the organization, which influences its profitability and financial health as well. These are the numbers pertaining to sick leave, replacement of ill personnel and staff turnover, as well as data from audits of work satisfaction, work-related stress and motivation.

Each of the indices and figures mentioned so far gives some indication about the performance and health of the organization. As such, a change agent should collect as many of them as possible. However, these indicators have their limitations. As they essentially simplify things, the history that leads to a certain numerical value and the context on which their meaning depends are left out. As a result, such an indicator can put a very illusory image of reality in our head. The weaknesses of these indicators signify that decisions should never be taken based on only one of them. Consequently, they should always be integrated into a set of other data, which together tell us the 'whole' story (Klein, 2003). For example, a high stock valuation in itself does not mean that the company is healthy and vigorous. Possibly the valuation has been much higher and is actually on its way down. Maybe also its competitors are doing much better. And the high valuation may also represent a bubble just about to burst.

Another warning is that organizational performance is not only a matter of clear-cut indicators. As it is, there are many matters that greatly affect the profitability and financial health of the organization, but which are very difficult to quantify. We deal with a great number of them under the heading 'sources of ineffectiveness' (see Chapter 4), but there are also more of them. Examples are the negative effects of matters such as:

- poor motivation of employees
- low trust on the part of employees
- internal and external disturbances in communication with all stakeholders
- internal conflicts
- external conflicts
- missed opportunities
- low or decreasing product quality
- diminished attractiveness to potential new employees
- undesirable publicity

As each of these in themselves can be devastating to the organization, it is wise for change agents to be alert to such phenomena as well, and to study them more deeply when there are signals indicating that such matters might play a role.

Index numbers are often used to set goals for an organization, because they are clear-cut and relatively easy to measure. Moreover, some increases and decreases are easily associated with improvement. At the same time, those at the top of the organization should understand that it is important to be selective when they set such goals, and that they must have good reasons to pick those they do. Good selection makes the goals more specific, more positive and more realistic. In Chapter 6 a number of criteria are discussed that can help to improve the quality of goal setting. In any case thoroughly discussing this selection within the top team is paramount, the more so as it may surface radical differences of opinion, which have to be sorted out first, for instance in dialogue sessions (see Chapter 5).

STRUCTURAL ELEMENTS OF CULTURE

The structural elements of organizational culture – as discussed in Chapter 1 – are, of course, also important strategic phenomena when we want to change the organization. This involves the following aspects:

- the history of the culture
- the type of culture
- the peculiarities of the culture

History

A historical sketch of the organization and its culture can provide important information about issues such as:

- the developmental stage of the organization
- the consequences of important and traumatic events
- the organization's founders and other important people
- the mythology of the organization

The *developmental stage* of an organization has important implications for both its structure and its functions. A new organization usually does not have much structure, while its main functions tend to be less clearly divided over different employees. As a result, the organization can operate quite flexibly, though there is the risk of wheels being invented time after time. Such a state of affairs does not only cost a great deal of time and money, but can also be exhausting for the employees involved. This can limit the efficiency and effectiveness of a new organization when it comes to serving the end customer in the cheapest, quickest and best way. In a fully mature organization, on the other hand, the danger exists that the structure and the division of functions become so rigid that changes in the environment cannot be adapted to. Consequentially, a change agent should always take the developmental stage of the organization into consideration. As a rule of thumb, providing more structure and a clearer division of roles can be an appropriate intervention for organizations that have outlived their first pioneering stage. Likewise, readjusting the structure and role division in such a way that the organization is better attuned to its environment is a standard intervention for organizations at a later stage of their development.

A study into the history of an organization can reveal different kinds of *important and traumatic events*. Examples are radical reorganizations and mergers, massive layoffs and all kinds of ethical transgressions. Such traumatic events are dealt with in Chapter 4 as sources of ineffectiveness resulting in a lack of safety, which interferes with effective functioning. By studying these events, change agents get some insight into what is possibly still sensitive in the organization, and what may limit the range of possible interventions they want to use.

When these events turn out to be very limiting, it may be wise to address the issues, bring them out in the open and discuss them (Ryan & Oestreich, 1988). Though addressing the 'skeletons in the closet' may be scary to the change agent – and to the other stakeholders! – it may be the only way to overcome its interference with organizational functioning. By properly acknowledging – preferably in a workshop that really addresses the matter – what has happened, finding out what went wrong, what mistakes were made and how these mistakes can be prevented in the future, those involved can make their peace with the event.

Examining important and traumatic events can also teach the change agent how the organization typically responds to such events. After all, a radical change of culture can be traumatic to some people. In any case, an intended culture change might evoke memories and feelings attached to such events. Essentially we are talking here about personal transitions, processes of change that require sufficient time, information and attention to deal with (see Chapter 6). These memories and feelings can then almost unconsciously color the responses to the current change. If relevant, the change agent should address this issue. Apart from bringing the event out into the open in a dialogue-like session (see Chapter 5), the change agent can explain the differences and similarities between the present change and the previous traumatic event. Moreover, if the employees reacted well to the previous traumatic events, the change agent can also point that out, to evoke a similar response to the intended cultural change.

A historical study of the organization should also involve its *founders and other important people*. They are probably still influential, as they laid out the guidelines for the conduct of the members of the organization, at a behavioral as well as an ethical level. Apart from explicitly stating these guidelines, they have served as a model to their employees. The effects of these guidelines on employees are similar to the effects that parents have on the conduct of their children, namely unconscious imitation of the attitudes – mentally as well as behaviorally – in different situations (see Chapter 3). As a result, both children and employees follow certain scripts that determine their behavior (Berne, 1966, 1972; see also Chapter 6). Though these scripts involve a rather strict determination of their behavior, this usually happens in such a self-evident way that the employees are completely unaware of this influence. The nature of the scripts can vary greatly, though, as can their effects. So some scripts are very productive, while others may lead employees into trouble. If the founders or other important people have laid down guidelines or scripts that bring the present employees into trouble, the change agent can address these guidelines or scripts. An example of such a guideline may be the assignment to do anything that furthers the immediate interests of the organization, without paying any attention to the ethical implications and undesired side effects of what people are doing. These scripts are what we, as change agents, are after when we study the influence of the founders or other important people. So it makes sense to ask what these founders and other important people did and how they did that.

Moreover, knowledge of the ways of the founders and other important people can save change agents from approaches that go needlessly against how things are done in the organization. On the other hand, such knowledge enables us to come up with an approach that is much more in line with what these people did before. As a result, we can even use the founders and other important people as examples or even protagonists of the kind of intervention that we are introducing.

A study of the organization's history can also examine its *mythology*, or its 'further' mythology, as the founders and important people are usually also part of the mythology. This is the lore or stories about critical events, victories, happy moments, close calls and disasters in the organization, featuring the founders and other important people as the heroes, and their adversaries as the villains. The mythology provides extensive principles for good and bad behavior. Here too, studying these stories enables the change agent to avoid going against the ethics involved in them, as well as to tailor the proposed approach to these ethics. In addition, the principles involved in the mythology can also reveal practices of questionable morals, which still negatively affect the actual conduct of the members of the organization. When such an influence interferes with the appropriate functioning of the organization, the change agent must address it, preferably in a special dialogue-like workshop.

Though the past cannot be changed, history can, for example by digging up new material and changing emphases. History can also give rise to ideas about changes to be made, as well as to differences of opinion about that. However, the emphasis on solutions and goals here is less prominent, and the same applies to differences of opinion.

Typing Cultures

There are all kinds of ways to type cultures into several categories. Though some of them reflect more the theoretical stances of the people studying the cultures than the character-istics of the cultures themselves, several typologies prove to be quite useful in practice. Charles Handy, for instance, describes an appealing typology in *Gods of Management* (1987). Handy distinguishes four types: bureaucracies, social clubs, networks and gather-ings of soloists. Though, of course, these are four ideal types while most organizations are of a mixed nature, they give change agents some indications of what they can and even should do, as well as what they had better not do. They also give change agents some leads about the kinds of organization where they can be more and less productive and successful.

Bureaucracies – represented by the Greek god Apollo, the god of the sun, the official arts and the sun's clarity – are organizations where clear rules are the main instrument of control. Rules prescribe what everyone does, as well as who relates to whom and how things should be done. In bureaucracies, everything has been described as clearly as pos-sible: the hierarchy, individual responsibilities, as well as rewards and sanctions for all kinds of conduct. Underlying values are clarity, objectivity, rationality and justice. Fre-quently occurring problems in bureaucracies are a lack of flexibility, a lack of feeling and emotion and a neglect of – or sometimes even contempt for – productivity (see Chapter 4, where too much orderliness is discussed). When we want to change something in a bu-reaucracy, this change – at least if we want to implement it successfully – must not go against the underlying values, while its implementation must be anchored and secured by the right rules. Attempts to install alternative values such as flexibility and profitability in such a culture usually fail. In fact, it has proved to be difficult to 'privatize' governmental institutions such as railroads, national airlines and all kinds of research institutes, which were once part of the government. This is not to say that it is completely impossible to change a bureaucracy into a more flexible and goal-directed organization. However, such a change does require a more radical approach, which will take much time, attention and communication.

In cultures termed *clubs* – represented by the higher god Zeus – personal relationships are all important. This concerns who says what, who we know and how we stand with X, Y and Z. Things happen here only when we assemble sufficient clout. In a club, personal influence, power and loyalty are the important concepts, rules don't mean much, and lack of coordination and goal directedness, as well as treason, are the pitfalls. When we, as change agents, have to bring about some change in a club culture, we should pay a lot of attention to the power positions of the different players and the nature of their affiliations and other relationships. Finding out what the different players think and want is crucial, and we have to lobby and strike a lot of deals to create a solid platform on which to base the change. Proposing goals and solutions that go against the opinions and interests of the top players is often useless, if not downright suicidal. Going along with the power is all important here. In practice, this means that the change agent has to present solutions in a way that is acceptable and agreeable to the top cats.

Networks – represented by the goddess Pallas Athena, standing for schooling and science – are primarily pragmatic, profession driven and goal oriented in nature. They are concerned with working in projects in changing teams, the quality of solutions, and accomplishing objectives in the best possible professional way. Important values are quality, creativity and professionalism. Pitfalls are high costs, problems with communication and power, difficulties with time limits, neglecting routine activities such as administration and the financial side of things, and sometimes forms of groupthink and placing too much trust in standard methods. To successfully implement cultural change in such an organization, the change agent must gain respect for their own professionalism, pragmatism and creativity. Also they should make clear what the objective gain is of the new approach, instead of trying to secure their interventions by merely installing rules or lobbying.

In *gatherings of soloists* – represented by the god Dionysus, the god of wine and intoxication – performance is based on the qualities and networks of the individual 'partners' of the organization: free people, who act as professional experts, each of whom is doing their own thing. Core values are originality, artistry and individualism. Pitfalls are egocentricity, *l'art pour l'art*, vanity and solutions that are too idiosyncratic. Tactically influencing the 'partners' entails personally involving these people in the proposed goals and solutions, which can boil down to a kind of dialogue that demands inquiry and advocacy (see Chapter 5). Another possibility consists of showing the disadvantages of the pitfalls of this culture; that is, the lack of effectiveness, losing contact with clients and the lack of synergy. Examples of gatherings of soloists are to be found in consultancy firms, and in hospital departments organized around medical specialties.

Broadly speaking, when one of the four types gets into trouble, it often can be helped – at least on paper – by installing some of the characteristics of the other types. So a bureaucracy *can* be helped by bringing about more flexibility and goal directedness, a club by installing some structure, a network by more emphasis on speed and profitability, and a gathering of soloists by more cooperation and synergy. However, all of these 'solutions' go against the grain of these cultures and will evoke a great deal of resistance, which may turn out to be very effective, as it will not be an individual matter but a well-concerted group activity (see Chapter 1).

An example comes from the changes in Dutch hospital departments, where specialists used to work as basically free entrepreneurs in a partnership context, which can be called a gathering of soloists. However, now they are paid as normal employees by the hospital, which is essentially a bureaucracy. Consequently, their work is now determined by all kinds of rules, and it has lost most of its autonomy when it comes to planning, cooperation and communication. On many occasions, this loss has given rise to all kinds of friction and conflicts, as well as to totally ineffective work situations and – unfortunately– some needless deaths as well.

All in all, when it comes to changing these types of culture, just giving their members some rules, urging them to be more flexible, communicative or dependable, will not do the trick. Such a change demands a much more radical approach, which will only work if the need for change is deeply felt, and such a deeply felt need will only arise when the present working situation has become fully ineffective and counterproductive. This more radical approach will be discussed in Chapter 5.

Recognizing Cultural Peculiarities

Within each culture, there are of course a great number of *forms* that are typical of the specific culture. These are out in the open for anybody who wants to perceive them. These are the typical ways of doing, saying, thinking and feeling things, as well as the – often implicit – dress code that the members follow. All of these forms can be used to 'wrap up' propositions to change the culture. In other words, the change agent must not only be able to speak the language of the organization and use its forms, he must also use this knowledge to be maximally effective.

By determining the forms of what the members of the organization do, think, feel and say, the culture also determines what they don't do, think, feel and say. As a result, they 'cannot' apply certain solutions, approaches and policies. For example, when living healthily or unhealthily is regarded as a private matter, organizations do not get involved in this matter, which means that they cannot influence the health of their employees. However, the costs of unhealthy living by these employees may be very high to these organizations. Hunting for such *impossibilities* should be a standard pursuit for change agents who want to bring about a cultural change. This is often simply a matter of asking 'why' and 'why not' and probing a little more, when we, as a change agent, do not understand why employees aren't doing what appears to us to be only logical and obvious thing to do.

Something similar occurs when certain complaints, solutions, approaches and policies are articulated to close colleagues, but not to those who can make a difference on this issue. For example, employees may complain among themselves that their manager is doing something stupid, while they do not share this with the manager in question. This is often the case if a small gathering of employees at the coffee machine suddenly disperses when the manager passes by. Such '*unspeakables*' (Ryan & Oestreich, 1988) are not only interesting in themselves, but especially also for the reasons they are used. What is so risky about being open with someone who can make a change? Often big improvements can be made here, as such unspeakables are most of the time clearly dysfunctional to organizational effectiveness.

Both cases – the inability to apply a certain approach, as well as withholding a comment from those who can make a difference – can be difficult to spot for an outsider. After all, spotting something that is not present is always difficult. However, once the change agent has noticed such an occurrence – or non-occurrence – he may be tempted to comment on its incongruity, which then would trigger undesirable forms of resistance. This does not mean that the change agent should not ask for clarification, on the contrary, but the change agent should certainly refrain from making derogatory remarks about such occurrences. Instead, they could say something neutral like: 'I noticed that... Can you comment on that?' The way to go here is to surface the underlying ideas, which later can be discussed in a dialogue session (see Chapter 5).

Because a culture can be regarded as a set of fixed approaches to standard problems, it comes as no surprise that cultures have their own unproductive standard explanations and ways to tackle problems, as well as their own blind spots.

Often *standard explanations* can be recognized by their imploring rhetoric. In the verbal realm, this is characterized by the frequent use of terms such as 'normal', 'really', 'truly', 'actually', 'simply', 'just', 'only', 'always', 'all', 'never' and 'nothing' (see Chapter 8). Non-verbal clues involve a display of self-evidence by facial cues (corners of the mouth, eyebrows), hand gestures, sighing, stressing certain words, being 'declarative' by lowering one's voice at the end of a sentence, rhetorical questions and so on. It is as if the effects of a law of nature are explained, which actually are too simple to need explanation. This also implies that in such explanations the causes are often rather general in nature: 'That is only a matter of simple economics', 'It is all a matter of bad morals', 'That is just the culture here'. Some of the explanations also make use of stereotypes and prejudices: 'The locals here are just not that smart', 'It is simply their age', 'What else can you expect of a woman?' A collection of good examples can be found in van Krieken (2006). Change agents must be alert to standard explanations, but must keep in mind that the ways of formulating described here are of course not reserved for standard explanations. Moreover, standard explanations are sometimes right.

The most characteristic feature of *standard solutions*, either productive or unproductive, is that they are just that, standard. They may be valid or not, but it is still important that a change agent can recognize them as standard. After all, many people are tempted to use a standard solution when they don't know exactly what to do, or when they want to win time. Examples are:

- 'I'll contact X.'
- 'Just take some days off.'
- 'Don't pay attention to it.'
- 'Let's do a study first.'
- 'This study is no good, we need a better one.'

As it is, some highly respected research institutes live on the last two solutions.

Blind spots are similar to the forms of individual denial that I describe elsewhere (Schabracq, 1991) as 'holes in our everyday reality'; that is, places or issues that are not attended to by the person in question, but that can be and are attended to by others. In short: blind spots. These holes in our everyday reality are not necessarily subconscious. Blind spots also can be a matter of strategically installed 'borders', which are substantiated by remarks such as:

- 'That is not my business.'
- 'For that you have to be in our HR department.'
- 'They certainly would not inform me about this.'

As many of these blind spots obviously are not particularly functional for the common good of the organization, change agents must be alert to their (non)occurrence. Supposing that an organization really wants to prevent trouble, the question arises why people sometimes display their blind spots so blatantly, especially when there is a serious system error at work. Why do people behave like that, when they also could mend the situation in various ways? Apparently we find it very important to leave the illusion of a flawless culture intact, more important even than mending the real trouble at hand, which would jeopardize that illusion. Moreover, for many people being the bringer of bad news is not the most popular role. Examples of well-advertised blind spots are:

- 'This is not an issue at all here.'
- 'Everything is going just fine.'
- 'It will go away by itself.'
- 'At least in my department, everything is all right.'
- 'Nobody told me so.'
- 'Actually, we are a very warm community.'

Some organizations harbor values that can be counterproductive from time to time. Good examples of such *counterproductive values* are expressed in phrases such as: 'not invented here', 'just talking about it doesn't lead to a solution' and all kinds of prejudice and stereotyping. Surfacing such values is highly important, even when it is unwise to address them directly. However, they can be a good reason for organizing a dialogue session (see Chapter 5). Values that are incompatible with the personal values of organizational members are a special case. These incompatibilities make up an important source of organizational ineffectiveness and are discussed in more detail in Chapter 4.

FUNCTIONS

After having dealt with the measurement of the structural characteristics of culture, this section and the following ones concern themselves with studying and measuring the functions of culture, as they were described in Chapter 1. The measurement here is a rather loose one. It consists for each of the three functions of a series of questions intended to map how the function is achieved. In addition, there is a 'report mark' on a five-point scale, which gives an overall evaluation of how that function is realized. Of course, it is important to be as precise, considerate and honest as possible when one gives such an overall mark. These questions are meant for the change agent. If the change agent answers them after the intervention as well, they may help him to evaluate the intervention and to pinpoint the issues on which he brought about real improvement.

Another possibility would have been to make scales of multiple-choice items and let you fill out a neat questionnaire resulting in one or more overall scores. Though this would have saved you time, and maybe even would have given you some sense of security, it would also have had some grave disadvantages. For starters, it would have curtailed your own thinking in a big way. Filling out a questionnaire prevents you from assessing what is important in the specific organization and from making use of that information when you take a decision. As it is, our brains are rather good at amassing a great deal of diverse information and coming up with an overall assessment. Moreover, denying yourself the possibility to think about single issues would also deprive you of the possibility of coming up with specific improvements and solutions. After all, this is not easy, and making it easy would do a huge injustice to the organization.

Reason for Being There

The questions the change agent must ask about the organizational reason for being there examine the topics discussed in Chapter 1. This involves the following questions:

- What problems does the organization help to solve for its environment?
- What improvements does the organization bring about in its environment?
- How can that be done more effectively and efficiently?
- In short, how can the organization offer its customers the greatest possible added value?
- To what degree does the organization contribute to something that goes beyond the life of its individual members, in the sense that it will be valuable to those who live after them as well?
- To what degree does the organization offer opportunities for belonging; that is, to what degree can the employees feel at home and part of the organizational community?
- To what degree does the organization provide its employees with a cause, a purpose beyond themselves; that is, does the organization aim at making the world a better place?
- What does the organization do best?
- Are the organization's policies primarily of a long-term nature?
- Does the organization know where it is going?
- To what degree do the organizational members know its goals?
- Is the work challenging enough?
- Are the wages sufficient for the lifestyle the employees desire?
- Are the work and the organization pleasurable enough?
- Can the employees live from it as they want?
- To what degree does the organization succeed in doing something that is attractive and self-evident to all parties involved?

What is the strongest point of the organization's reason for being there? What is the weakest point? Give the organization a report mark for its reason for being there on a five-point scale:

1. Insufficient
2. Just sufficient
3. Quite sufficient
4. Good
5. Excellent

Adaptation

The questions the change agent must ask about organizational adaptation examine the topics discussed in Chapter 1. This involves the following questions:

- How well is the organization attuned to the needs of its clients?
- To what degree is the organization an attractive, easily accessible, inexpensive and self-evident supplier and interaction partner to its clients? What systems do you share with them?

- What is the quality of the organization's relations with its suppliers? What systems do you share with them?
- What is the quality of the organization's relations with its shareholders?
- What is the quality of the organization's relations with its fellow organizations in the trade – including its competition? What does it learn from them? What alliances are there?
- What is the quality of the organization's relationships with the government and its legislation?
- What is the quality of the organization's relationhips with its geographical neighbors and with the surrounding community at large?
- To what degree does the organization have an effective early warning system in place to detect relevant changes in the environment?
- To what degree can the organization effectively respond to relevant changes in the environment?

What is the strongest point of the organization's adaptation? What is the weakest point? Give the organization a report mark for its adaptation on a five-point scale:

1. Insufficient
2. Just sufficient
3. Quite sufficient
4. Good
5. Excellent

Coordination

The questions the change agent must ask about organizational coordination examine the topics discussed in Chapter 1. This involves the following questions:

- To what degree are the members of the organization aware of, and care about, the effects of what they are doing on their colleagues in other departments?
- To what degree are the members of the organization aware of, and care about, the effects of what they are doing on customers?
- To what degree are the members of the organization aware of, and care about, the effects of what they are doing on the organization as a whole?
- What improvements can you bring about in these respects?
- To what degree does the organization operate as a well-coordinated whole?
- To what degree is there real synergy in the organization?
- To what degree do departmental and individual interests prevail over the organizational common good?
- To what degree are the mutual expectations of departments, as well as of individuals, clear to all involved?
- To what degree will the members of the organization help and support each other if that is needed?
- What are the main constraints in the production process of the organization, and how can these be taken care of?

What is the strongest point of the organization's coordination? What is the weakest point? Give the organization a report mark for its coordination on a five-point scale:

1. Insufficient
2. Just sufficient
3. Quite sufficient
4. Good
5. Excellent

EMPLOYEES' EVALUATION OF THE CULTURE

Lastly, three scales are presented that give an evaluation of the culture by the organization's individual employees. These scales can be used as pre-test and post-test measures to help evaluate the effects of the intervention from the perspective of the employees.

The three concepts – that is, manageability, comprehensibility and meaningfulness – have been borrowed from Antonovski (1987), who grouped them together under the denominator 'sense of coherence'. However, Antonovski used these three variables as personality measures. High scores on these scales indicate that the respondent has a high degree of resilience to stress. The idea was that as long as people see possibilities to manage, comprehend and give meaning to their life, they are able to cope with the stressors inherent in it. Antonovski developed these three concepts while studying survivors of the horrors of the Nazi concentration camps. He discovered that these three traits made the difference between being able to live a valuable life and being too traumatized.

The current three scales are not about life in general, but about the organization in which the employees work and its culture. Most of the items are totally new and the remaining ones are fully rephrased. High scores on these three revised variables imply that the employees can feel at home and function appropriately in the organization. Low scores mean that the employees feel alienated from the organization. This alienation can be of two kinds: either the employees feel that something has changed, or they do not feel much at all (Schabracq & Cooper, 1993).

The scales do not pretend to be highly reliable and valid measures. They are merely meant to provide relative data, and can be used to evaluate an intervention by comparing pre-test and post-test scores, as well as to compare different groups.

Manageability

Being able to work well in an organization – that is, to be successful and effective there – depends on whether we can manage what we have to do in the organization. Manageability thus stands for the degree to which we are able to do what we want and have to do in the organization, in a way that we can feel in control. As such, appropriate manageability involves experiencing sufficient control over our own functioning and goal attainment within the context of the organization. This experience of control implies having the right skills as well as the right means at our disposal. Concerning the organization, appropriate manageability means that the organization must give us sufficient freedom, enough 'room to move', as well as enough ways and means to influence what happens inside and outside the organization. It also means that we are not hampered in our work by all kinds of needless and unwanted regulations and other hindrances.

Manageability Scale

(a) Whether I do a good job in this organization is fully up to me.
(b) There is no real solution for many problems here.
(c) Planning is pretty good in this organization.
(d) The things that I need to do a good job here are just not in place.
(e) Doing something really well is very difficult here.
(f) When I do my best, I can accomplish anything here.
(g) I have all the freedom I need to do my job well.
(h) Without the right breaks, it is impossible to be successful in this organization.
(i) Everything that can go wrong does go wrong in this organization.
(j) It is relatively easy to implement improvements in this organization.

The answering possibilities are:

Yes: 1
No: 0

The manageability score is computed by adding and subtracting the scores for the items in the following way:

$$a - b + c - d - e + f + g - h - i + j = \text{the manageability score.}$$

It can vary from 5 signifying very manageable to -5 signifying very unmanageable.

Comprehensibility

Comprehensibility here means the degree to which an organization and its culture make sense to us and the degree to which we understand it. In a comprehensible organization, the way things happen must be clear and transparent. We must know why we do the things we do. Also, the effects of different lines of conduct must be sufficiently clear, while the behavior of relevant other people must be satisfactorily predictable as well.

Comprehensibility Scale

(a) When I talk to people in this organization, I get sometimes the feeling that we live in totally different worlds.
(b) Essentially, I do not really understand this organization.
(c) The organization is often in a puzzling way contradictory in what it says and what it does.
(d) When I do something in this organization, I know pretty well what consequences it will have.
(e) I pretty much know what I can expect from my colleagues.

(f) I really don't understand what my manager wants.
(g) I know what quality and quantity of work are expected of me.
(h) The feedback I get on what I do enables me to improve my work.
(i) It is not at all clear to me what exactly most of my colleagues do.
(j) I know what I have to do to do a good job.

The answering possibilities are:

Yes: 1
No: 0

The comprehensibility score is computed by adding and subtracting the scores for the items in the following way:

$$a - b - c + d + e - f + g + h - i + j = \text{the comprehensibility score.}$$

It can vary from 5 signifying very comprehensible to -5 signifying very incomprehensible.

Meaningfulness

Meaningfulness here means that what we do in the organization has intrinsic value and purpose. We can show our true worth in the organization; that is, we can prove ourselves. This involves our profession and the status of the organization, as well as the greater good we stand for. This is concerned with how much working in the organization adds to the meaning of our lives.

Meaningfulness Scale

(a) Working here means a lot to me.
(b) I find working for this organization not so interesting.
(c) Working in this organization has a clear purpose for me.
(d) I often ask myself why I am working here.
(e) The sense of some of the things I do here escapes me completely.
(f) Working here does not make my life more meaningful.
(g) By working here I feel like I am contributing to a greater good.
(h) I know exactly what I am doing here and why I am doing it.
(i) Making something out of my work is a frustrating and difficult undertaking.
(j) My colleagues significantly add to the quality of my life.

The answering possibilities are:

Yes: 1
No: 0

The meaningfulness score is computed by adding and subtracting the scores for the items in the following way:

$$a - b + c - d - e - f + g + h - i + j = \text{the meaningfulness score.}$$

It can vary from 5 signifying very meaningful to -5 signifying very meaningless.

Evaluation

Evaluation is concerned with assessing the effects and value of the intervention and taking care of the results of the project. This assessment involves questions such as:

- How effective is the intervention?
- How efficient is the intervention in producing the intended result?
- What are the critical incidents and main bottlenecks during the intervention and how can they be dealt with?
- What is the project's added value?
- Which desired side effects does the intervention have?
- Which undesired side effects does the intervention have?
- How can the intervention be improved?
- How can the intended effects of the intervention be secured? How can they be anchored in the habitual management cycles?
- How can the results of the intervention be used to advocate similar interventions elsewhere?

Essentially, evaluation is not a separate step in an intervention, but takes place during the whole project. Evaluation consists of gathering relevant data in a more or less systematic way, but without excluding relevant data that fall outside the scope of the regular procedures. These data are then ordered, in such a way that this ordering results in relevant information: frequencies, averages, measures of variation, significant differences and correlations. The next step then entails interpreting that information and giving it meaning. Relevance here implies that we must place ourselves mentally in the positions of all parties involved and examine what are the important outcomes for each of them, without losing sight of the goals of the interventions. Essentially this is about empathy.

Evaluation can also encompass comparing pre- and post-test measures, as well as comparing these results with those of one or more comparison groups. Other options are determining the effects of the intervention on a number of other variables, such as productivity, turnover, sick leave, work satisfaction and the variables described in the previous section. Moreover, post-testing can involve several measures at different times, to examine whether the effects are stable or need some reinforcement.

Evaluation is a part of knowledge management. By looking closely at the procedures followed to bring about the cultural change and their results and recording them, the organization gains a knowledge advantage over its competition.

CHAPTER 3

Everyday Reality, Attitude and Leadership

This book is about changing culture. As everyday reality is the product of culture, changing culture will change our everyday reality and by that ourselves. Then again, aren't we the ones who make our own everyday reality and our culture? In this chapter we examine the relationships between ourselves and our reality somewhat more closely and address how we can change this reality. First, we focus on what our reality is about.

REALITY AS ILLUSION

Wittgenstein preaches in the first sentence of his *Tractatus Logico-philosophicus* (1961) that the world is 'everything which is the case'. Though this is a rather ambiguous statement – for example, what does the case mean here? – it does suggest that the world is all-encompassing. After an evocative description of what such a total sum of everything that now is and happens might consist of, William James stated:

> But can we think of such a sum? Can we realize for an instant what a cross-section of all existence at a definite point of time would be? (...) Yet just such a collateral contemporaneity, and nothing else, is the *real* order of the world. It is an order with which we have nothing to do but to get away from it as fast as possible. As I said, we break it: we break it into histories, and we break it into arts, and we break it into sciences; and then we begin to feel at home. We make ten thousand separate serial orders of it. On any one of these, we may react as if the rest did not exist. (James, 1890/1950, Vol. II, p. 635)

William James came across something important here: we really do respond to a minuscule part of all that is the case, and then act as if the rest, by far the major part for that matter, does not exist at all. We feel perfectly at home within a fraction of the whole, without having the idea that we are missing anything. On the contrary, we perceive what we are witnessing as the full and only possible reality. Such a reality may be an obvious case of illusion, but it does correspond to the human measure and we share it with the other people involved. So we approach our world as a succession of separate situations and the broken-up realities within them, the situated realities.

The etymology of the word 'world' is more or less in line with this view. World comes from *weorold* or *woruld*, in which the first part, *weor* or *wor*, means 'man' (*vir* in Latin) and the second part, *old* or *uld*, stands for 'old' and 'age' (Weekley, 1921/1971). Thus, the world as a man's lifetime. Here too, the emphasis is on man as the measure of things, though this of course relates to time rather than space. In essence, situations are by nature more temporal than spatial. After all, situations can be seen as unrolling scenarios or, put differently, as the result of enacting culturally determined standard plays with standard roles and a standard role division for standard players. By enacting the play time after time, each time the participants accomplish the same situational goals. Situations thus involve enacting procedures in time. Buying a loaf of bread at a bakery is an example of such a procedure, having sexual intercourse with our partner is another. Of course, there are also all kinds of spatial elements. A situation has a definite place, a 'where', and in many cases there are spatial elements of the architecture of that 'where', its interior design and the behavior of the players involved. However, these spatial features have a part in the temporal sequence too, for they serve as signs that indicate where to look and what to do next. These signs signal to us where we are in the sequence of the situation at hand. As such, they are there to indicate where we are in time.

Besides knowing that taking part in a situation as if it were the only possible reality is an illusion, we can experience its illusory qualities directly as well: from time to time, there is simply nothing. Reality exhibits hiatus. Its omnipresence and continuity are suspended for the moment. Popping out of reality is not even such an unusual experience:

> We have all experienced the instant amnesias that occur when we get too far on some tangent so we 'lose the thread of thought' or 'forget what we were going to do'. Without the bridging associative connections, consciousness would break down into a series of discrete states with as little continuity as is apparent in our dream life. (Erickson, Rossi & Rossi, 1976, p. 299)

This actually happens to everybody many times a day, for instance when something startles us (a so-called orienting or novelty response, see Chapter 7), when we can't concentrate on our work and even – at least when we pay attention – every time we blink our eyes:

> I imagine, sometimes, that if a film could be made of one's life, every other frame would be death. It goes so fast we're not aware of it. Destruction and resurrection in alternate beats of being, but speed makes it seem continuous. But you see, kid, with ordinary consciousness you can't even begin to know what's happening. (Bellow, 1982, p. 295)

All kinds of incidents may evoke comparable experiences. For example:

- A negative experience (Goffman, 1974), the feeling when we realize that something that we assumed to be present is actually missing, for instance when we look at the empty spot from where our car just has been stolen.
- A shock caused by the transition of one reality to another, for instance in falling asleep, awakening or being disturbed while reading (Schutz, 1970, p. 254), accompanied by somewhat theatrical statements such as 'Where am I?' (after having been unconscious), 'What time is it?' (awakening from having fallen asleep) or 'What did I do?' (after having been very drunk).
- Being between scenes and between activities and not having sufficient situated activity at our disposal to provide complete involvement (Goffman, 1963, 1971; Schabracq, 1991; Vrugt & Schabracq, 1991), for instance while walking, waiting or on public transport. The popularity of the use of cellular phones in such situations, which make them more personal, indicates that many people actually are uncomfortable with not being sufficiently 'situated'.
- The idea of some unexplainable cross-connection in reality, the suspicion of a 'wormhole' in physical terms, such as 'déjà vu', the feeling that we have experienced a certain event

before but not knowing when and where, or a strange coincidence, possibly helped by some overly enthusiastic pattern recognition on our behalf.
• Realizing that we have made a mistake in interpreting reality, for instance when we see two people together when we assumed they were one and the same person, which by the way is a rather unsettling experience.

The illusory character of situational reality is so often described from all kinds of perspectives that it has become a cliché. Still, we handle our everyday life as if we do not know anything about this. This is remarkable, certainly when we realize that we never do something for nothing. Going along with this illusion, subscribing to it as it were, apparently brings us important yields. First, going through the routine provides us with the outcomes of the situations, such as a meal, sleep, company and so on. In addition, there are the yields of control. Apart from the feeling of being on top of things, repeatedly dealing with just a fraction of reality involves knowing what to look for and what to do next, knowing where danger lurks and what to do about it. As a result, we keep our head free for what we deem important and we can avoid needless risks, while we experience acceptance by others and quiet. These yields have proved to be highly addictive, as will be described more elaborately in Chapter 7. Here, we pay attention to how this illusory reality is brought about and how we pass it on.

THE DISCIPLINE OF ATTENTION

Breaking up reality into manageable chunks, to subsequently stick to such a chunk for the time being and experience it as the whole reality of that moment, does not sound easy. How do we do it? Apart from all the repetition involved, which will be dealt with in the following section, this essentially boils down to a form of self-discipline: we systematically attend to what is relevant to us within the piece or play of the moment, while ignoring the rest. We do this by observing 'rules of irrelevance' (Goffman, 1972a). These are tacit rules, derived from a format that we share with the other players. These rules are cultural achievements, which in a given situation determine from moment to moment what we do and do not attend to. We have mostly familiarized ourselves with these rules without recognizing them as such, primarily by unintentionally copying others' attitudes (see later in this chapter).

Our culture helps us in this way to limit our personal reality. By sticking to the rules of irrelevance, we avoid needlessly losing ourselves in other plays and landing in all kinds of inconvenient contacts with strangers. For example, on the way to work we do not get lost in explorations of the world to the left and the right of the shortest journey, and we don't lose ourselves completely in the eyes of the person who is selling us a loaf of bread on the other side of the bakery counter. In this way we keep our head – and our life – free for what we apparently do find more important.

Sticking to one reality and ignoring all other possible situations can be seen as a shared, culturally determined way of coping, an approach by which we prevent stress, even without realizing that stress would have been a likely outcome otherwise. Of course, there is a biological substrate underlying this culturally determined way of coping. Many animals do similar things, for instance looking away from an unnecessary stress-inducing stimulus (Chance & Larsen, 1976). Nevertheless, the forms and ways by which we manage this are a cultural matter.

When other mental contents – thoughts, images, feelings – that don't belong in the situated reality still intrude, the feeling of self-evidence and reality disappears and automatic dealing with these things is no longer possible. Such an intrusion occurs, for example, when thoughts about losing our job or oncoming disaster intrude while we are working, eating or trying to sleep. Such intrusions can lead to stress.

The discipline to limit our reality can take several forms. First of all, there is the example of finding ourselves in the vicinity of others with whom we have no further business, such as in an elevator or train. There, we hardly pay any attention to the people we don't know personally, not even when their faces are familiar to us. We merely display what Goffman has called 'civil inattention' (Goffman, 1963; Schabracq, 1987). This often implies that we let our gaze wander over the others for a moment as a sign that we are aware of their presence and that we don't object against that presence. Then we look away, without having given any proof of recognition, to indicate that we do not want any further contact. It is a form of civility by which we show to others that we do perceive them as full people, though we do not have any special intention to engage in contact with them.

Displaying civil inattention is the normal way of doing things in such situations and it usually does not strike us as anything special. The existence of rules in this respect comes only to the fore when we violate the relevant rules. This happens when a stranger catches us secretly studying him or when we notice that a stranger is staring at us. In both cases, such an intrusion may evoke feelings of uneasiness.

Another more elaborate variant, which demands considerably more effort, occurs when the number of people per square meter becomes too big, such as in a crowded bus or elevator. As Hall puts it:

> The correct behavior is to be as immobile as possible and, when part of the trunk or extremities contact another, to withdraw if possible. If this is not possible the muscles in the affected areas are kept tense. (. . .) it is taboo to relax and enjoy the contact. In crowded elevators the hands are kept at the side or used to steady the body by grasping railings and overhead straps. The eyes are fixed at infinity and should not be brought to bear on anyone for more than a passing glance. (Hall, 1969, p. 118)

By tensing our muscles, to a certain degree we switch off the feelings of being touched. Furthermore, we also prefer not to sniff the bodily smells of these unknown others or hear their bodily noises. All in all, we are blocking all sensory information that emanates from other people.

A more conscious form is 'discrete blindness', ignoring inappropriate events or people with a deviant appearance (Goffman, 1972b, p. 18). My father, for example, was very impressed by the civility and discretion of a noble family at whose house he was invited to dinner once as a teenager and who didn't move a muscle when he dropped his spoon in his soup. Another example is a military parade at which a soldier faints and then is completely ignored. Another of Goffman's examples relates to life in psychiatric institutions, where nurses, visitors and patients alike heroically ignore the deviant behavior of some of the other patients (Goffman, 1968). A similar behavioral pattern with a kindred function occurs in religious people who gaze downward during social encounters, in order not to lose themselves needlessly in the faces of other people and the worldly affairs that occupy them.

All these examples are instances of a culturally determined discipline of attention, which allows the members of a culture to keep their particular situational reality. Discipline of attention, however, can be also a purely individual matter. This amounts to not noticing certain things that other people in the same position would notice immediately. Such inattention is called 'denial', a way of suppressing experiences, partially or fully, which we can apply in a precisely measured way (Breznitz, 1983). This also enables us to deal with a situation and keep our mind on the immediate goals. In the case of drastic forms of denial, we tend to fill the resulting emptiness with something less threatening, disturbing or unpleasant (Dorpat, 1985).

This discipline of attention contributes to the 'all-or-nothing' character of situations. In practice, it turns out that we can experience only one situation fully. That situation we then experience without much critical sense, reserve or suspicion, while all ideas about other possible situations are effectively inhibited. We just play our situated role. In that way, our own behavior, and with that our own discipline of attention, serves as a situational stimulus to other players; that is, as a compelling signal that the situation is actually enacted. In this way we clarify to them how we see the reality at hand, which to them is an implicit but powerful invitation to share the reality of the situation with us.

All in all, this discipline of attention is an important technique for not letting ourselves be diverted from our occupations, though we are barely aware of the fact that we use it. The discipline of attention enables us to be in a situation and inhabit it as if it were the only possible reality. We do this by shielding ourselves off from all other possible situations, namely by not paying attention to any other situation whatsoever and by showing that we do so. In that way, we actively prevent going needlessly through unexpected events, while we provide our everyday reality with clear borders. We seldom transgress these borders, even though we usually do not experience them as such, simply because we do not pay attention to them. Staying within these borders has become a matter of habit.

Though habit is a powerful phenomenon, it is not an unchangeable datum that is given to us by some higher power that we cannot influence or control. In a sense, we installed it ourselves, we embraced it, subscribed to it and made it part of who we are. Once we become aware of a habit we can allow ourselves to change it, provided that we want to. Changing habits implies changing our reality, as well as the reality of the other people involved. Changing culture is about changing habits.

However, before going into changing culture, which is what this book is about, we first pay attention to all the repetition resulting from our discipline of attention and the way in which we have incorporated all these habits and made them part of who we are and want to be.

REALITY AND REPETITION

Etymologically speaking, the word 'reality' goes back to the Latin word *realitas*, which in its turn stems from *realis*, 'factual' or 'thing-like', the adjective derived from the substantive *res*, meaning 'matter' or 'thing'. Reality, then, is the whole of facts or things as we know and recognize them. Most of these matters and things are not naturally given, at least not directly. Things, or material objects, are mostly man-made or 'man-altered', in a very specific way to give them their 'proper' forms and functions. As such, these things are subject to decay and have to be taken care of, maintained, cleaned, repaired and replaced when they are beyond repair.

Another kind of 'matter' also exists. These are events, activities, ways of doing things, procedures and routines, which also have certain forms and functions. As behavioral phenomena, which are not of a permanent nature, they must be re-enacted time and again. And to make them recognizable and functional, their forms must conform to rather strict specifications. In plain terms: we have to repeat their forms precisely time after time, for as long as we live. In this way we manufacture normality and reality, for ourselves but also for the other players. Examples are buying bread, having a drink in a pub and doing our work tasks.

All this keeping things in shape and enacting procedures involves an awful lot of unbelievably monotonous work. It is no coincidence that in some Germanic languages the word 'work' takes a central place in the word for reality, such as *werk* (i.e. work) in *werkelijkheid* in Dutch and *Wirk* in *Wirklichkeit* in German.

Reality then becomes the sum of the settings that we choose to use, help to arrange, equip and decorate, help to maintain and take care of, and also – not unimportantly – what we do, think and feel in these settings, again and again. We do all of this most of the time in close collaboration with the other players who are there: we re-present reality, re-cite it, re-think it (Moscovici, 1984, p. 9). Here, too, reality is something that conforms to the human measure, and again something that does not correspond at all to Wittgenstein's 'everything that is the case'.

Failure to reproduce the right action sequence at the right moment means to everyone involved, including ourselves, that we are doing something wrong. In principle, this can be repaired by explaining our actual intentions, excusing ourselves for the failure and producing the intended sequence after all. The important point here is, however, that this indeed is a matter of 'right' and 'wrong': essentially, it is an ethical or moral issue. Culture always involves evaluations in terms of good and evil, as well as the follow-up procedures triggered by its outcomes. As it is, it is no coincidence that in Greek the word *ethos* ($\eta\theta o\varsigma$) means 'custom' or 'customary place to be', as is still used in the word 'ethology', the biology of behavior. The same goes for the stem of 'moral', the Latin *mos*, plural *mores*, which means customs as well.

Repetition has always caught the attention of philosophers and psychologists, but mostly as a factor that strengthens associations between different items in the form of a learning principle. Repetition as a learning principle has, for example, been described by Aristotle (in his 'De anima', ca. 350 BC, in Aristotle, 1941), the seventeenth-century empiricists, behaviorists such as Thorndike ('connections are reinforced by exercise and weakened when exercise stops': Thorndike, 1911) and the French suggestion psychologists of the era before the Second World War such as Baudouin ('suggestion is facilitated by exercise': Baudouin, 1924, p. 127). Also, it was recognized that repetition may have motivational properties: 'habit becomes drive' (Woodworth & Schlosberg, 1954). Still, there has been little or no attention whatsoever on the all-determining role of repetition in itself, when it concerns what we actually do in everyday life. Put more strongly, we are almost blind to the simple fact that we endlessly repeat ourselves every day. Nor are we bothered by the consequences of this repetition: its limiting effect on the variation in our repertory, and the fact that it prevents other forms of behavior from appearing.

Why? If we were asked whether a life of endless repetition would appeal to us, we would probably say that we would not find such a life particularly attractive. It would sound more like a punishment than our normal way of life. After all, aren't we primarily free and creative? Aren't we able to choose what we want? We are fond of excitement and like to think that we lead challenging lives. Continuous repetition, on the contrary, sounds like the sad fate of slaves and prisoners. We probably just do not notice the repetitiveness in our lives because it is so omnipresent, familiar and normal. Repeated forms are simply always there. Repeated forms form a constant factor, while our perception is more focused on variation and novelty than on constancy. Isn't the fish the last one to discover water? And wasn't oxygen only detected in the eighteenth century?

An example: the first hour of a normal working day. Each day you awake at the same time, probably helped by an alarm clock, which you have set yourself. Next to you lies somebody else or no one, and in either case you are not overly surprised. What then follows is a series of utterly familiar routines, by which you provide all your senses with a multimodal bombardment of normality. Besides the thoroughly familiar sensory information that emanates from the receptors in your muscles and sinews when you perform your familiar acts, there is the input of the other senses. So there are the usual smells of – if present – your partner, your urine, your toothpaste and soap, your deodorant and perfume. Moreover, as long as all is well, you don't smell yourself and your own breath, just because these smells are so utterly familiar that you don't notice them any more. The same applies to the smell of your house, which you notice only when you come home from a holiday. Then there is taste: the tastes of your toothpaste, your coffee or tea and your breakfast, which always is more or less the same, as you eat and drink what you like, and so on. Concerning vision, looking around you see a highly familiar environment, which you designed yourself in a way that appeals to you, with stuff that you yourself have selected. In the mirror you see a very familiar face and, when there are other people around, they look quite familiar too. They also sound very familiar. When nobody else is around, you may put on the television or the radio, which broadcast familiar programs with familiar people as well, until it is time to go to work.

This goes on throughout the day, each day anew. We have chosen places and activities in line with our own tastes and preferences. This leads to fixed routines and familiar ways of dividing our attention, which we repeat with a calm kind of fanaticism, time after time. So we enact our own reality, in daily, weekly, monthly and yearly cycles. We meticulously expose ourselves to utterly familiar thoughts, feelings and sensory stimuli, while our discipline of attention sees to it that other matters do not get a look in. In this way we spiral forward through space and time: a case of forced labor, which takes a great deal of effort and energy. When we honestly look at it, we can only be surprised. Of course, people differ in what they repeat. However, the point is that all of us repeat ourselves constantly and by that greatly limit the possible variation in our life. This limitation of variation becomes even more apparent when we consider the endless possibilities of variation, which – at least in principle – are all open to us.

SITUATIONS

The occasions in which we display our routines are not of our own making or design. We are talking here about the chunks of reality, mentioned before when we talked about repetition. These chunks of reality are cultural achievements called situations. Situations are 'pieces' or 'plays' in the theatrical sense, with a recognizable identity. We can enact such a situation alone, but most of the time we do this together with others, namely with the other players and possible onlookers. By enacting a situation, we make it part of reality, for ourselves as well as for the others involved. Situations are separated in space and time from their environment and their transitions can be more or less gradual or abrupt.

Enacting a situation excludes all other possible situations and their realities at that moment. Without noticing it, we limit ourselves to a very small part of what else would be possible. In this way, we design our life as a series of separate situations that we can share with others. Sometimes situations have their own name, such as a workshop, dinner or cocktail party, but even if situations do not have a name, they can be described in a few words.

All in all, this reality can be described as an *Umwelt*. This term of von Uexküll, an Estonian biologist who died in 1944, is difficult to translate. With it he is referring to the limited reality that results from attuning perception and behavior to the structure of the outer world in which the organism lives, and to which it has fully adapted. To von Uexküll this implied, among other things, that an organism does not occupy itself with neutral objects; that is, with matters that are of no meaning to that organism (von Uexküll, 1909). Meaning here resides in the relationships with survival and reproduction. This emphasis on usefulness fits in with James's conviction that intellectual abilities are primarily pragmatic and not aiming at the acquisition of objective and disinterested knowledge (James, 1978). This emphasis is also in line with Gibson's concept of 'affordance', the idea that perception and behavior are determined by what they yield (Gibson, 1979). In addition, this is also compatible with the phenomenologists' position, going back to Franz Brentano, that every act is intentional (http://en.wikipedia.org/wiki/Franz_Brentano).

In the first section of this chapter, the illusory nature of situational reality was discussed. Moreover, I also explained earlier that by adhering to our situational realities, we imprison ourselves in a narrow spiral of repeating situations, excluding all other possibilities in the process. At first sight, such a way of living makes little sense as it has important disadvantages. Still, this is how we live through our days. Yet as people do not do something for nothing, certainly not each time afresh, this approach apparently provides us with sufficiently rewarding outcomes. These outcomes primary consist of the 'fruits' of these situations: we enter situations to collect their yields. Thus we go to a shop or a restaurant, because we want certain goods, e.g. we want to have a meal. We enter into these situations willingly, knowing what we want to give and take, though the outcomes, of course, vary by situation.

Examples of outcomes are a place to sleep, money, education, quiet, sex, services, company, amusement and so on. These outcomes serve as so many rewards for the right use of our attitudes and behavior in these situations. In this way we let ourselves be conditioned like little Pavlovian dogs: we develop skills and act in the right way, both in a technical and a moral sense. We learn what we should learn. This applies to all parties in these situations. Situations offer us, and the other players, clearly marked and practicable ways of acting to satisfy permanent or ever recurring needs in fixed ways. In that way we can satisfy these needs almost without paying any attention. Doing errands without getting into a row, walking along a crowded pavement without bumping into somebody, asking an employee to do something without twisting their arm, feeding my grandson without making him cry, making love without landing in jail – these are all outcomes of situations that presuppose the kind of everyday practical skills that we so obediently acquire.

Situations are thus the basic forms that culture brings to everyday life. They provide the infrastructure of the cultural division of roles. Almost everybody can play his own role in a way that makes sense; that is, in such a way that the role fits meaningfully in the situation, which provides complementary roles to other people, roles that get their meaning from being played in that situation as well. As such, situations provide – among other things – the infrastructure of the division of labor. To be the playground of all this skill display implies that situations must have stability. This stability is attained by the participants carefully enacting their situated roles each time afresh in a more or less fixed way. A situation then can be described as a format for fixed procedures, equipped with signaling systems to coordinate these procedures to attain the situational goals. In this way, situations provide stability and structure, the more so as we do most of what is involved out of our awareness. The secondary gains of living a life of situations consist of staying in a comfort zone that provides for control, a feeling of reality (no alienation), quiet, avoidance of risks (experienced safety, see Chapter 4) and acceptance by the others involved, and are described more fully in Chapter 7.

On the one hand, the unconscious nature of situations and the powerful rewards involved make situations appear to go their own way and are difficult to change. On the other hand, situations can be changed. They are human-made and thus can also be altered by humans.

ATTITUDES

In the previous sections I argued that we confine our attention to what is relevant in a situation and each time we repeat the behavior appropriate for that situation. In this way, we enact that situation. Basically, this is a matter of assuming the right attitudes. The word 'attitude' refers to a mental stance or mindset as well as to a corresponding bodily posture.

Using the same word for a bodily and a mental phenomenon highlights the inextricable connectedness of the two phenomena, a typical instance of the kind of phenomena that gave rise to the 'embodied mind paradigm' (see Damasio, 2003; Lakoff & Johnson, 1999; Varela, Thompson & Rosch, 1991). This approach to human functioning sees activity as a gradually developing, inextricable unity of doing and knowing in a certain environment. This activity results in behavior that is tuned in to that environment, as well as in knowledge about that behavior in that environment. The knowledge is 'incarnated': 'And the Word was made flesh' (John 1:14). This implies that within this paradigm there is no such thing as a separate intelligence.

Attitude also determines how we take up space. It shows our orientation toward the people and objects in our environment, but also our energy level and tension, as well as how unambiguous or divided we are. So our attitude expresses whether we are relaxed, depressed, angry or tired, as well as whether we like the other people or not. Our attitude communicates all of this and much more, just like others' attitudes do. As such, our attitude gives information about how we experience the world and what meanings we ascribe to it. We give that information in a way that is comprehensible to other people, so that they can respond to it.

Because we sustain an attitude for some time, an attitude also implies a certain stability in time, again in both a bodily and mental way. As long as we hold on to an attitude, everything stays more or less the same. By sustaining an attitude, we create a stable environment for anything we do and experience. As a result, our attitude can provide a relatively stable basis or ground from which we feel, think and act.

As relatively stable grounds for our functioning, our attitudes are not once-only phenomena. On the contrary, when we have appropriated a proper and usable attitude, we repeat it time after time, whenever and wherever we can use it. In practice, this means that we assume certain appropriate attitudes each time we take part in certain recurring situations. In this way, we function in and from a string of familiar attitudes, the relatively unchanging unities of our life. Each time we assume a certain attitude again, everything is more or less the same as the previous time we did so and it even feels as if nothing has happened in between. As such, attitudes can function as 'grounds' within the figure–ground paradigm, originally introduced within Gestalt psychology by Edgar Rubin around 1915 (http://en.wikipedia.org/wiki/Rubin_vase).

An attitude is not only a recurring form, but also has an intention. We don't assume an attitude just like that but do so for a reason: either to attain a goal in the longer run or because assuming a certain attitude is in itself the goal to be attained. Thus observing an attitude – someone else's or our own in a mirror – teaches us something about the intentions of the person being observed.

We have appropriated our attitudes by mirroring the people to whom we have been exposed, without realizing that we were doing so. Babies adopt attitudes automatically (Gopnik & Meltzoff, 1997). Babies are like copying machines, as are adults, for that matter. By copying attitudes and movements from our earliest childhood on, we got involved in the world of others, the reality we shared with these others. Once we had copied their attitudes, we were able gradually to appropriate this reality from within by, step by step, filling in the structures provided by the attitudes. This of course began without any idea of meaning and without any words, but slowly the meanings and words were put into place within the structure of these attitudes. In this respect we were greatly helped by the people who felt responsible for us. Familiarizing ourselves with all the ins and outs of a particular attitude and its inherent reality went hand in hand with getting a grip on the situations in which this attitude was appropriate.

Most of our attitudes are already very old. As we copied them from our parents and they probably copied them from their parents and so on, their origin goes back a long time, long before our birth. These attitudes and the world view they represent are transferred from generation to generation. They have survived, however, because they still do their job. Moreover, we do not question them, even though different and better attitudes are conceivable. As a result, our repertoire can contain less than adequate attitudes. Examples are attitudes that are loaded with intense anger or chilliness and feeling nothing. Another example is withdrawing from a situation and retreating into ourselves. We may have adapted these attitudes from our father or mother or from a sibling. These attitudes have once, in tough times, proved their value, when we or others were abused or neglected, for example. Now their intensity, or even their goal, is most of the time out of proportion, but they still can be evoked by a single word or image. This state of affairs will remain that way as long as we do not want to face these attitudes or to be on speaking terms with them.

How does it come about that we adopt these attitudes so easily? The answer to that question is surprisingly simple. Mirroring somebody's attitude is a normal element of paying attention to that person: when we focus our attention on somebody, we imitate or simulate the attitudes and movements of that person. This is probably an outcome of the activity of the so-called mirror neurons, nerve cells that at the same time are involved in the perception of other people's movements and the control of our own movements (Rizzolatti & Craighero, 2004). Apparently, experiences are less separated from actions than Descartes taught us. It really looks as if our experiences are embodied.

The degree to which we take over the behavior of another person whom we attend to differs. When we are fully lost in the other, we fully or partially match their attitude and movements, usually without noticing it. When our attention is less intense, there usually is only a mental simulation of movements and attitude (Schabracq, 1987, 1991).

When there is no factual imitation of attitudes and movements, it is often possible to demonstrate the electrical activity in the muscles that would bring about these movements; that is, if the movements were not suppressed. Gibson, for example, showed that understanding spoken speech is accompanied by electrical activity of the muscles that would have led to echoing the words if we abandoned ourselves fully to that activity (Gibson, 1979). The initial impetus to imitation is thus present at the neurological and muscular level.

During our first two years of life, we engage much more in fully imitating movements and attitudes than we do as adults (Gopnik & Meltzoff, 1997). When we get older, we learn to suppress the complete imitation and stick to a more superficial simulation, except when we fully lose ourselves in the other person, for example when we are in love. Something similar, however, occurs in martial arts such as boxing and fencing, as long as the opponents are of equal ability and strength. This mirroring can also be a matter of jointly tuning into a given external rhythm or melody, for instance in singing, making music and dancing together, or in drilling an army unit. In all these cases there is a heightened sense of 'we' and 'together', even in fighting. This is also what drilling is about. As long as the drill is sustained, an individual decision to call it quits is less likely: there is too much 'we' present to abandon the situation.

Certain forms of brain damage can take away the suppression of complete mirroring, leading to the phenomena of echopraxia and echolalia, the unresisting mirroring and echoing of everybody who comes into our field of attention (Schabracq, 1991; Vrugt & Schabracq, 1991).

By imitating someone else, we feel from within the other's attitude. In this way we get all kinds of information about what he is doing and intending, as well as how he is feeling. By simulating or mirroring someone, we tune in to him. We put ourselves in the other person's position and look at the world through their eyes. We open up to what moves him, by exploring in ourselves what we experience.

ATTITUDES AND ASSUMPTIONS

We say that we assume an attitude. In this way, we talk about attitudes as well as about assuming them. Of course, assumption also has the meaning of an underlying idea or basis. The English language here points to the crucial relationship between the concepts of attitude and assumption, just as Dutch (*een houding aannemen* and *aanname*) and German (*eine Haltung annehmen* and *Annahme*) do as well.

What are assumptions? Our assumptions are the ideas from which we depart and from which we reason and act. Assumptions are a matter of faith or belief. We believe that our assumptions apply or, put differently, we believe that they are usable and true. When we take our attitude to be an effect of the assuming – or the assumption – of the attitude, that attitude reflects a belief as well. This is a well-proven belief, because we have already assumed that attitude many times before and successfully so. Success here means that in this way we actually got the outcome we had assumed the attitude for, namely the outcome of the situation of which our attitude was a part. In this way, our attitudes have become thoroughly familiar to us, forming an important part of our self-manufactured, solid and seamless reality, in which everything is normal and safe and in which the others accept us. In short, our attitude has become a reality in which we love to believe.

My attitude thus tells how I believe things are, a belief that I fully embrace, because it is the only firm ground to stand on when I want to understand the world: Anselm, who became archbishop of Canterbury in 1093, said, 'I believe in order to understand' (Störig, 1966). Among philosophers this way of thinking is not unusual, though – of course! – they are not of one mind about it. So Hume also saw belief as the basis of our knowledge about ourselves and the world, while Hamann, taking this one step further, spoke about belief as a mental habit (Berlin, 2000).

When we assume another attitude, our belief has apparently shifted or changed entirely. When we are in doubt about what to believe, we tend to change our attitude frequently, for example by shifting our weight from one foot to the other and back. In such a way we demonstrate loudly and clearly that we don't know which attitude to assume.

All these forms of belief concerned the best way to handle the situation at hand. Usually, we don't test the value of such a belief. Most of the time it feels so self-evident that we experience it as a logical part of the only possible reality. What is nice is that in this way our attitude actually becomes the only possible reality. By automatically assuming an attitude, all other options are gone for that moment because, as it is, we can assume only one attitude at a time. After all, we have only one body and our consciousness is so organized that we can be fully aware of only one situation at a time. So when the attitude we assume does not evoke resistance in the other people present, it has tacitly become part of the current reality. Our faith operates as a self-fulfilling prophecy: our belief about how we think things are makes itself true. In this way we invoke a complementary attitude from the other players, while we might have evoked completely different attitudes by assuming a different attitude ourselves, without spending any thought on it. Magic works! Before becoming too enthusiastic about our influence on things, we should realize that the attitude that we assumed fitted the situation to start with, and therefore it was one of the very few attitudes that was appropriate there. Maybe it was the only one in our repertoire that fitted that situation!

Assumptions determine what can and cannot be 'the case'. Wittgenstein revisited after all? Maybe, but we can change our assumptions – somewhat. Such a change, however, changes our reality as well, as may be demonstrated by the following anecdote.

Three orthodox Jews disagree about whose rabbi can work the greatest miracles. The first relates that when it rains, his rabbi remains completely dry: 'Before the rabbi it rains, behind him it rains, on both sides of him too, but no drop falls where he walks.' 'Nice, but nothing compared to our rabbi,' the second one says. 'When our rabbi walks through the dark, it is dark before him, it is dark behind him, and it is dark on his left and right as well, but where the rabbi walks it is light, always.' The third one shakes his head gravely, smiles sadly and then says: 'Nice, but that is next to nothing. Our rabbi, he is a real miracle worker: he works on Saturday! Before him it is Sabbath, behind him it is Sabbath and next to him it is Sabbath. Everywhere it is Sabbath, except where the rabbi works.'

ATTITUDE AND SITUATION

Our attitude thus reflects the reality that we believe to be 'the case'. As a result, our attitude implies a proposal about how we see reality and how we, based on this, want to relate to other people. It is about who has to do what, the division of power, the emotional hue of the relationship and the depth of our engagement in it. In short, attitude serves as a situation or relationship proposal (Watzlawick, Beavin & Jackson, 1968).

The proposal implied by my attitude is most of the time not perceived as a proposal. That is, as long as my attitude fits the situation as all those involved see that situation, nothing unusual happens and everything goes like we want it to. Instead, the reality suggested by my attitude is treated as if it concerns the only possible reality. On the one hand, this acceptance of my attitude is a consequence of the fact that the attitude I display is just a normal one, while there are only a few attitudes possible here. On the other hand, the acceptance of my attitude is probably related to the fact that people simulate others' attitudes, so they feel my attitude from within and experience the proposal inherent in it as originating from within as well. As a result, the situation implied by my attitude is then taken as a solid fact, a logical part of how things are. The others merely respond by assuming complementary attitudes. In this way my proposal is promoted to the status of reality. My situation proposal has been accepted without anyone wasting a word or thought over it. We just deal with the rest of the situation as if it is the most normal affair in the world. And that is precisely what it is.

This course of affairs makes attitudes in practice very compelling situational proposals, also because all parties in such situations know what they are going to get and give and what advantage a particular course of affairs holds for them. Doing errands, walking along a busy sidewalk without bumping into anyone, asking an employee to do something, making love, quarrelling, being left in peace – these all originate from compelling situational proposals.

However, what is so compelling when we all get our way? Many authors have already given the answer to this question: we don't communicate or discuss, but take part in a communication or discussion, a piece in which we obediently play our role. Albert Scheflen (1982), for example, stated that we don't inter-act, but co-act, together enacting a piece. Is it coincidental that the meanings of the original Latin terms (*coactus*, compelled; *cogĕre*, to compel) are all related to coercion? *Coactor* even means tax collector. The piece, the situation, is the compelling instance here. The situation determines our attitudes. Though these situations and their role divisions with their prescribed attitudes are nothing without us, we apparently have convinced ourselves to embody them and let them exist. We are the ones who, with the forced labor of our attitudes, make the situations into our joint reality, by each time forcing ourselves like convicts through the narrow tunnels and caves of their dimly lit mazes.

In a way, the situations taught us our attitudes with their specific functions and meanings. We observed how other players in these situations assumed these attitudes and registered what they got out of that. In that way we learned when and how to use these attitudes, a typical case of vicarious learning Bandura (1977) or of suggestion (Tarde, 1890), as it used to be called. The situation in which our attitudes are connected to those of other people is, after all, the instance that enables us to get something. By assuming the right complementary attitudes in a given situation, we can buy bread, walk along the street and so on.

Assuming the right attitude boils down to agreeing with the assumptions of the situation we are in. The suppositions that underlie our attitudes are then the same as those of the situation we enact. With our attitude we indicate our assumption that the situation is indeed 'the case' and that it will bring us what we expect of it. We show that we believe in the reality of the situation. Put more strongly, we demonstrate that the situation is for us the only possible reality right now. The message to outsiders is: this is the way things are done here.

Attitudes are the building blocks of situations and therefore of our collection of recurring solutions for our recurring problems, which ensue from periodically satisfying our basic needs. Together these solutions form our culture. By appropriating the right attitudes, which for the greater part happens by itself, we become part of the culture, our shared reality. At the same time, we mold and model the culture, we help to maintain it and to transfer it to other people, without realizing that we are doing that. Is it a consolation to realize that all the work invested in sustaining our reality benefits other people as well? They incidentally do the same and that again benefits us.

All in all, person and culture coincide in attitudes. Personal behavior can be described as a string of attitudes through time, in which each attitude is reinforced by the gains from the plays or situations of which these attitudes are a part. At the same time, our culture can be regarded as the whole of the standardized configurations of these attitudes in definite plays or situations, where each offers a solution for an ever recurring problem.

Children sometimes make a game out of mirroring. The ones who are mirrored, children and adults, usually find this obnoxious. The same applies to being mirrored by somebody in a Charlie Chaplin outfit, preferably in front of a pavement terrace. What is so irritating about this? Or the other way around, why do children find so much fun in doing this? Why can an unemployed person complement his social security benefit in this way? And why are impersonators a sure part of a variety show? Keep in mind then that this is about gloating, about the hilarious fact that others abandon themselves so seriously to the forced labor of their everyday situations, trying to give it a personal touch after all.

ATTITUDE AND DEVELOPMENT

Do we surrender completely and defenselessly to the attitudes as they have presented themselves to us? Not necessarily. We can position ourselves in front of a big mirror and study our own attitudes. What do our everyday attitudes look like? What assumptions do they reflect, about us and about the world? What situation and relationship proposals do they imply? Do we want to take responsibility for the attitudes we see in the mirror? Are they just excellent? Are they good enough? Or do we still prefer something else? What is good is that we may make the choice ourselves. Nobody forbids us from adjusting our attitudes. Nobody compels us to do so either. We really are free in this respect. Assuming attitudes we would love to subscribe to for a change, leading an undivided life and enjoying some self-esteem, all of that certainly sounds attractive. However, developing our attitudes is far from simple. Every now and then it does not go well. Still, it is worth trying. Stand in front of a big mirror and learn about your attitudes (see Chapter 8). Maybe you owe that to yourself.

There is more. When we develop a more refined attitude, it can – thanks to its highly contagious nature – spread to other people as well. The speed of that spread depends on the degree that the refined attitude demonstrably contributes to better solutions, and in this way makes the old solutions obsolete. It also depends on the amount of attention we receive: the more attention, the more contagious our attitudes will be. When we have developed new attitudes and we want to spread them, we should make sure that we get sufficient attention. This is one of the ways to change culture, the direct way, as I call it.

Spreading effective attitudes is essentially an evolutionary process. The attitudes then serve as units of – or even vehicles for – the transfer of personal and cultural information.

Considering the ease of imitating and simulating attitudes and how their use, if successful, is reinforced in situations, they act as Dawkin's (1976) *'memes'*, a kind of non-hereditary genes that shape cultures as well as personalities. As transferable units of our identities and culture, our attitudes succeed each other in periodical ways, attuned in standardized ways to others' attitudes, making up what can be called a 'periodic system of attitudes', which underlies all the possible strings and combinations of attitudes.

So really changing culture involves getting acquainted with our attitudes, in order to be able to surface the assumptions inherent in these attitudes. It also involves questioning these assumptions and what is so terrible in adjusting or extending them a little; that is, questioning the assumptions on their pretense of being unchangeable. As it is, assumptions can change, though not in any arbitrary direction. The best way to change an assumption is to extend its meaning by combining the assumption with another valid assumption, for example one underlying someone else's contradictory opinion about something. However, you cannot take assumptions out and replace them by completely different ones just like that.

When changing attitudes and assumptions is at stake, there are always two basic ways of perceiving, namely looking from the inside and looking from the outside, and it is important to make a distinction between the two.

Looking from the inside means going through the moves of the attitude, for example the moves of the familiar situations in the organization, and looking at what is happening from that perspective. Looking from the inside is the only way to be able to function within the everyday reality defined by our attitudes and assumptions, and those of the other members of the organization. When we are actually busy bringing about a change we may never completely lose this perspective. Losing it would imply that we lose the other members of the organization and that we cannot properly communicate with them any more.

Looking from the outside means looking from the perspective of an outside observer. From this point of view, we can see the greater picture in which the event in question is only part of another whole. This way of perceiving can be necessary to overcome an impasse and to ask the right questions. What is the greater good? What are the limiting factors when we want to realize that greater good? What kind of changes does this imply for our assumptions and attitudes? This feels like a very free way of perceiving, but at the same time it is a very lonely one and with that a vulnerable one.

For a real change, we need both ways of perceiving; that is, we must be able to alternate at will and quickly between perceiving from the inside and perceiving from the outside. The obvious risk here is losing ourselves in one of the two and neglecting the other.

ATTITUDE AND LEADERSHIP: THE DIRECT APPROACH

The relationship between attitudes and assumptions, as described earlier, is so important because it clarifies where many of our assumptions come from. By adopting the attitudes of the people to whom we have been exposed, and on whom we were dependent in the first years of our life, we adopted their assumptions too. In this way, we took part in their ways of living, including all their ideas, stories, images and feelings, which were attached to these attitudes. These 'attachments' were not at all clear to us then, but – as discussed in Chapter 7 – they had the opportunity to gradually unfold and develop within us. These assumptions are now part of our 'basic trust' (Erikson, 1968) – that is, as far as we developed such a 'basic trust' – that we developed in our first years of life, the trust that life is (at least to a certain degree) manageable, comprehensible and meaningful (Antonovsky, 1987). Attempts from the outside to change these attitudes can then easily be interpreted as intrusions into this basic trust, with all the intense reactions that might be evoked by all that.

By adopting the attitudes and assumptions of the people who raised us, as well as of the other people who have influenced us, we have literally and figuratively identified ourselves with them. We relate in comparable ways to the world, without noticing that for one second.

Another interesting point here is that somebody's power position determines the amount of attention they receive. That is, more powerful people almost automatically draw our attention. As a result, we tend to adopt their attitudes and consequently we tend to look at the world from their perspectives. This is in practice a matter of biology. The same also happens in other ape species (Chance & Larsen, 1976). A well-known example of this phenomenon is that hostages, who are fully dependent for their survival on the whims of their captors, tend to adopt their captors' views. This so-called Stockholm syndrome helps the hostages to survive, because by adopting this mindset they can better predict what the captors are up to. The adoption of the captors' point of view often happens without the hostages noticing that they are completely changing their views of the world.

It is interesting to realize that small children are equally dependent on others for their survival as are hostages. Anna Freud (1971) spoke in a comparable context about 'identification with the aggressor'. This makes it all the more understandable that we have adopted our parents' attitudes – and assumptions – to such a great degree. We just have taken them up in our body: we have 'in-corporated' them (literally put them in our body, as *corpus* is Latin for body).

This adoption of the point of view of the 'more powerful' person has important implications for leadership. As leaders are by definition powerful, they draw much attention. As a result, their followers tend to take over their attitudes and assumptions without question. Leaders then become by definition strong role models who can use their attitudes to influence their followers' motivation and behavior. The downside of this is that a leader who displays inadequate attitudes can have a devastating effect on his employees' motivation and behavior. So leaders should be aware of their modeling function and be very careful about their attitudes. They should walk their talk, strongly and perceivably.

In order to be maximally contagious, an attitude should be energetic and show clear intent. High energy makes attitudes more vivid (Nisbett & Ross, 1980) and salient (Taylor & Fiske, 1978) – that is, more likely to attract attention – because it appeals more strongly to the observer's emotions (James, 1890/1950). The most distinguishing characteristic of Mao Zedong, for example, appears to have been his unbridled energy (Spence, 2000). Clear intent refers to being undivided in one's attitude; that is, not showing mixed objectives or restraining oneself too much. It also means displaying a clear focus and purpose, being determined, certain and optimistic. Unclear or mixed intent has a self-disqualifying effect: don't look at me, I don't know either. Clear intent is also perceived as a sign of sincerity and authenticity (Heidegger, 1962; May, 1969), of being the same on and off the job (Bennis & Thomas, 2002).

Being authentic is most of all a matter of knowing and being convinced of your own suppositions and goals. This may take a lot of work and exercise. Mahatma Gandhi, for example, put in a great deal of effort and reflection to be as clear and undivided as possible (Nair, 1998).

Essentially, authenticity is a special case of a more general pattern: the leader as hero (Campbell, 1988; Smit, 1997). Heroes enter the stage when things are not good. Exemplary heroes usually retreat from society to a secluded place for some time, where they don't need their intellect for everyday concerns. Some – Jesus, Moses and Mohammed – preferred deserts. Ignatius of Loyola chose a grotto. A prison-like environment, such as in the cases of Sadat, Lenin and Mandela, and even a desolate garret – Hitler – can do the trick as well. In such an environment, heroes have room to face the painful difference between how things are and how they ought to be. Their hero-like capacities manifest themselves most in enduring this discrepancy and all the inherent aversive feelings as long as necessary. To this end, they descend to the level of the assumptions. Here they slay their dragons and find the seeds of the new approach, which take them to visionary heights where the new vision can fully unfold. Most of the time, this vision is a vigorous new combination of well-known elements, which turn out not to be completely obsolete after all. Lastly, heroes step down again to the world of everyday life, armed with the blueprint of a new approach to overcome the discrepancy. Once returned to society, heroes try to implement this vision there. Though this sounds like a purely individual affair, it doesn't need to be. As the stories about the Argonauts and the Trojan War demonstrate, heroes can band together. A group, a management team for example, can do the same and, when things are very complicated, to probably even better effect.

When leaders know their modeling power, they can use their attitude deliberately to propose to their people what they want them to do. This implies that they must pay special attention to their own attitudes. The first step here may literally consist of looking in the mirror and inspecting their habitual attitudes. What relationship proposals do they imply? Do they communicate what the leaders want them to communicate? By carefully modifying habitual attitudes and experimenting with them, it is possible to be more in control over those attitudes; that is, to display the attitudes that one wants to display. This enables one to take more responsibility for one's attitudes and to be more precise and effective in what one wants to get across. The main guideline here is to be honest with oneself (see Chapter 5).

Some leaders exaggerate their attitudes, make them larger than life and supporting them with elaborate gesturing, in order to make them more salient. Infamous examples are Mussolini and Hitler, as caricatured by Charlie Chaplin in *The Great Dictator*. Hitler also put up a display of near frenzy when addressing big crowds. A modern variant can be seen in the performances of pop stars, though spreading frenzy there appears to be more of an objective in itself.

Energy and clear intent are part of charismatic leadership, energizing and steering follow-ers. In an organization, this implies a direct confrontation with the members. Charismatic leadership then represents a classic, up-front approach to leadership. This approach is char-acterized by much repetition: displaying the positions one wants to display, time after time, in all relevant situations. It also involves advertising a strong moral stance: I act as I do because this is the best way to act. However, what is the best way to act? This is the line of action that maximally furthers the *raison d'être* of the organization, its mission, in a morally sound way.

An important instrument here is a convincing story (Postman, 1999), preferably one with catchy metaphors, acting as a self-fulfilling reality and indicating action guidelines. So good leaders are more than averagely successful storytellers, casting themselves as protagonists. A good mission must also apply to the longer term and picture a destiny worth taking risks for. When a mission is well embedded in the organization's history, it gains an extra sense of logic and self-evidence. Furthermore, it should provide a visual component – as the word 'vision' already implies – as well as a feeling of adventure and challenge. Moreover, the success of a mission is partly a function of its novelty, triggering curiosity and creativity. A good mission lastly leaves enough room for personal interpretation, adaptation and transformation, is flexible enough to be applicable in a changing environment and allows for a choice to take it or leave it.

Essentially, championing a mission is an incremental approach, a serial, remedial and fragmented process, which takes a great deal of effort and stamina. Essentially, this is the task of the leader. In everyday practice this *toujours frapper*, as the French call it – keep on pushing, in English – boils down to the rules of thumb in the following sections. Though the rules given are intended for leaders, they also apply to consultants and all other change agents.

BEING AWARE OF YOURSELF

- Study yourself hard, maybe not as hard as Gandhi did (Nair, 1998), but ensure that you make time for some self-reflection.

This self-study concerns both our motives and the attitudes that we, knowingly and un-knowingly, assume. Studying our motives and attitudes may be done in different ways. It may involve a daily routine of questioning the motives for our actions and objectives, each morning before work for example, which then boils down to inner dialogue. A similar approach when a new project or plan is at stake is explicitly to make time to examine our motives and attitudes concerning that project or plan. This may, for example, consist of taking a walk to have a longer inner dialogue (see Chapter 8). Also we may spend some time in front of the mirror and play with our attitudes (see Chapter 8). To study our attitudes, we can also consult the people who know us best and can be fully trusted. This may be our partner, a parent, our child, a good friend or a trusted colleague, or also a professional coach. What impression do our attitudes make on them? What can they say about our motives?

- Don't fall into role playing, not even when you are developing your attitudes. Don't force yourself to assume attitudes that are completely incompatible with who you are.

When we are developing our attitudes, they still remain our own. We may play with them, by all means, but we should also remain true to ourselves. What is interesting, though, is that we can display many more different attitudes, and experience the accompanying mindsets, than we may have expected. So we can display radiant optimism, trust, decisiveness, passion and hope, as well as despair, indifference, reticence and reluctance, even though we usually exhibit quite different attitudes. The important point here is that we must display these attitudes in our own way, even though that may take some exercise and practice.

- Be aware of your modeling role. Do it your way, but know that you are fully responsible for what you are displaying.

We are not allowed to do just anything only because we want to do it. We are not God. We must think about what we may and may not do. A leader or an change agent who defies these limitations can have a devastating effect on his employees. Such a leader will either radically undermine employees' feelings of safety in a way that this badly affects their effectiveness (see Chapter 4) or evoke similar untoward behavior from them, or both. These limitations may imply some infringement on our personal freedom, but that goes with the territory. If this infringement is hard for us, this may be a good occasion to examine our motives somewhat more. If that is too hard, thinking about another occupation may be an option. All in all, we must learn to be at ease with the limitations of the freedom stemming from our leadership.

- Fully connect yourself with what you are doing and consequently be undivided in your attitude.

First, this rule implies that we should display our attitudes with sufficient energy. Having sufficient energy at our disposal involves – among other things – taking care of your health (sufficient rest, sufficient exercise, eating healthily, not too much coffee and alcohol, no smoking, no recreational drugs, living a well-balanced life). Essentially, all of this boils down to proper self-management.

A second issue here is staying focused and involved. This happens all by itself when we really want to do what it takes and are interested in what we are busy with. If staying focused and involved is less self-evident, this again is a matter of self-examination and reflection. Why are we so easily distracted? What makes it so hard to focus? Sometimes, it can be useful to apply a form of self-suggestion. Let the attitude we want to display sink in by giving ourselves an assignment to that effect in a state of mental quiet.

Another point in this respect is our consistency. Consistency is also a matter of reflection. Are we fully consistent? What causes a possible inconsistency? How can this be solved? More seriously, are we completely honest? In general, lying is very dysfunctional: do not ever lie (Hammer, 2001)! Being caught lying undermines not only our leadership in a big way, but also our self-esteem (Branden, 1987) and with that our effectiveness and well-being.

The point of all this is that being undivided in our attitude directly concerns our strength as a sender of situational proposals, and may make the difference between being followed and not being followed. Being divided also negatively affects our credibility.

- Don't block experience: make it a point to experience everything that is relevant and don't suppress feelings of aversion, intuitions and hunches.

Often it is very tempting to subdue our feelings and hunches, especially when they are less than pleasant. Though subduing them is sometimes the simplest, and even the best, way to handle things, there can be important drawbacks. Subduing our feelings and hunches habitually leads to a state of alienation, which may result in damage to our well-being and health. Moreover, subduing feelings of aversion deprives us of important information: such feelings are often acute signals that something is wrong. By ignoring these signals, we considerably decrease the effectiveness of our functioning (Schabracq & Cooper, 2003).

The previous rule must be even extended somewhat, namely: Actively explore your feelings and reflect on these feelings on a regular basis. Overcome your apathy to do so.

The idea behind this rule is that reflecting on our feelings teaches us about our suppositions and assumptions. This active exploration is a matter of inquiring into the causes of our mood: why we feel angry, sad and so on. Answers will then pop up sooner or later. These answers then may give rise to further questioning. This is not to say that we will always like the answers. They may concern sources of frustration, dealing with uncertainty or our need to be liked. We have to learn to tolerate the feelings stemming from this. Only when we are able to cope with these feelings can we do something about the factors that evoked them. Other items that may have a role here are dealing with exaggerated admiration and ascribed stardom (see Chapter 4) as well as with our vulnerabilities: though we might wish otherwise, we are far from invulnerable, yet at the same time it is important not to be paralyzed by that knowledge (Lencioni, 1998).

PREVENTING AND DEALING WITH STRESS

• Plan and evaluate your day.

To deal with our own stress, it helps to start the day by briefly thinking about what we are going to do and what is pleasant about it. In addition, we can systematically insert pleasant activities as well as shorter and longer pauses, and intentionally use traveling time and waiting periods (for example in elevators and between tasks) as pauses to calm down and think things over. When the work is finished, when we go home for example, we can determine what we actually accomplished during our working day and 'celebrate' these accomplishments. In this way, we compensate for our tendency to dwell on what did not go well and what still has to be done.

• Monitor your stress reactions, determine and do something about their causes.

In addition, we can systematically monitor our different body parts to check for the presence of tension in them. We can relax tense body parts and loosen them up by moving them – like a boxer with his neck by shaking his head before a fight. We also can breathe 'through' these body parts; that is, by inhaling deeply and imagining that all the energy involved goes through the body parts in question in a nice and comforting way. In addition, we can 'think of nothing in particular' (see Chapter 6). What evokes this tension? We can draw up a top five of its sources. Subsequently, we can reflect on these stressors and come up with better ways to deal with them. We can use thinking of nothing in particular also in a more systematic way, to periodically relax and rejuvenate ourselves.

• Generate sufficient social support.

Another way to prevent stress is to generate sufficient social support. We can find out how to make contacts with customers, colleagues and bosses more pleasant and rewarding. It is a well-known fact that sufficient social support of the right kind is an important way to prevent and counteract stress. Being given the wrong kind of social support is being treated as a weak, dependent and essentially immature person. Of course, generating social support is not only a matter of getting support, such as actual help, care, protection, information and personal attention. Giving social support ourselves is one of the best ways of generating social support in the longer term.

• Guard the balance between your work and private life.

Guarding the balance between our work and private life is still another way to prevent stress. Apart from spending sufficient time and attention on the rest of our life (our relationships, leisure time, public involvement, general knowledge and philosophy of life), guarding the balance between our work and private life also means paying so much attention to these matters that they really get an existence of their own.

• Take enough exercise.

Lastly, stress can be effectively counteracted by taking enough exercise. Running, swimming, cycling and walking are good ways to do this.

STEERING AND BEING AWARE OF WHAT IS HAPPENING

• Prepare your actions, know what you want to do and where you want to go next.

To be effective as a leader, we always must be prepared before actually undertaking an action of any significance. Being prepared involves the exploration of options and difficulties, planning, and securing the necessary resources and support in advance. Just rushing into things is asking for trouble. We should know exactly why we are doing something, where we are going and what we can expect to find there. In this way, we can also prevent needless stress. The next step then consists of actually undertaking the action in a wholehearted and undivided way, and knowing already precisely what we want to do next if we are successful. In order to be successful, it is also necessary to know what the other parties want to do, why they want to do that and who will support them. All this preparation is concerned with acquiring overview and vision, which are essential elements of leadership. This overview is not a magic quality, but only the outcome of paying attention to the right things, which actually is the outcome of a learning process. All of this may sound like a collection of truisms – and maybe it is – but it is a fact of life that by far the majority of people in leadership positions do not live up to these truisms. As it is, I derived them from Sun Tzu, a Chinese strategist from the fifth century BC (see Sun Tzu, 1993).

• Don't change too much at a time. See to it that all change can be labeled with one concept (Hammer, 2001).

In Chapter 1 I explained that it is an essence of culture to keep things the same and to provide stability. People need stability to function effectively. Consequently, changes that are too extensive tend to upset human functioning. Too many changes at once may jeopardize the functioning of the whole organization. In order to avoid doing this, it is only logical to implement changes in a well-measured way. The provision that all change can be labeled with one concept is intended to structure the change process, to simplify it and also to demonstrate the impression that there is really only one change going on, the success of which can be easily monitored by applying only one overall criterion.

• Don't do the work of your employees, not even when they do it badly. Just provide clear direction.

Leading is a task in itself and needs all the attention we can mobilize. The task involves having oversight over the organization and its environment, developing a vision, initiating activity, making sure that everybody does what they are supposed to do, monitoring the progress of everything and following up its outcomes. Essentially, appropriate leadership is such an extensive task that it does not leave any room for helping out employees who do not meet their targets. Helping out will simply be at the expense of our own tasks. Moreover, helping out employees sends the wrong signal to those involved: essentially, they should solve the problem themselves. If, after all, it turns out that meeting their targets is an impossible assignment, we can assign somebody else to help. Even then we should resist the temptation to help out personally, in spite of the fact that this may seem the nicer and even more natural thing to do.

• Stress common interests.

Leading an organization also consists of balancing the interests of the different individual employees, the different departments and the overall organization. Usually, individuals and departments look after their own interests. If they do not, it may be the leader's task to step in and to protect these interests. However, the primary leadership task here is to balance individual and group interests in such a way that the organization as a whole benefits the most, but still so that the interests of individual parties are not neglected. Essentially, the leader is the one who primarily is responsible for guarding the interest of the overall organization. Emphasizing the interest of the overall organization is an important task, as individual departments tend to go for their own goals and often are rather shortsighted when the overall interest is at stake. It can thus be recommended that a leader speak now and then in terms of 'we' and 'our'.

• Define and advertise your goals and mission in clear and positive, general and generic terms.

Leaders should always be clear about what they want and stand for. The easiest and most logical way to do this is to communicate clear goals and a clear mission, in which the culture change is strongly anchored. The goals and the mission can give then clear guidelines to everybody involved. To emphasize the importance of these goals, we can show a vision of what will happen when these goals are fully accomplished (see Chapter 6). In addition, we can make the most of what would happen if these goals were not accomplished. Both techniques should be repeated time after time, but with different wording. In this way a sense of urgency can be created. Something similar should be done with the mission, though this is more of a general guideline and less of a clear target to be accomplished. Awareness of the mission is built into the organization by advocacy, as well as by questioning, challenging and probing (Senge *et al.*, 1994). The same can be accomplished by making what we do into a symbol of the mission and advertising that. We can do that too by showing that we use the mission as an explicit guideline and touchstone in our decision making, as well as in the selection of new personnel.

• Support and reward what adds to the change.

Many managers are inclined to respond only to what does not go well: they limit themselves to correcting and punishing. Though, when they are needed, correcting and punishing are a legitimate part of managing that no manager should avoid, exclusively correcting and punishing can be very damaging to employees' motivation. The only attention the employees then get is negative, and this may feel to them as if they only make mistakes. For that reason, it is important to consistently reward things that go well, especially when they contribute to the intended change. Moreover, learning psychology teaches us that rewarded behavior tends to be repeated. Rewarding and supporting the intended behavior thus will actually strengthen and stabilize the intended change. So acknowledge well-focused industry and toil, show sympathy and give tokens of appreciation. In more general terms: celebrate and feed success, and starve failure.

• Make clear that there are different ways to accomplish the intended change.

Acknowledge that accomplishing the mission is no linear process and that different approaches are feasible: let people find out themselves what the mission implies for them and make enough room to discuss this in progress meetings. Letting people find out themselves what they can do can involve asking questions as well.

• Ask questions.

When too much correcting and punishing is to be avoided, asking questions can be a good alternative, at least if it is done in time. This implies that the leader introduces and monitors everything that is going on and from time to time has talks about progress. Besides just asking how things are going – which by the way is a very good question to ask regularly (see Chapter 6) – this is also about discussing problems and solutions:

• What is the most difficult point right now?
• How are you dealing with that?
• How can you do that better?
• How can you do that in a more innovative way?
• How can you do that in a more satisfying way?

Another technique that can be used here is Klein's 'premortem' technique (Klein, 2003). This consists of imagining that a project goes bust, then discussing what the main reasons were for it going wrong and how we could have prevented it. Asking questions does not imply at all that we ourselves must have all the answers. Asking questions explicitly also ensures that we explore new territory.

Asking questions is also the preferred technique in the case of resistance. Fighting resistance has proven to be completely counterproductive. Instead asking the right questions – 'I see you are not happy with that. Can you please tell me what would be better for you?' 'What is the problem here?' 'OK, if you were in charge, what would you do?' and so on – is a much better approach.

• Give protagonists of the intended change enough room and authority.

Protagonists of the intended change by definition are your allies. It is only logical to put them in positions where they can help you most; that is, if they are good enough to do the job well. Putting allies in the right positions implies that you should – if appropriate – put them in key positions, in positions where they can further change the most. One of the ways to accomplish that is to make them responsible for the model projects you initiate to further the change mission. When such a project is successful, it is important to consolidate that success by anchoring it firmly in the organizational cycle (Kotter, 1996).

• Take ample time to reflect on how you are doing and how you can improve things.

When you are very busy bringing about all kinds of changes, you are perceiving things from an internal perspective. In itself this is good, but it is not enough, because you must from time to time look at things also from an external point of view. This is both true at the individual level and at the group or organization level: some reflection is indispensable. Techniques and exercises to that effect are discussed in Chapters 6 and 8. It is also advisable to reserve from time to time a longer period to think things over, for example in the form of a long walk (see Chapter 8). The errors you undoubtedly will make are issues for reflection as well. Errors should not be perceived as annoying or disastrous, but rather as excellent learning material. So find out what exactly went wrong, why it went wrong and how the errors in question could have been prevented. In short: learn from your errors.

Essentially this is all about a direct approach, following what seems to be the shortest way. It is for example in line with the list of leaders' characteristics from the *Field Manual of the US Army* (McNeilly, 2001). This list consists of the following concepts:

- integrity
- will
- flexibility
- endurance
- coolness under stress
- justice
- assertiveness
- sense of humor
- bearing
- tact
- maturity
- self-discipline
- confidence
- decisiveness
- initiative

However, as Sun Tzu has taught us, the shortest way is not always the best one and is often not even the quickest either, even though direct approaches may be an indispensable element of the overall strategy (McNeilly, 2001). What is meant here is that a frontal approach organizes the attitudes of the people you are confronting: the other people imitate it or assume a complementary attitude. At the least, they subliminally simulate it (see earlier in this chapter). When their attitudes are successfully organized in such a way, this leaves the others exposed to the more indirect approaches that are examined in Chapter 5. A combination of direct and indirect approaches is thus the most likely route to overcoming resistance and preventing conflicts and damage (McNeilly, 2001). Two of these indirect approaches are discussed in the following two chapters.

CHAPTER 4

Mapping and Taking Away Ineffectiveness

Everyday work, like every form of reality, depends on the attention we pay to that work. When we focus our attention on something else, either through our senses or just in our thoughts, the reality of the work stops right there: we occupy ourselves elsewhere. As a result, the work no longer determines our actions, which, of course, negatively affects the effectiveness of our work: to work well, our work must be the exclusive object of our attention for a considerable time, without too many interruptions. The easiest and best way to pay the necessary attention to our work is to do it more or less automatically, at least without having to force ourselves: the work has to engage us as if by itself. To engage us in such a way the work has to meet certain conditions, while at the same time the environment of the work should not provide too much in the way of diversion that will needlessly demand our attention. As far as these conditions are met, the working reality is effective.

We experience functioning in an effective work reality as self-evident. Such functioning is accompanied by a sense of trust and control, feelings we hardly experience as such, though we do experience their absence. The effect is that we experience performing the task at hand as the only possible reality at that moment. William James (1890/1950) speaks in a comparable context about faith; that is, faith in the reality of what occupies us (see also Chapter 3).

THE REALITY OF EVERYDAY WORKING LIFE: STABILITY AND CHANGE

As discussed in Chapter 3, and in the section about resistance against change, the reality of our everyday work life provides us with important outcomes, which turn that reality into quite an addictive comfort zone. We also have invested a lot in bringing about and keeping up this reality: it took effort to acquire the necessary skills; it involved, and still involves, a lot of highly repetitive work; and it demands the strict discipline of our attention. As a result, we tend to perceive this comfort zone as something of our own, a part of our identity, and a self-evident part at that. Consequently, we experience pressure to change these adaptations as an infraction, certainly when such a change is forced on us from the outside. Such pressure may evoke all kinds of unpleasant emotions, which we prefer to prevent and avoid. Moreover, we do know our present outcomes, but we do not know what outcomes the future holds for us.

Though we experience this comfort zone as private, and even as a part of ourselves, the comfort zone is a part of culture as well. In fact, we share the unpleasant emotions and concerns evoked by impending change with many of our colleagues. These shared concerns, and the emotions triggered by them, often turn our attempts to hold on to our comfort zones in the organization into a collective undertaking: it feels only logical to support each other in this respect. The mutual support can make the collective resistance to fight off change surprisingly effective and well coordinated (see Chapter 1). This resistance even occurs when it concerns changes for the best; that is, as seen from an outside perspective. The collective fighting off of change is of course not particularly surprising. When we define a culture as a repertory of standard solutions to standard problems, it is only logical that cultures strive for stability and continuity (see Chapter 1). Only as far as a culture accomplishes this objective can it provide reality and normality to its members.

Fighting off change involves collectively taking refuge in the shared organizational reality, as well as identifying with its 'unspeakables', 'undoables', standard explanations and standard solutions (see Chapter 1). Regardless of the validity of these 'unspeakables', 'undoables', standard explanations and standard solutions, they turn out to be components of a seamless reality, because the members of the organization are convinced that they are valid. The reality forged in this way provides a solid base for fighting off impending changes (see also Chapter 1).

To the change agents involved, clinging to what they see as a bunch of unwarranted and invalid ideas often looks weird, if not completely disturbed. In their eyes, the employees are acting like little children. However, seeing and treating the employees as little children, or disturbed people, doesn't make it any easier to convince them. Treating them in such a way only helps to start up a conflict with them, with all the emotions that involves, followed by the employees' refusal of all communication. In such a way, the organizational culture can successfully stall the intended change or stop it altogether. What exactly will happen, of course, depends on the power base of the change agents. If that power base proves to be sufficient, the change will be brought about anyhow, much to the employees' dislike. They have lost, apparently betrayed by their colleagues and managers. Such a course of events can have serious and long-lasting negative effects on the effectiveness of the employees' functioning, as well as on their well-being and health.

Though it is only natural for cultures to fight change, this resistance can be a deadly course, because it can interfere with their adaptation to changes in the outside environment. As it is, the occurrence of change there has increased in an unprecedented way and still is increasing, at an accelerating pace (as we saw in Chapter 1).

As a result, many companies have only one option, namely to adapt to the changing environment as quickly and radically as they can. Adapting here means attuning to the demands of customers, making use of state-of-the-art technology and applying other ways of organizing and working. All these options boil down to more or less radical changes in the employees' reality of their everyday work life. Adapting to these changes requires new skills and knowledge, which in their turn demand permanent re-education and new ways of training and learning. Though this kind of change of course does not occur to the same degree in all organizations, employees everywhere are confronted more and more with changes that they did not ask for.

All these changes must be integrated into our everyday behavior in a manageable and effective way. One can – with some right – state that such an adaptation is a sheer perversion of our culture. After all, is it not the main objective of a culture to provide standard solutions to standard problems? Though such a statement may feel right and justified, it is not particularly helpful in adapting to these changes. Moreover, humankind has a long track record of adapting and it makes no sense to be overly pessimistic up front.

Still, if adapting implies changes in our work, it will set back the effectiveness of our functioning. Even when we are able to adapt to such changes, it does take time. Too much change in our work in too little time is thus a crucial factor in the effectiveness of our functioning. That is why a checklist of some of these changes is presented here. What changes have occurred to you? And how have you been affected by them?

Checklist 4.1 Changes affecting effective functioning

	Yes
Reorganization(s)	...
Merger(s)	...
Outsourcing	...
Changes in the legal-political external environment	...
Implementation of new technology and computer hardware	...
Highly competitive outside environment	...
Job change	...
Implementation of new computer programs	...
A different organizational policy that is of influence on your work	...
Quickly changing management	...
A new manager, doing things differently and stressing other things	...

WORK AND WORK ENVIRONMENT: THE MIDDLE ZONE

The degree to which we can believe in our everyday reality of work, and by that the degree to which that reality can be effective, depends on three factors: the work itself, the work environment and ourselves.

Effective work is a matter of the challenge that the work demands: the challenge should be neither too little nor too much, because effective functioning only takes place in a kind of 'middle region'. Something similar applies to an effective work environment. Here such middle regions play a role as well, though several variables are involved. Here too, 'too much' or 'too little' of a variable implies a lower level of effectiveness. Taking 'task challenge' as an example, it is obvious that we can't perform a task that is too challenging; that is, too difficult, too extensive and so on. On the other hand, a task that challenges us too little causes problems in the longer run too. We get bored, our attention is diverted and so on. However, the right degree of challenge, the middle region – the nature of which of course varies with each individual – makes it possible to function effectively.

We can consider this middle region as an illustration of a very old and widespread ethical concept, namely 'the narrow path of virtue' or 'the golden mean', a central concept in the thinking of Aristotle and Christian philosophy, as well as in classical Chinese philosophy. Wasn't China the empire of the middle?

Regarding the work environment, four variables are discussed here. The middle region of each of these variables is a necessary condition for an effective work environment. These conditions are probably indispensable for every kind of reality. The variables are derived from the work of Salomon Asch (1971). Asch incidentally formulated these conditions for the reality of hypnotic trance, with the distinct purpose to prove that such a trance really is a very common phenomenon. We here discuss the following conditions, which now and then overlap somewhat:

- orderliness
- social embedding
- compatibility of values and goals
- safety

THE WORK ITSELF

Our work is organized functionally and effectively to the degree that it is easy to keep our attention on it. Put differently: our work must be challenging enough, while at the same time we must be able to handle the challenge. As discussed before, handling the challenge well is a matter of a golden mean, and where this mean is located is strongly individually determined.

Work that Implies Insufficient Challenge

When work does not challenge us sufficiently to hold our attention although we still have to perform it, we have to switch over to another kind of attention: we have to force ourselves to keep our mind on our work. Such a forced form of attention soon becomes very tiring. We can only go on this way for a limited period. Then our attention is diverted, we become strangely sleepy, we have to yawn and it gets more and more difficult to do the work. This makes us less effective. Several causes of insufficient challenge are discussed here.

Too Few Activities to Fill the Time

For many people, having insufficient activities to fill the time in a work situation, while not being allowed to leave either, is intensely unpleasant. Too little to do is the stuff of which imprisonment is made. The same goes for too slow a work pace. In the longer run, we become drowsy, we get bored and have difficulty concentrating on the little work we have to do. We become less effective and chances are that we are going to make more mistakes. Social contacts often play a crucial part here in keeping us focused and effective.

Lack of Demands

Older employees often find themselves in, or have steered themselves into, situations where no one expects a great deal of them and they reflect that in their attitude. In addition, younger managers often do not stress older employees' responsibilities, even when those employees' performance becomes less than acceptable. The due respect for these elderly employees, who have won their spurs in the organization a long time ago, often makes it hard for a manager to treat them in the same way as they do younger employees. Correcting these older employees may evoke feelings of uneasiness and guilt. As a result, the older employees hardly feel any demands, which makes good performance less meaningful.

Work with Insufficient Meaning

Work without much meaning appeals insufficiently to our talents and motives. The effect is that it is hard to keep our mind on the task's execution, which makes us ineffective. Insufficient meaning can have different causes. Some tasks have very little variation and consist of infinitely repeating short episodes. Examples are assembly tasks at a conveyor belt (such as assembling one simple, tiny part), working at a counter selling tickets or at a call centre. In the last two examples the personal contact involved may still appeal to us somewhat. Often such tasks are quite easy, which is not good for concentration either ('Because you really can do this work when you are almost sleeping, I have been thinking whether someone like you may make something out of that idea'). The lack of meaning can also stem from the remoteness of the task's contribution to the final product ('I see to it that these little things here are in the correct position when they enter the machine over there').

Too Little Decision Latitude

Some tasks are so regulated that there is no freedom to influence the course of affairs in any way ourselves. Everything – breaks, the sequence of partial tasks, work pace and so on – is fixed. This lack of freedom occurs for example at counters or call centers, as well as when our work links us up to some machine or assembly line that we cannot influence.

Often such work is strictly supervised as well, with or without the help of electronic devices. For example, some cash registers produce receipts that do not only show the stuff paid for, the prices and the final sum, but also the number of seconds it took the cashier to execute the whole transaction. Together with the date, the time of day and the cashier's number, this small slip of paper becomes legal evidence of the cashier's performance. Moreover, strict supervision can also interfere with the possibility of social contact during the work. Because strict supervision usually is characteristic of tasks that also fit under the heading 'tasks with insufficient meaning', it becomes obvious that this kind of work, when things do not go so well, can make us highly ineffective.

Moreover, tasks with little meaning and decision latitude as well as monotony and repetition often have to be done in large quantities and at a fast pace. As a result, these tasks also can be too challenging.

Very Formalized Work

In some organizations, the way tasks are performed becomes more important than their results and outcomes. The task then turns into painstakingly sticking to time-consuming formal procedures, checks and double checks, a ritual way of working, capitalizing on following conventions without paying attention to, or even disdaining, outcomes and

results. The task itself may become empty and devoid of meaning. To get anything done
is almost impossible: too many rules, too much hierarchy, too many people who have to
approve first, too long communication lines. This degree of formalization may make it
hard, if not impossible, to keep our attention focused on the task. This formalized work
occurs frequently in big bureaucratic organizations, such as ministries and other public and
semi-public organizations, but also in big companies and other organizations with a strict
hierarchy, such as (para)military organizations and some churches.

Checklist 4.2 Too little challenge in your work

	Yes
Too few activities to fill your time	...
Too few job demands	...
Too easy tasks	...
Meaningless tasks	...
Irrelevant tasks	...
Work that demands much less knowledge and skill than it used to do	...
Too much repetition	...
Too little variation in tasks	...
Works in which painstakingly sticking to formal procedures is more important than outcomes	...

Tasks that Imply Too Much Challenge

Work can also demand a level of challenge that is too far beyond our competence. Either
everything happens too quickly and we cannot keep up with it, or the task gradually
becomes too complicated for us and demands more knowledge, skills and abilities than we
can mobilize. We then start to make mistakes. We are not able any longer to deal with the
task in a systematic way or survey things properly. We experience mental chaos and task
performance breaks down. When we still have to perform our task, we become completely
ineffective. The following issues can play a part.

Too Many Things to Do in Too Little Time

Doing things at high speed can be very pleasurable, especially when everything goes well.
In this sense, deadlines can be pleasant challenges. We can surprise ourselves, be proud of
our accomplishment and enjoy relaxing afterwards – if everything goes well. It becomes a
different story when things are not going well, for example if we:

• are not in the mood
• are angry about the way in which our manager allocated the work to us
• are tired
• cannot keep our mind on our work
• feel that we are not really doing very well

When on such an occasion the deadline is difficult to meet, it becomes harder to work
ourselves up to it. In general, deadlines should not be too hard nor too numerous. However,

the concept of 'just-in-time' management has increased the number of hard deadlines in all kinds of work. 'Just-in-time' management is based on the idea that things should be ready or available just in time, not too late and not too early. This prevents stocks of materials, half-products and completed products from piling up, getting in the way and demanding extra storage room while they are not generating any returns.

Tasks that Are Too Difficult

Difficult tasks that we can only just handle have similar effects to those mentioned above, in a positive as well as a negative sense. It is a different scenario, however, when some parts of the work are already too difficult to begin with, due to the fact that we lack the necessary experience or training, for example in the case of new tasks. We then make a lot of errors and task performance becomes chaotic. Attempts to repair the mistakes take time and are not always successful. We can then try to work around the problems and get some of the work done anyway, if that is at all possible. Things become especially annoying when the tasks that we are finding difficult used to be relatively straightforward. An example is a new word processor or other computer program that we are not used to and where commands for all kinds of familiar tasks are almost, or completely, opposite to those of the former program.

Serious Consequences

The challenge presented by a specific task becomes greater in proportion to the degree that the consequences of doing it wrongly become more serious, for example when we have to take decisions that have serious consequences for different parties. In the latter case, this difficulty does not need to be only a matter of mistakes. As it is, often we simply do not have all the necessary information. Still, we do not want others to suffer from this and we want to do everything correctly, which is impossible. This dilemma becomes even more acute when a choice is involved about where the burden of a certain development is to be laid (see under 'Incompatible responsibilities' below). Because of the fact that organizations have become flatter and more responsibility has been pushed down to the shop floor, people who were used to doing what the boss said now have to take such decisions themselves. For these people, having this level of discretion to take such decisions can make their work more challenging than they like it to be.

Ambiguities

In many jobs, it is not completely obvious what is expected of us. The challenge then is to do well anyway. When the ambiguities are too great or when we take them too seriously, it is much harder to carry out the task effectively. Ambiguity can take many forms. Sometimes the goals of the task are unclear: 'I more or less manage things around here.' Sometimes it is the way in which the goals have to be attained: 'How you do it doesn't interest me much. I don't even want to know, as long as you do it.' Sometimes also it is a matter of insufficient feedback: 'Did it work out?' 'We'll know more in five years.' Other issues that can affect our effectiveness are a lack of clarity of responsibilities ('I think you should take this up with Peterson.' 'No Johnson, I must have you'), appointments ('I told you it would be soon'), criteria for performances and quality ('You meant something like this?') and so on.

Too Many Divergent Responsibilities

When a task brings too many divergent responsibilities, the result may be a decrease in effectiveness too. To begin with, such a task demands that we mentally change gear a lot concerning both problems and people. Such a task also means that we are doing very different things, have to keep many loose ends in our heads and are never ready, because each time, as if by itself, the next responsibility emerges. Consequentially, we cannot really relax and recover. Furthermore, the ways in which we deal with the different responsibilities may interfere with each other from time to time, for example when the timely completion of the one makes the timely completion of the other impossible and vice versa.

Incompatible Responsibilities

A special case of divergent responsibilities is role conflict or incompatible responsibilities. A familiar example is the position of the lower or middle manager. When such persons please their superior by increasing production, they may evoke a conflict with the department's employees. This conflict is not only a matter of employees not wanting to work harder, but they also may see their manager as the advocate of their interests. However, when our poor lower or middle managers take on such a role, they risk a conflict with their management. The dilemma is obvious: what is good in the eyes of one party is wrong in the other party's and vice versa. Though a completely perfect and correct task performance, to the full satisfaction of both parties, will always be problematic, the managers in question have still been hired to do as good a job as they can.

Checklist 4.3 Too much task challenge

	Yes
Working under continuous time pressure	
Too many deadlines	...
Too much overtime	...
Being understaffed	...
Too difficult tasks	...
Too many decisions	...
Having to work too fast	
Too many responsibilities	...
Incompatible responsibilities	...
Tasks that disturb each other	...
Work in which you always have to be on your toes	...
Work that you never can do completely right	...
Work that demands creativity when you cannot deliver it	...
Lots of demands for immediate action	...
Insufficient feedback on the results and outcomes of your work	...
Unclear criteria for performance and quality	...
Having to keep in mind too many instances of unfinished business	...

THE WORK ENVIRONMENT: ORDERLINESS

The orderliness of the work environment has a physical component as well as a behavioral or procedural one. Both components have to be 'in order'. That means that both should be arranged in a way that makes them effective; that is, contributing optimally to the goal attainment inherent in our work. To that end, the environment should facilitate our work and be relatively free of irrelevant elements that demand attention and interfere with task performance. Being in order implies also that the work environment should be relatively constant and stable, so that we get the chance to become fully familiar with it and optimally attune to it. Too much change, on the other hand, can seriously diminish this orderliness and occasionally might give rise to a counter-reaction that in a forced way leads to too much orderliness. Of course, there are significant individual differences in the degree of orderliness.

The physical component of orderliness of our work environment involves its architecture and interior design, as well as the available furniture, machinery and other equipment. Preferably, all equipment is accessible and in the right places, including provisions to prevent disturbances, ideally in a way that meets the priorities inherent in the task, so that we at all times can do automatically what needs to be done, even when something goes wrong. When something breaks down it should be repaired or replaced, so that all equipment is in working order. In addition, it must be well maintained and clean. Maintenance and cleaning imply that we actively and habitually have to reinstitute the order of the work environment: this order has to be reconstructed and tidied, time after time.

Physical orderliness is often accentuated somewhat by emphasizing and marking distinctions and relationships (Ashcraft & Scheflen, 1976; Kaplan & Kaplan, 1982). An example is grouping objects that belong together. Moreover, we can mark objects that belong together by giving them a common background, color and label, and by enclosing them in some frame that functions as a visual border. We can also provide kindred objects with another marker such as a text, lines, thresholds, arrows, pictograms, special materials, special lettering and so on. With the help of these artifacts, we can highlight certain borders and points that need our special attention.

This kind of orderliness helps us to keep our environment easy to scan and survey, by providing us with clear 'set points' of what is normal (Frijda, 1986). This orderliness facilitates the automatic intermittent scanning of the task environment for possible intrusions and disturbances, because intrusions and disturbances stand out more in this way. This effect is probably also one of the reasons tidying and cleaning can have such a pleasant centering effect: once finished, we have apparently tamed all irregularities and disturbances.

Such a stylized display of orderliness suggests that our environment is ruled by a well-considered purpose, the outcome of a plan that takes care of everything: apparently, everything goes as it is meant to go, for things are not supposed to be in this kind of order by themselves. Such a display suggests the kind of control that excludes surprises. Many organizations even go further and have designed everything in their company style, in their own colors and with their logo on all kinds of objects, to make sure that nobody forgets which club is running things here. Here too the message is clear: everything goes as it is meant to go and we are on top of things.

As an orderly work environment draws no special attention, we hardly notice it. We can thus 'blindly' proceed with our tasks. Though every working environment needs some orderliness, it is logical to assume that especially difficult and complex tasks, as well as tasks with many unpredictable elements, profit most from an orderly and stable environment, because these tasks demand more of our undivided attention.

Overall, this physical layout should provide good physical work conditions, in the sense of lighting, sound, temperature, seating comfort, effort in using the equipment, air quality and so on.

The relationship between the physical environment and our habitual behavior is of a dialectical nature, in the sense that the way in which we design our environment and how we behave mutually determine each other. So the way our workplace is designed very much determines how we walk, where we sit, as well as what we see, hear and feel (see Chapter 3). The other way around, we design and furniture our workplace in a way that accommodates our preferred routines. As we saw in Chapter 3, we manufacture normality and everydayness in our life by continuously repeating ourselves and by a strict discipline of attention. As we repeat ourselves in a remarkably strict, more or less ritualized way, our habitual behavior becomes an all-important source of orderliness as well, to ourselves but also to others.

Too Little Orderliness

Too little orderliness may seriously hamper our effectiveness, for example when several issues fight for our attention, making it impossible to attend to a single issue long enough to deal with it properly. In such a situation, we are supposed to keep all loose ends in our head so we can return to them when we get the opportunity later on, while many tracks just stop somewhere. Also, we are exposed to ambiguous and inconsistent cues, which may put us on the wrong track. Furthermore, things around us go wrong, are changed, still do not work and are changed again. We witness some colleagues handling things badly and we step in, or at least are tempted to do so. Some people just love chaos and are very good at handling it. To others, work degenerates into an endless succession of daily hassles (Kanner *et al.*, 1981), which destroys the effectiveness of their functioning.

Too little orderliness can be found in all kinds of professional firms, stock exchanges, dealing rooms of merchant banks, advertising agencies and in the media (television studios and editorial offices). Too little orderliness is often caused by change as well, for example in times of (successive) reorganizations and mergers. In reorganizations and mergers the old rules no longer apply while new ones still have to be developed, which of course implies the breakdown of orderliness. Moreover, in such cases there are all kinds of rumors about changes of jobs and departments, early retirements and layoffs, which easily divert our attention from our work. Too little orderliness may have very diverse causes, which can reinforce each other as well. We discuss some examples below.

Dysfunctional Work Conditions

If a work environment does not provide the right lighting, temperature, auditory and olfactory conditions, as well as the proper furniture and equipment to do the job properly, it interferes with the proper division of attention for the tasks and can disturb the effectiveness of operations. Such an environment can disrupt our well-being and health too. Moreover, it signals that the organization is not in order and does not care much for us. Something similar is the case when we are annoyed by the dirtiness or disarray of our work environment.

Broken or Ill-Functioning Tools and Apparatuses

When a tool or apparatus that we need for our work is functioning poorly or not at all, we can't go on with our task as planned until it is mended. Apart from the fact that this can be very frustrating, can ruin our mood and in the longer run can damage our health too, it obviously disrupts the effectiveness of our functioning.

Flexible Workplace

In order to make maximal use of the available work stations in offices where employees are only present part-time, some organizations use flexible workplaces. Apart from the fact that having to work at a different work station in itself can interfere with orderliness, not all places are equally appealing to everybody and it does happen that all stations are occupied. All of this may interfere with effective functioning.

Flexible Working Hours

Flexible working hours can interfere with the orderliness and effectiveness of our work in several ways. First, our working hours have a variable place in our daily rhythm, which influences our activity and alertness, certainly when we have to get up early. Secondly, flexible working hours can lead to being unable to reach the colleagues and staff we need to interact with to do our job properly. Thirdly, flexible working hours interfere with family life and periodic leisure activities and pastimes. All of this can be become worse when the daily work is divided in parts with 'free' periods in between.

Being a Member of a 'Pool'

Some organizations that place a high value on flexibility organize support staff, such as secretaries, in a pool so that they work for different people in different departments. This arrangement effectively prevents them from building up any thorough knowledge of the specific tasks of each department. Installing such a pool leads to an undesirable annihilation of useful knowledge as well. In practice, working in a pool can even mean that a secretary works every day for somebody else, without much possibility of properly finishing a somewhat extended assignment. Working in a pool also prevents support staff from building appropriate relationships with the people they work for. As a result, they only do the simplest of tasks for different employees, time after time, not using and developing their skills.

A New or Fast-Growing Organization

In a new organization, it is not unusual that everybody does everything. The same occurs in a rapidly growing organization. In both cases there is a lack of structure, standard procedures and specialist, well-trained employees. Consequently, everybody is terribly busy reinventing the wheel, while the pace at which things get done is far from impressive.

High Sick Leave, Staff Turnover or Many Temporary Employees

In an organization with high levels of sick leave, staff turnover or a high proportion of employees on temporary contracts, those employees with longer tenure are often exclusively busy filling holes and putting out the most acute fires in a completely unpredictable and chaotic order. In addition, they have to break in new people and hardly have any time left to do their own work. Moreover, many of the newly trained employees leave after a short time, which makes the efforts of breaking them in no more rewarding and meaningful. All these activities can have a cumulative adverse effect. Moreover, in an organization with high sick leave and staff turnover more things tend to go wrong: high sick leave and staff turnover can be considered a case of voting with one's feet.

Checklist 4.4 Too little orderliness

	Yes
Bad physical work conditions	...
A dirty work environment	...
A messy work environment	...
Being a member of a pool, working for different people or departments	...
Ill-functioning or non-functioning equipment	...
No clear place to work	...
Variable working hours	...
Many things around you going wrong	...
Too many issues in your environment that fight for your attention	...
A new organization	...
A fast-growing organization	...
High absenteeism	...
High staff turnover	...
Having to break in new (temporary) colleagues frequently	...

Too Much Emphasis on Orderliness

Too much orderliness in the work environment means that orderliness demands so much attention that it can obscure the original goal, namely getting the actual task done. Orderliness then turns into a goal in itself. Sticking to time-consuming orderly procedures, with their checks and double checks, leads also to a severe limitation of what we are allowed to do. As a result, it may interfere with work being carried out effectively and efficiently, which manifests itself, for example, in problems of internal and external communication, 'political' relationships, slow decision making and stagnation of projects. These problems present themselves as unchangeable data, ruled by relentless and indifferent natural laws, and are characteristic of bureaucracies.

People working in such organizations develop a good eye for rank, status symbols, movements up and down the hierarchy and the possibilities and dangers that these imply. There is much political jargon, of a somewhat legalistic nature, some difficult words and little concrete content. This is the language of a permanent conspiracy, with its inherent suspicion and fear of outsiders: when too much orderliness makes it impossible to deal with issues in a forthright manner, it has to be done otherwise.

When a outsider asks an employee of a bureaucratic organization – with whom he gets on quite well – a factual question about their work, the outsider often experiences a kind of *praecox Gefühl*, the feeling that it is impossible to make contact and relate. This pre-war term was used as indication that the other person was suffering from 'dementia praecox' or schizophrenia, as it is now called (Grube, 2006).

At the individual level, too much orderliness leads to hiding emotions, denial of problems and conflicts stemming from annoying occasions in the past. Too much orderliness is characterized by a ritual way of working, just going through the motions, following conventions, disapproving ostentatiously of deviations, without paying much attention to – or even disdaining – outcomes and results. Moreover, many colleagues are bored and will not take any risks, afraid as they are to make a bad impression. Nevertheless they want everything to go their way and such a system offers many possibilities for this. Many people, however, eventually cannot stand such a way of working. They complain about a high workload, and many suffer from alienation and aversion. Because deviant moods and activity states are contagious (Hatfield, Cacioppo & Rapson, 1994; Kiritz & Moos, 1981; Meerloo, 1972; Schabracq, 1987, 1991), this may have a serious paralyzing effect.

This condition of too much orderliness is common in big bureaucratic organizations, such as ministries and other public and semi-public organizations, but also in multinational companies and other organizations with a rigid hierarchy, such as military and paramilitary organizations and some churches. The causes are obvious: too many rules and too strict a hierarchy with very precisely delineated communication lines and responsibilities. Such a culture has much to offer to people who want to reach the top, just to obtain power (status, prestige and influence), certainty and, in some cases, money.

Checklist 4.5 Too much emphasis on orderliness

	Yes
Too many regulations	...
Too strict a hierarchy	...
Too rigid job descriptions	...
Too little room to make your own decisions	...
Too strict supervision and monitoring	...
Having to get approval from too many people to get anything done	...
Colleagues who are very afraid to make a bad impression	...
Too precisely delineated communication lines	...
Colleagues who just go through the motions	...
A taboo on displaying emotions	...
Suspicion of strangers	...
Denial of problems	...
Emphasis on conventions	...
Colleagues who do not want to take any risks	...
A very formal way of working	...

THE WORK ENVIRONMENT: SOCIAL EMBEDDING

Work implies social relationships; that is, the relatively stable ways in which specific people relate to each other. The form of relationships is of course determined by their history. For their construction, however, more or less standardized cultural units and formats are used, while their development follows culturally determined scenarios. Within a relationship we know more or less what the other party expects us to do and attend to, as well as what we may expect from the other. As such, relationships are important in bringing repetitiveness and stability into our work environment, which in its turn contributes to orderliness.

First, there are relationships with the people with whom we relate regularly and frequently. These people form our social network. A good network is big enough, extends over different organizational levels and departments and also includes people from outside the organization, such as customers, suppliers, government representatives and colleagues in the same line of work. The network consists mostly of people we more or less trust and like. The main outcome of a network consists of making everyday business manageable. As the interactions in most relationships are often highly repetitive in nature, such relationships give us an opportunity to develop and apply a familiar repertoire of activity for them, in principle to make them as effective and pleasurable as possible. The development of and care for a network thus takes time and effort: to be optimally effective, relationships need history.

As working together means sharing experiences, for the good and for the bad, an important outcome of a social network in an organization is the opportunity for pleasant and meaningful contacts. Moreover, because we are in the same line of work, the chances are that we have similar interests and hobbies and even that we are of like mind, all well-known conditions for getting along well. As a result, some relationships grow out into personal and even intimate ones (Hall, 1969). We find protectors, as well as favorite subordinates, colleagues and people elsewhere with whom it is pleasurable to interact. No wonder that when we lose or quit our job, the loss of these relationships and their outcomes is often felt to be the most unpleasant consequence. The need for such relationships also turns out to be one of the primary reasons for taking on a job again at a later age (Krijnen, 1993).

The pleasant contacts inherent in such relationships can result in emotional support and a general sense of belonging. As such, these relationships can help to reduce tension and aversion. This effect is brought about by entering the different kind of reality of just socializing, a time out from the sterner and more impersonal reality of work. The emotional support and sense of belonging probably are also a matter of exposing ourselves to emotional contagion (Schabracq, 1991); that is, letting ourselves be 'infected' by the other person's pleasant mood and livelihood, a phenomenon that Montaigne described as long ago as in the sixteenth century (Montaigne, 1580/1981).

Apart from pleasurable contacts, belonging to a team or a group can be rewarding in itself. Doing things together and being part of a greater social system, being part of a 'we', can be gratifying in itself. The fact that the others are there as well and do their work too also suggests that there is some meaning and logic to our presence and activities at the work site. Moreover, the other people at the work site usually are familiar to us, which adds to the predictability of our work environment and by that to its orderliness. As it is, unfamiliar people are habitually introduced in such a way that their presence becomes understandable and normal (Goffman, 1971, 1972a): 'This is Joanna, from sales, she will join us today because...'

Another outcome of a good network is that it enables us to get and give strategic information, warnings, advice, factual help, protection and feedback about our own performance and position. A good network also allows us to team up with other employees to fight our battles. All these outcomes make a well-developed social network an important tool for controlling our own work and work environment: the network determines – and is determined by, for that matter – our own informal power position in the organization and the organizational politics. This power position, its direct outcomes and the sense of control resulting from it are of considerable importance in keeping our functioning effective.

All in all, having a well-developed social network at our disposal helps us to develop an optimal freedom of acting, which enables us to focus more or less automatically on our work. Here too, however, when the social network becomes too important and takes too much time, this interferes with the effectiveness of our work.

Being embedded in the organization as a whole can also bring us important outcomes. The embedding gives us, for example, a consistent and continuous background that enables us to experience our being in the organization as normal and real, and also adds to the orderliness of the work environment. The embedding too is a matter of continuous repetition, in this case displaying 'normal' patterns of behavior and keeping up normal appearances, to show that nothing special is going on. Most of the time, this display entails a conduct and appearance that are considered to be normal in the external environment of the organization too, though they are almost imperceptibly styled by the specific organization. By displaying this conduct and appearance, we show how well socialized we are. We demonstrate that we belong there and are true members, who can be trusted not to do anything irresponsible or unexpected. We can actually use the word 'we'.

By styling our behavior and appearance to a certain extent, we also point tacitly to our place and function in the organization, as well as to the kind of relationship we are in at the moment (Vrugt & Schabracq, 1991). This styling involves our body language, linguistic usage, clothing, hairdo and the use of accessories such as glasses, bags and jewelry. Though this styling is not explicitly worded most of the time, a transgression (wrong conduct, wrong clothes or wrong shoes) is usually obvious at once to all parties. By following prescribed conduct, we continuously supply each other, in a completely self-evident way, with the right cues to allow each other to act in a self-evident way as well (Schabracq, 1991).

When something goes wrong, in the production process or in the social realm, we also have available a standard repertoire of ways to repair the normal state of affairs and by that to restore orderliness. For example, when we are slipping we may act in a way as if everything is under control 'really', for example by smiling and pulling a funny face. Other examples are reassuring each other verbally that nothing serious has happened, or by explaining to each other that these things do happen, are nobody's fault and do not undermine the reality of our projects. Goffman presents a wealth of other examples (Goffman, 1971, 1972). In this way, our relationships provide us with a continuous, highly redundant but implicit series of situational or relational propositions about what is expected of us and what we can expect from others (Watzlawick, Beavin & Jackson, 1968). This bombardment with situational and relational proposals is so redundant and omnipresent that it suggests a solid reality, where everything is under control and nasty surprises are excluded. Harré (1979) even speaks of 'social musak' (musak being the music in elevators and supermarkets that is supposed to soothe us into feeling at ease).

Another outcome of being embedded in organizational social relationships is that it serves as a stage. Being embedded in an organization allows us to use our work to show off highly valued work-related qualities, such as professional skill, diligence, collegiality, persistence, a sense of humor, courage and creativity. We even can use the organization as a theater where we can be good in general. The terms 'stage' and 'theater' are not accidental here. An organization offers more distance and privacy than a family, a bigger audience, as well as more off-stage opportunities and time for preparation. We can use our work in this way to develop and demonstrate a beautiful 'public' character of a more general kind. Organizations in general are especially fit for such self-expression. There we can play out our nice and lofty characters, ostentatiously driven by the highest of values, while the risk that our less noble sides are exposed is much smaller than at home. Consequently, we may demonstrate shamelessly our great needs for perfection, helping others, conducting the perfect project, being creative, knowing everything, making it all possible, coming up with the latest developments, being the perfect boss and creating a wonderful atmosphere. All in all, we can project a good image of ourselves, suitable to be commemorated during the official speeches when we celebrate a jubilee or when we leave the organization. This self-expression also may have offshoots in wider circles; at least it is good exercise material.

Too Little Social Embedding

Too little social embedding implies that we must work without some or all of the outcomes of that embedding, such as pleasurable contacts, belonging to a group, a comfortable, informal power position, a solid social reality and a stage to perform on. Without these outcomes, many people find it hard to keep their attention on their working task and become less effective in their work, especially when the task is not very interesting in itself or doesn't have other outcomes that they value highly. Many people, moreover, experience isolation and the anonymity resulting from it as unpleasant. As it is, social relationships are to many people the main reason for coming to work every day.

The sudden partial or complete loss of this embedding can be very painful and often is experienced as a real life event – that is, an event that unsettles our fixed ways of doing things and paying attention – and demands a further adaptation from us. As a result, a loss in this area may interfere with our effective functioning. This may be a matter of our own departure from our department or organization, as well as the disappearance of other people. Such a loss of social embedding may evoke feelings of grief and alienation, just as in the case of the loss of a loved one. Insufficient social embedding and losses in this area may have very diverse causes. We give the following examples.

Lack of Feedback, Appreciation and Support

Many employees get little feedback about their performance, little appreciation for what they do and no support at all from their manager. This lack of feedback, appreciation and support may be a matter of their manager's poor social skills and their being too busy with other things. In many organizations, however, such a lack is part of the culture, as it is routine to give only feedback about things that go wrong. This lack of feedback, appreciation and support may be of negative influence on our motivation and therefore on the effectiveness of our functioning.

Role Transitions

Examples of role transitions in an organization are entry, job change, dismissal, retirement and work disability. Of course, these transitions are very different, as is the degree to which they go together with impairment of functioning. However, in all these cases we have to part from a certain position, its activities and its inherent social relationships. How this parting is experienced varies, depending on the specific nature of the transition, the degree to which it is voluntary and the person involved. It can be experienced as a serious loss, with all the inherent emotions (see for example Allen & van der Vliert, 1984), but can also be felt as a relief. In general, impending transitions interfere with the effectiveness of functioning in the last stage of the old job. In the case of retirement, this last stage may take many years, the phenomenon of 'getting in lane' (Henkens & van Solinge, 2003), characterized by rejecting training programs and letting go. When feelings of loss play a significant role, these feelings can also interfere with effectiveness in a new job or with finding one.

Decay of Social Networks

When elderly employees work in an organization for a long time, their social networks tend to decay. The people who hired them and their patrons and sponsors have left. Gradually, almost all their favorite, familiar colleagues, superiors, assistants and outside contacts also disappear from sight for different reasons: replacement, leaving to join another organization, layoff, accident, retirement and death. This leaves them with an impoverished social network, because they often are not inclined to fill up the empty spaces. Older employees often are more reserved and less outgoing than younger ones in this respect: 'Getting to know people is something that just happens, not something you do' (Winnubst & Schabracq, 1995). This implies that elderly employees must abandon an important part of the outcomes of such a network, which can seriously interfere with their effectiveness.

Massive Layoff

When an organization slims down – which has often happened recently – and lays off or outsources many employees, those who stay behind experience the problems mentioned above to an intensified degree. Moreover, such a course of events can lead to feelings of unpleasantness and guilt for them ('What have we done still to be working here?'). Furthermore, there is a good chance that the people who stay will lose their trust in the organization, especially when it comes to its further intentions ('You ask yourself, will I be next?'). This negatively influences employees' commitment and motivation and, by that, the effectiveness of their functioning. However, this so-called survivors' sickness (Kets de Vries & Balazs, 1997) can also be categorized as a case of too little safety (see Chapter 6).

Physical Barriers that Impede Social Contact

Physical barriers, stemming from the organization of production and the work itself, can cause social isolation. One example is noise, or the protection against noise, which makes it impossible to have a conversation. The lonely position of a crane driver high above his mates on the ground provides another example. A third one is the work cubicle, the crude partitioning device to subdivide a larger room, which has become widely known from the Dilbert comic strips. Especially in simple work – in which personal contacts can actually make an important contribution to work satisfaction – such physical hindrances can make for an often unnecessary disturbance of work satisfaction and motivation.

Communication Problems Between the Top Team and the Shop Floor

Social isolation at the top of the organization is a serious problem. Apart from interfering with the effectiveness of the managers in question, it harms the quality of organizational communication in general. This applies to bottom-up communication ('The management hasn't a clue about what we are doing here and it seems a good idea to keep it that way') as well as top-down communication ('Some things you cannot explain to them, they just don't get it'). Here the quality of leadership and management are at stake.

The causes of communication problems between the top team and the shop floor differ. On the one hand, there is the idea that it is impossible to interact in an open and personal way with employees because of their possible hidden agendas and intentions. Often this is a manager's defense against the greater attention that employees pay to their manager, a point we deal with in the next section. On the other hand, employees tend to feel fearful and unwelcome. Moreover, groups that have incompatible interests often perceive each other in a distorted way and entertain prejudices and stereotypes. Lastly, both parties can usually improve their social skills considerably.

This kind of poor communication and the resulting lack of management negatively affect the effectiveness of everyday working life. Something similar may occur in communication between departments or teams, and this also can disturb effective functioning. When interdependent departments do not communicate well with each other, this can for example lead to unpredictable fluctuations in the work flow of one of them, resulting in all kinds of unexpected temporary task overload and underload.

A Climate of Distrust and Conflicts

A climate of distrust and conflicts results in contacts remaining limited to the few people we trust, so that life becomes rather isolated. We can characterize such a climate also as one with an insufficient sense of safety (see below). A similar outcome may be the consequence of an organization characterized by too much orderliness.

Checklist 4.6 Too Little Social Embedding

	Yes
Impossibility of communication due to noise	...
Physical barriers that hinder social contact	...
A physically isolated work position	...
Loss of key colleagues	...
A climate of distrust	...
A climate of hidden conflicts	...
Being isolated by being much older than your colleagues and executives	...
Being lonely at the top of a department or organization	...
Too little appreciation from your executives	...
Having a manager with poor social skills	...
Poor or too little communication between management and work site	...
Poor or too little communication with other departments	...

Too Much or Undesired Social Embedding

Our social environment can involve all kinds of undesired effects, such as territorial infringements, undesired intimacies and conflicts. As these primarily affect our sense of safety, we deal with these in the section about that specific issue (see below). Here we limit ourselves to some other examples. The mechanism each time is that the social embedding just demands too much conscious attention from us. Our attention to social affairs then is at the expense of attention on performing our real working task properly. We look here at four examples.

Lack of Privacy

A good example of too much and undesired social embedding lies in the unlimited mutual accessibility and lack of privacy in an 'office garden'. Apart from being aggravating and distracting in its own right, this lack of privacy may also lead to self-consciousness, embarrassment and even anxiety about failure. From this perspective, installing Dilbert's cubicles (see above) would be an act of mercy. Essentially, lack of privacy is an issue in every work environment that exposes us too defenselessly to the supervision of our executives, or their electronic devices, and to the perception of others in general. We experience a special case of lack of privacy when we are exposed to stressed and highly emotional colleagues. Under the heading of 'Too much emphasis on orderliness' we already described the way in which deviant activity levels and emotional states can be highly contagious, which is the case here too. As a result, we can be infected with the emotional state of our stressed and highly emotional boss and colleagues, which will disturb the effectiveness of our functioning.

A Culture that Is Too Person Oriented

In some organizational cultures, it is usual to share all life's joys and sorrows, both work-related and private ones. This mutual self-disclosure may easily interfere with the appropriate division of attention needed for work and hamper our effectiveness. This interference especially occurs when the stories are really harrowing, we happen to be very busy, or when failing to pay attention to our colleagues is interpreted as an unkind lack of interest. This frequently happens, for example, in social work and nursing organizations.

Imbalanced Social Exchange: Getting More than We Give

A special kind of imbalanced social exchange results from being a 'star'; that is, getting much more attention than we give. Stars are people who attract a great deal of attention and feeling, sometimes also through the media. As a result, their everyday reality has become much larger than life, while as human beings they are able to cope only with a life of a normal size. For many of them, this dilemma interferes with the manageability of their everyday work situations, especially when they derive their star status from their work. The latter happens primarily when they have come to believe in their extraordinary status, which is more likely to happen when their self-esteem has not been well developed or has been damaged. This variant of imbalance is an important theme in world literature (Greek dramas, Shakespeare and so on) as well as popular media. In spite of the efforts of many religions (or maybe thanks to them, since religions also need their deterrents), 'something for nothing' and 'what happened next' remain themes that stimulate our imagination probably more than the reverse form of exchange imbalance, giving more than we get. We shall deal with the latter form under the heading of 'Too much similarity of values and goals' (see below).

Continuously Changing Social Settings

Having to work all the time in different and changing teams or projects, with different managers and diverse people and with divergent priorities and competencies, can interfere with the effectiveness of our functioning. This interference occurs a lot when we work in a matrix organization or a consulting firm. When we work for a multinational organization, this may also be a matter of working in different countries, with people from diverse cultural and linguistic backgrounds. Getting sufficiently acquainted and becoming more familiar with each other then becomes a necessary but time-consuming enterprise, which may interfere with our actual work tasks. A seemingly simpler variant of this in a relatively stable work environment is getting a new manager.

Checklist 4.7 Too much or undesired social embedding

	Yes
Lack of privacy	...
Too personal a work atmosphere	...
Having to listen too often to private, emotional stories	...
Attracting too much attention and emotion	...
Being continuously exposed to other people	...
Feedback about your performance that is too extensive, too fast or too directive	...
Highly emotional colleagues	...
Stressed colleagues	...
Too much communication with too many people	...
Too many ignorant and incompetent colleagues	...
A new manager who sets different goals and priorities	...

THE WORK ENVIRONMENT: COMPATIBILITY OF CONVICTIONS, VALUES AND GOALS

We have convictions, values and goals, and in a sense the same applies to our organizations. In general, convictions specify how things are and how they come about, while values delineate how things should be and goals designate what you and the organization want to attain. In their verbalized forms, convictions and values can act as guidelines for setting goals and for the actions to accomplish these goals. Broadly speaking, the organization's convictions, values and goals and our own stem from the same pool of social representations (Moscovici, 1984) prevailing in the surrounding societal culture. As long as our personal convictions, values and goals and the organizational ones are compatible, which usually is the case, they jointly determine and shape our everyday work and relationships.

In some cases, however, the organizational convictions, values and goals and our personal ones may differ, in spite of the fact that they originate from the same pool. This is mostly a matter of the priority of their differential relevance and importance. Still, these differences can be so big that they may amount to contradictions at the behavioral level. Such a contradiction then interferes with the optimal division of attention that is needed to act in a self-evident way and therefore with the effectiveness of our functioning. Rather simple examples here are the problems of a teetotal bartender and a vegetarian butcher. A more realistic example is somebody doing a completely innocent job for an problematic organization, for example being a concentration camp's telephone operator.

The fact that both the organization's and our own convictions, values and goals apply also in the surrounding society implies that we share many deeply rooted ideas about what reality is and should be with the other members of that society. Of course, there may be differences of opinion about some matters, but our everyday life would be impossible unless we all took a lot of common assumptions for granted. For example, we all know and agree about what houses, shops, bars, police stations, offices, schools and churches are, as well as what they are for. Also we understand, and mostly respect, social relationships such as marriage and friendship. Furthermore, we habitually use the rule systems that regulate traffic, everyday conversations, work and all kinds of other transactions, and tend to be quite successful at that.

Apparently, we willingly subscribe to the principles that regulate our everyday life. If something goes wrong in this respect, we explain our position by articulating these principles ('I came from the right', 'I was here first', 'That's my wife' and so on) and most of us are quite adept at this. Essentially, these are ethical or moral principles. By explicating these principles, we show that we tacitly assume that they apply to everyone around and also that everyone agrees about them. Most of the time we get an answer that is phrased in terms originating from the same ethical stock, which proves us to be right in those assumptions.

The point here is that all these ethical principles amount to an ethical system that is surprisingly effective in regulating our mutual relationships, at least when we all stick to it. In a sense, we all tacitly know about this ethical system and we have learned to trust it. When we relate to other people, we expect them to behave according to the common rules that the general system supplies for the different situations in which we meet these people. For example, we usually don't expect to be robbed, stabbed or kissed when we enter a shop. When we have been raised well, we have faith in the reality of this ethical system, which then is part of our more general basic trust.

However, when somebody else acts in a way that we feel to be completely inconsistent with the overall system and we cannot do much about it, the relevance of the whole system suddenly appears to dissolve into nothing. As a result, we don't know what to expect and find it hard to continue with what we were doing. In essence, this is what incompatibility of convictions and values entails: we fall out of the overall system that is supposed to regulate all our mutual relationships in a known and safe way. To proceed, we have to take it one step at a time, being alert to what might happen. This obviously interferes with the division of attention needed for normal and effective task performance.

Most of the time, we do not experience our convictions, values and goals as such. We usually are only aware of their existence when something happens that makes it difficult or impossible to use them as guidelines, for example as a result of changes in the organization or our work tasks.

To give some idea of the possible problems resulting from incompatibilities of organizational convictions and our own, we mention the following (not fully mutually exclusive) examples of issues that may give rise to such incompatibilities:

- What the organization is about, its reason for being there, its goals.
- How the organization should relate to its environment.
- What the constituent parts of the organization are and how these should relate to each other.
- What we talk about and attend to in the organization, or simpler: what really exists and what does not exist. This has of course all kinds of implications for what we are able and allowed to do, think and say, and for what we are not.
- What is good and what is bad in the organization. This is about virtues and sins and their relative importance and priority.
- How power is divided and exercised in the organization.
- How the organization sees, values and treats its employees and the relevant categories and criteria here.
- How the members of the organization are expected to relate to each other.
- The commitment, effort and productivity that are expected and demanded.

Generally speaking, a good fit of personal and organizational convictions, values and goals on the above issues is an important factor when we talk about the effectiveness of a work environment. A good fit allows us to deal with our work in a self-evident way, without putting question marks against everything that happens and everything we do.

From our individual perspective, a good fit means also that we can to a sufficient degree achieve our personal goals in and by our work. To the degree that such goal attainment is realized, the working task can appropriately captivate our attention, and only then do our task and its environment remain effective. Accomplishing and keeping a good fit is a complicated matter, which is seldom achieved fully and continuously.

The compatibility of personal and organizational convictions, values and goals usually comes about rather organically. First, organizations and potential employees select each other. Then the employees who have been selected are socialized; that is, they learn about and accept the organization's convictions and values. In the longer run, acceptance turns into identification and the organization's convictions and values become their own. The people who don't fit in often go away by themselves or are dismissed (Schneider, 1987), which of course doesn't exclude all individual problems.

Too Little Compatibility of Convictions, Values and Goals

It has become clear that too little compatibility between our own and the organization's convictions and values leads to poor effectiveness. The same applies to work in which we cannot sufficiently achieve personal goals. However, there are people who do experience such incompatibility. This can be a matter of a poor selection procedure or a disappointing individual choice. Also there are people for whom it is difficult to realize sufficient compatibility of convictions, values and goals in almost any organization. This is relevant too for some people with a different cultural background, as well as for anybody who differs too much from the norm in convictions and values or has non-realistic goals. From the perspective of the organization, many of these people simply disappear from view. Some of them still adapt to a certain degree and stay, under far from optimal circumstances. They remain because they see no other way to make a living, without having many illusions about achieving other personal goals. Often they perform all kinds of tasks that have little meaning to them and, essentially, they are far from effective. Here some descriptions of specific causes of too little compatibility are described.

Organizational Change

Often incompatibility of convictions, values and goals arises when organizations change radically, for example by reorganization, merger, privatization or the appointment of a new manager. Goals such as higher production, more flexibility and being more customer centered can become more prominent, while values such as technical perfection and professional freedom can lose their dominant role. However, the latter may well have been for us the very reason we chose the organization in question. The organizational change then leaves us with work that has been stripped of a great part of its challenges and meaning. Though it is easy enough to describe such a development as a matter of personal motivation problems and to deal with it accordingly, it is important to realize that its causes lie in the cultural change. Because changes are especially drastic to people who do their work for a long time in a certain way, we here pay attention to some issues that are important for elderly employees.

The most important problem with many organizational changes, especially for employees over 50, is that many of these changes go against what the organization used to expect of these employees. During their working life, many older employees have effectively learned not to act in the way the organization is now asking from them. Organizations nowadays have to become flatter, as well as more flexible, transparent, less product and more market oriented and so on. The principal consequence is that employees have to become more autonomous, decisive and creative: they have to act as if they were 'internal entrepreneurs' who work for themselves and not for an organization owned by other people. To some people – especially some older employees – the formula 'be free and serve us: make us rich' seems absurd. Moreover, older employees have often learned, mostly the hard way, to mistrust management intentions. Stories about employability and the disappearance of lifetime employment do not improve things. When a reorganization aiming for example at more autonomy is initiated, strong resistance may be evoked. Apart from the fact that this can hamper the implementation of the reorganization and the effectiveness of the organization, the whole affair is also more likely to be accompanied by all kinds of individual emotional and bodily complaints.

The Changing Perspective of Ageing Employees

The changing perspective of ageing employees implies also a change in their goals at work. Their new goals then may be incompatible with the organizational ones as perceived by their superiors. On average employees over 50, compared to their younger colleagues, are less focused on enlarging their income, as they know that it is improbable that their income still will increase substantially. Older employees have developed their own life style attuned to their income and are not strongly motivated on this point. They have realized that they only have a finite amount of time left and focus more on the here and now. As a result, older employees concentrate more on conserving what they have. That is why they also do not like radical reorganizations and the adaptations that those demand from them, the more so as they have gone through a lot of reorganizations already. Moreover, they have little cause to be impressed by the quality of their execution and results.

The Generation Gap

Employees belong to different generations, each characterized by its own value orientation; that is, the members of the different generations share the same values but prioritize them differently. These different priorities make the members of the different generations look at reality in different ways. The various value orientations and points of view of the different generations are not always compatible. The members of the so-called baby boom generation (born between 1945 and 1960), for example, think on average differently than the generations before and after them about many issues (Schabracq, 2003b). These differences can give rise to disagreements between generations, as well as to mutual prejudice and stereotypes, which can interfere with the effectiveness of work.

Checklist 4.8 Too little compatibility of convictions, values and goals

Resistance against: Yes
- disappearance of craftsmanship   ...
- increasing lack of interest in technical and professional perfection   ...
- having to be more autonomous and decisive   ...
- training   ...
- reorganizations   ...
- change of jobs   ...
- job redesign and changes in tasks   ...
- older generation's values   ...
- younger generation's values   ...
- rule violations   ...
- political games and a 'political' climate in general   ...
- being undervalued   ...
- rules that are more important than people   ...
- being thwarted in your objectives   ...
- not being allowed to use new solutions   ...
- work that is too much routine   ...
- work that does not allow for reflection, overview and understanding   ...
- work that has too few practical implications   ...
- the way your managers and team leader operate   ...
- work that is not up to the state of the art   ...
- intrusions on your position and your department   ...
- ways of working that go against your ideas about how people should   ...
  relate to each other.

Discrepancy Between Espoused Theory and Theory in Use

A last issue of incompatible convictions and values to be mentioned here is usually more problematic to younger employees than to older ones, namely the problems that may arise when the organization is ambiguous about its own convictions and values. This ambiguity mostly is a matter of depicting a much more pleasant image of its own convictions and values – the 'espoused theory' – than the convictions and values that determine the actual everyday reality – the 'theory in use' (Schon, 1983; see Chapter 1). When newcomers innocently identify with the better image, which can even be the reason they come to work there, they are bound for trouble.

Too Much Compatibility of Values and Goals

Too uninhibited a coincidence of values or too narrow a focus on the achievement of goals negatively affects the effectiveness of the work and the work environment, because it leads to work overload and a lack of recuperation possibilities. This often goes together with the disturbance of the balance between work and life as well.

Giving More than We Get

When we embrace organizational or job values and goals too intensely, we cannot say no to requests that appeal to these values or goals. For example, when we fully identify with the values and goals of nursing or social work, it becomes very difficult to turn down a request for help from a client. Instead, we see responding to the request as our calling and tend to take on more and more. Being unable to say no to our work can also be a matter of liking that work very much and being good at it. Well-known examples are the obsessed romantic artists in their attics, who in spite of hunger, cold, tuberculosis and other miseries only focused on their art, and their modern counterparts, the gray-faced computer nerds, who spend the whole night in front of the screen. As a result, people bite off more than they can chew, even to the extent that they do little else and their effectiveness diminishes. All these forms of imbalance can be characterized as 'giving more than we get', the mirror image of 'getting more than we give' or stardom (see earlier in this chapter). Giving more than we get is also a matter of organizational culture. Younger employees, who have not yet learned to develop and guard their own limits, are on average more susceptible to this imbalance than older employees.

In the long run, giving more than we get can even result in burnout (Schaufeli & Buunk, 2003) and all kinds of physical complaints such as ME or chronic fatigue syndrome and RSI (repetitive strain injury). These complaints can be characterized as functional; that is, they incapacitate us so much that they effectively take us out of the situation that caused them. The impersonal, and sometimes even antisocial, demeanor characteristic of burnout can be seen as an awkward form of self-protection against the tendency to give much more than we get.

Checklist 4.9 Too much compatibility of values and goals

Yes

Working too hard based on:
- setting no clear limits when it comes to work overload   ...
- finding it unacceptable to say no to requests to do something   ...
- a deeply felt obligation to accomplish a certain goal   ...
- seeing the work as intrinsically good   ...
- feeling obliged to meet the highest standards   ...
- the idea that other people are in much worse circumstances   ...
- striving for perfection   ...
- getting recognition   ...
- wanting to be a model performer   ...
- wanting to compete and win   ...
- wanting to be absolutely original   ...
- wanting to know and understand everything   ...
- not trusting others sufficiently to delegate tasks to them   ...
- being too eager to engage in new options and tasks   ...
- proving that one can take on anything   ...
- doing all kinds of work for everybody   ...
- wanting to keep the atmosphere sweet at any price   ...

THE WORK ENVIRONMENT: SAFETY

To be functional and not to attract needless attention, we must experience our working environment as safe. This need for safety is more or less a necessary condition for all kinds of reality. When a reality becomes too unsafe, we snap out of it. This principle applies equally to hypnosis, dreaming, being lost in a novel or movie and so on. It is relevant to our work as well. This safety involves our physical surroundings, such as the building, the equipment and furniture, as well as our social environment. A safe social environment implies for example trust in the intentions of our colleagues, managers and subordinates. Work simply becomes much more complicated when we know for sure that the others are out to get us.

Though safety is comparable to the previous variables – too much emphasis on safety and too little safety both disturb the division of attention needed for effective job performance – there is also a significant difference. Safety is an outcome of the others. Achieving the right amount of orderliness, social embedding and compatibility of convictions and values is probably the best way to evoke a feeling of safety, to keep away a feeling of being unsafe. For example, proper orderliness results in physical conditions and a thoroughly familiar reality that are both easy to survey. Appropriate social relationships lead to pleasurable contacts, feelings of belonging and control, as well as to what Harré (1979) called social musak, the ongoing stream of signals that everything is in order stemming from the behavior of all the participants (see the earlier section on social embedding). The same applies to appropriate compatibility of the organization's convictions and values and our own, as it suggests that everything happens in accordance with the overall ethical system, which makes our society a place where we can live without fear of our fellow humans. All three suggest that everything is under control and goes according to plan, while nasty surprises are out of the picture. In short, all three suggest that everything is safe.

But what does safe mean here? Does it mean being invulnerable to any threat? That would hardly be realistic. Vulnerability is one of our essential characteristics. We all know that we will grow older, that all of our functions must come to an end and that we will die. These thoughts are reminiscent of what was said in Chapter 3 about reality. There it was argued that our feeling of reality mainly springs from the way we deal with our environment, by limiting ourselves to a very small part of all possible options. Here something similar applies. Safety refers only to what counts in the present situation and its possible immediate consequences. Thus, feeling safe here means that it is – probably – harmless to lose ourselves in the stretch of reality at hand for the time being. This principle applies to anything we occupy ourselves with: our work, our thoughts, a conversation or whatever. The feeling of safety acts as a green light to enter that reality and to continue with it. Safety also implies that we do not have to go into the mechanics of what we are doing or going to do: it is safe, so we just do it or let it happen. In this way, the feeling of safety keeps us going in certain directions and keeps us away from other ones. It acts as a kind of semi-automatic, short-term steering device that guides us through the maze of our life.

A drawback may be that this 'steering device' retains us too much within our own comfort zones and keeps us away from new experiences, because these new experiences don't feel safe enough. However, exploring the world outside our comfort zones might broaden our horizons and further our development. It might take us out of our daily rut (Knope, 1998; McGraw, 1999) and help us to overcome 'just good enough solutions' (see Chapter 7).

Both reality and safety essentially are feeling states, though of a rather subtle kind, as we usually hardly notice them. However, we do notice their absence or disappearance. The absence of the feeling of reality evokes rather diffuse and 'unfocused' feelings, such as alienation, depersonalization, derealization or what Goffman (1974) calls a 'negative experience'; that is, the sensation that something is absent or missing (Schabracq & Cooper, 1993). The absence of safety on the other hand leads to more distinct feelings, including a readiness for certain actions. Examples of such feelings are apprehension, fear and anxiety. As long as we feel that things are safe, we can go on with what we are doing. The waning of this feeling makes that problematic, as we feel the urge to find out what exactly is going on and whether we can, and should, do something about it. This urge often goes together with the 'suspension' of the reality of what originally was going on. Obviously, reality and safety are closely related – though not identical – while both are also closely linked with trust and faith. For example, when our trust and faith have been violated in the past by some traumatic event, this may interfere with our present feelings of safety and reality.

All in all, to be able to work well we should not be continuously diverted by thoughts about danger or warnings such as 'pay attention', 'look out', 'behind you', or – even worse – the telling absence of these. For perceived or supposed danger interferes with the division of attention needed for losing ourselves in our work. Conversely, too strong a preoccupation with safety can also interfere with the smooth execution of our tasks. In the building industry, for example, the safety prescriptions are sometimes ignored because following these prescriptions is felt to be 'too much work'.

Too Little Safety

Feeling unsafe interferes with the division of attention needed for losing ourselves in our work. Perceived danger makes it difficult to keep our mind on our work and renders our work less effective. Some of these sources of ineffectiveness are discussed below.

Traumatic Experiences at Work

Traumatic experiences are events that endanger our life or imply another gross violation of our personal integrity. Traumatic experiences at our work site are an important cause of feeling unsafe there (Kleber & van der Velde, 2003). Examples are accidents, hold-ups and client aggression. Such events help us to remember that we are less safe than we thought we were, and may completely unsettle our trust in the safety of our work environment for a long time. Events that in themselves are harmless but remind us of the traumatic event then may evoke violent stress reactions. An example is the entrance of some suspicious-looking but actually innocent people to a bank that has been robbed three times already.

Daily Hassles

Some events negatively affect the feeling of safety without demanding a complete new adaptation of our life. These breaches of safety are called daily hassles and there is some indication that their effects are cumulative (Kanner *et al.*, 1981). Examples are:

- discourteous treatment and intimidation by clients or the general public
- conflicts
- unwanted intimacies
- serving as a scapegoat
- other confrontations with malevolent or unreliable colleagues and bosses

Concerning malevolent or unreliable colleagues and bosses, it should be emphasized that the presence of psychopaths in organizations is a rather common phenomenon (Hare, 1993; Stout, 2005). When talking about psychopaths, I am referring to people who use others mercilessly, only to disappear to the next organization when there is nothing to take any more or when things get too risky for them.

Some daily hassles have long-lasting effects. Besides being painful, they may unsettle our trust in the organization, the more so as nobody has done anything about them and they have never been settled in a satisfying way. Examples of daily hassles that may have occurred a long time ago but still interfere with our feelings of safety are:

- being a survivor of a slimming-down operation (also mentioned under the heading of too little social embedding, see earlier in this chapter)
- being passed over (repeatedly) for promotion
- loss of rights and privileges
- broken promises
- other kinds of injustices, offenses and humiliation by colleagues or managers

Apart from the fact that these memories in themselves negatively influence our effectiveness, it also implies that we do not experience pleasant things as such any more. Moreover, it means that we approach innovations with suspicion and skepticism.

Uncertainty About the Future of One's Job and Organization

As stated before (see Chapter 1), the increased turbulence of the environment has a huge impact on organizations. One of the effects is that the survival of organizations and jobs is much less certain. This uncertainty about the future and the accompanying rumors can unsettle our personal feelings of safety as well. Taking into account the growing number of radical changes and their accelerated pace, this uncertainty is becoming an increasingly important factor. Lifetime employment, for example, is a gradually waning phenomenon. Uncertainty about the future may evoke all kinds of disaster scenarios, also about the fate of other people, inside or outside the organization, for whom we feel responsible. All of these forms of uncertainty can negatively affect our effectiveness at work. For example, one of the nasty effects of mergers that go together with slimming down is that hardly any work gets done at all.

Checklist 4.10 Too little safety

	Yes
Hold-ups	. . .
Accidents	. . .
Client aggression	. . .
Having survived massive layoffs	. . .
Intimidation	. . .
Sexual harassment	. . .
Being pestered	. . .
Witnessing others being pestered	. . .
Malevolent or unreliable colleagues and executives	. . .
Open conflicts	. . .
Being passed over for promotion in an unjustified way	. . .
Losses of rights and privileges	. . .
Broken promises	. . .
Being offended and humiliated	. . .
Uncertainty about the future of one's job	. . .
Uncertainty about the future of one's organization	. . .

Too Much Safety

Paying disproportionately too much attention to procedures that are supposed to result in more safety may be at the expense of the attention to our task performance. Forced compliance with such procedures may also lead to ignoring some of the safety prescriptions, because following these prescriptions is experienced as 'too much work', which, of course, can be very dangerous.

Another treacherous point is that an overly safeguarded work environment can make us feel 'too' safe. This kind of work environment may have undesired outcomes. First, such safeguarding may work as a sedative. It lulls us into a state in which we are no longer alert enough to deal appropriately with the dangerous eventualities that always may happen. Good examples are traffic situations that are so overly regulated that they completely take away our watchfulness. Secondly, just like most sedatives, too much safety also turns out to be addictive. We cloak ourselves in its comfort and tend to forget that this feeling of being completely safe may not last for ever. As a result, we don't take new initiatives and don't care about our further development. However, the effect may be that we sentence ourselves to life-long imprisonment in our present job.

As a result, we get stuck in our job, even when staying in the same job is no longer rewarding at all or safe either for that matter. As it then becomes difficult to keep up the right division of attention for effective job performance, diminished effectiveness may ensue. Staying too long in the same job is particularly a problem for older personnel. There may be a number of different causes, which also can occur in different combinations, but the constant factor is clinging to the present job, though it is not rewarding or safe any more. Many of these mechanisms occur especially – though not exclusively – in organizations that avoid competition, conflict, feedback about inappropriate task performance and open communication in general. Here I give some examples.

Experience Concentration

In general, we want to be good at something. We invest in skill development and learn how to perform well. To accomplish that, we specialize and develop a stable repertory of successful behavior. In this way, we develop ourselves solely within the narrow limits of our job: we learn more and more about less and less and unfortunately cannot be deployed elsewhere any more. This process is called 'experience concentration' (Thijssen, 1988). Experience concentration makes our job less captivating and leads to qualitative task underload and loss of effectiveness. Experience concentration becomes most damaging when the organization changes so that our job disappears. Essentially, experience concentration is also a consequence of a failing career policy. Timely horizontal mobility, further training and education could have prevented it. Several studies show that experience concentration occurs rather frequently, certainly among employees over 40 (Boerlijst, Van der Heyden & Van Assen, 1993; Groot & Maassen van den Brink, 1997).

The 'Golden Cage' Syndrome

A good salary can also contribute to too much safety. When we earn a high income it is often impossible to make the same amount of money elsewhere. As a result, we may remain in a position that does not challenge us any more, which is at the expense of our effectiveness.

The Peter Principle

The scenario of being promoted as long as we do well in our successive jobs and getting stuck in the first job where we are not doing so well because it asks too much from us is known as the Peter Principle. If this scenario were fully valid, incompetent people would in the long run occupy all key positions in every organization. Though organizations exist where this principle has actually played a part, this scenario is not so realistic in most organizations as it is based on rather unrealistic assumptions. The Peter Principle, for example, treats careers as being exclusively vertical in nature and sees a job as an unchangeable datum, which we cannot adapt to our needs. Moreover, the Peter Principle takes proven competence for the sole determinant of promotion. Lastly, it passes over the possibility of appointing a competent assistant who can do the things that we cannot do. As such, the principle is based on blind faith in the truthfulness of a drawing board design of organizations, which in some bureaucracies may be more or less realistic.

Being Kicked Upstairs

Some organizations solve problems with incompetent or unpopular employees by promoting them to formally higher but factually empty positions, where they cannot do much wrong. Seemingly, there is no loss of face. After all, they have been promoted and get a higher salary. However, everybody involved knows that they have been side-tracked and they often are perceived as being ridiculous. Though such a position offers, at least in principle, opportunities to somebody who flourishes in the freedom that it provides and loves to design their own job, in practice most of the time it does not lead to much effectiveness.

The Glass Ceiling Effect

The glass ceiling refers to the phenomenon that it is nearly impossible for certain groups of employees (women, employees of different cultural, religious, racial or ethnic backgrounds) to rise above a certain organizational level, although this was not at all clear to them when they joined the organization. The word 'glass' refers to the ceiling's invisibility: the unreachable levels are clearly visible and seem easily reachable too. The phenomenon stems from deeply rooted cultural premises about the underlying division of power and roles (see the section 'Too little compatibility of values and goals' earlier in this chapter). Employees troubled by the glass ceiling often have the capacities as well as the ambition to work at a higher lever. They work hard and perform well, only to find out later that this was not as important as they had been told. At the same time, they witness how colleagues and subordinates who come from the right group do progress in their careers. Consequently, many of these employees become frustrated and cynical, which may harm the effectiveness of their functioning.

Too 'Secure' an Organizational Culture

Most of the previous examples – the last one is different – predominantly occur in organizational cultures where a 'friendly' climate has become the norm. In such a culture, performance and failures are hardly addressed. Often there is also a taboo on mutual competition. Such an environment can be very disheartening to some people, as it makes no difference what we do or don't do: it is OK anyway. Too 'secure' an organizational culture can make it hard to keep our mind on our work and to perform effectively, certainly when others experience good performance as threatening and see it as showing off.

Checklist 4.11 Too much safety

	Yes
Attention to safety procedures that interfere with attention to the real work	...
Being stuck in your job because of overspecialization and lack of skills to do something else	...
Having been side-tracked	...
Having been 'kicked upstairs'	...
Staying in a job only because you would earn less money elsewhere	...
Friendliness and a nice atmosphere as an obligation	...
Enjoying a protected position	...
No appeal to your responsibilities	...
Not being addressed when your performance is below par	...
Absence of all kinds of mutual competition	...

USING THE CHECKLISTS

Working through the checklists described in the previous sections is good preparation for workshops to improve the effectiveness of teams and departments. Such a workshop is facilitated by one or, preferably, two change agents. The participants in the workshops are all members of a team or department, including the team or department manager. The maximum group size lies somewhere around 16 people. For bigger groups a system of representation can be developed, under which each workshop participant represents one or two colleagues. Representing others then implies that the one who represents one or two other people goes through Step 7 below with those they represent.

The everyday reality of the shop floor here is the point of departure. Essentially, this is a bottom-up or grass-roots approach. The approach consists of mapping the main sources of ineffectiveness within the team and department, finding out about the causes of these sources and their mutual relationships, devising as many solutions as possible, determining the best solutions, implementing these solutions and monitoring and improving them. This approach encompasses the following steps:

1. The members of the organization individually read the text of this chapter and fill out all the checklists of sources of ineffectiveness.
2. Each member who has filled out the checklists composes a top five of sources of ineffectiveness in their own team or department.
3. If possible, all the data can be assembled and then analyzed with the help of some basic statistics and data-mining techniques. This can give the change agents some insights into (patterns of) recurring causes of ineffectiveness. This step can be very helpful, but is not strictly necessary.
4. The change agents interview key representatives of the team or department. The information generated by Step 3 can be used as a point of departure. If this information is not available, the personal top five of the key representative in question serves as the point of departure. The interviewer tries to surface underlying causes of the sources of ineffectiveness, as well as relevant assumptions and goals. Step 3 and 4 are meant

as a preparation for the change agents, which also may help them to custom-tailor the workshop.

5. The workshop will take one to two whole days and can be extended by separate day parts to work out particular issues. The workshop takes place in a venue outside the organization, with good catering and, if necessary, sleeping facilities, where the members are not disturbed by other stakeholders.

6. The workshop starts with a short discussion of the text by the change agent(s) and answering all possible questions about the text.

7. The members of the workshop divide themselves in groups of three or four and discuss their top fives for 45 to 60 minutes, to find a common top five of sources of ineffectiveness.

8. The subgroups of three reassemble and their top fives are pooled on a whiteboard or flip chart. A number one gets five points, a number two four points and so on. The points of similar or the same sources of ineffectiveness are added. The intention is to pool sources, to come to as small a number as possible of sources of ineffectiveness arranged in order of importance.

9. The causes of the different sources of ineffectiveness and their relationships are examined by the whole group. Just as in Chapter 2 the Pareto principle applies: usually 20% of causes account for 80% of effects. This is also about underlying assumptions and goals. When underlying assumptions and goals can be distilled and when they diverge – and most of the time they do – the members can try to find a 'win–win' solution. Consequently, this part of the workshop has many characteristics of a dialogue (see Chapter 5).

10. The workshop first examines what can be done about the most important source of ineffectiveness and its causes. Then the next most important one is discussed. The intention is to find as many interventions for each source of ineffectiveness and their causes as possible. This is a matter of brainstorming: generating as many solutions as possible, combining them and testing their feasibility and practical value (see Chapter 6).

11. The next step is to look for better, more pleasant and more intelligent solutions. Team members can implement some of these solutions themselves. Other solutions demand actions of a manager, a human resources officer or an external consultant.

12. The team or department divides the responsibilities for each of the actions among the different members. This is primarily a matter of voluntarily taking responsibility for a certain activity.

13. For each action, a time path is developed (sub-goals and deadlines). Essentially this involves who, what and when.

14. A date is set for the next meeting. Each of the members agrees to keep track of everything that goes wrong, or not completely right, and promises to think of solutions for these issues. These problems and solutions subsequently are the input for the next session.

15. During the next sessions the change agents facilitate as well, but during the session after this they remain more in the background, while the manager now is the facilitator.

16. The next step can then consist of the change agents coaching the manager, who is now in full control.

The essence of this approach is inciting the team and department members to solve their own problems, creating support and a platform for their solutions in the process. The main problems to be solved here are in communication and planning. Important underlying causes often lie in the area of ethics. Significant issues are responsibility, honesty, courage, fairness, justice and love.

CHAPTER 5

Dialogue

A dialogue is a kind of discussion, either between two or more people or – in the case of an internal dialogue – within one person. The reason for starting a dialogue is usually that the existing reality has become obsolete and does not work any more. The reality has become dysfunctional: its situations no longer provide their proper outcomes and some of its participants no longer believe in it. The dialogue's objective then consists of coming to a new common ground, a new reality.

The obsolescence of the everyday reality that is the reason for starting a dialogue can be a matter of a sudden critical incident, such as a conflict, an economic crisis, a new competitor, a new general manager or a technological innovation. It can also be the outcome of a more gradual development, such as the ageing of the personnel, a slowly declining market share and so on.

The dysfunctional character of the old reality manifests itself in a disturbed relationship with the organization's environment and stagnated organizational functioning. There are serious problems with the daily course of affairs and the existing reality clearly needs a fundamental adaptation. Everybody usually agrees on that. However, what should be done about it? This question tends to give rise to fundamental disagreements. Different groups form and things get tense. Still, the parties are somehow aware that they depend on each other for their future. That is, the costs of either breaking up for good or solving the problems by force and violence are deemed to be unacceptable. The parties participating in a dialogue thus initially don't agree with each other. However, they are willing to talk, because their interests are at stake and they rely on each other for a solution. Still, they usually are initially far from enthusiastic about the whole enterprise, also because it is fully unclear what the outcome of the dialogue will be.

Before there can be a dialogue, something has to be done about the initial skepticism and distrust. The situation requires a certain fundamental attitude, which encompasses the following elements:

- the will to solve the problem together
- the will to reflect together on different opinions about the situation
- the will to accept each other as equals
- being in a position to take decisions
- taking together responsibility for good progress in the dialogue

This introduction may sound overly worried and cautious, but when the dialogue succeeds all participants can look back on a meaningful course of action. They speak about valuable, impressive and now and then also unexpectedly pleasant experiences. Progress is made. Everybody has memories of discussions that went extremely well, discussions that opened up new horizons, made us feel fully alive and enthusiastic. Remember how good that felt! There is a good chance that these discussions contained many elements of dialogue (Dixon, 1998).

Dialogue can be very useful in organizations. As it is, most organizations find themselves permanently forced to adjust their realities, because their environments show unprecedented change and turbulence (see Chapter 1; Schabracq & Cooper, 2000). In almost every organization there are individuals and groups who disagree with each other and are at the same time dependent on each other for their own survival and the success of the organization. Moreover, all these people apparently still think it is important to work in the organization and dedicate a considerable part of their life to that work.

Although most of the time organizations meet a number of conditions for successfully applying dialogue, most organizations are not an ideal environment for the fundamental attitude demanded by such a discussion. To make a dialogue possible, a lot has to be done. I will deal with these issues later on. Here I limit myself to mentioning that the most 'pure' forms of dialogue are probably not a real option for most organizations. At the same time, elements and derived forms of dialogue provide for many organizations the difference between flourishing and perishing. This is a matter of comparative advantage: to survive and flourish we don't need to be perfect, as long as we are better than the competition.

A name that often pops up when dialogue is discussed in organizations is Peter Senge, who gave an important impulse to the present interest in this way of working with his books *The Fifth Discipline* (Senge, 1990) and *The Fifth Discipline Fieldbook* (Senge *et al.*, 1994). Senge himself refers to the physicist David Bohm (2004) as the source of inspiration in this respect. An obvious precursor is also Chris Argyris (for example Argyris, 1990), who has done a great deal of pioneering work about distorted perception and defense mechanisms in organizations. A philosopher often mentioned in this context is Martin Buber (for example Buber, 1978). Lastly, an excellent overview is to be found in Dixon's *Dialogue at Work* (1998). Another related approach is the 'Socratic discussion', mostly based on the work of Leonard Nelson (www.friesian.com/method.htm), a German philosopher (1882–1927) who came to a kind of discussion derived from the techniques that Socrates displays in Plato's dialogues. A similar approach, called 'Socratic talks', is practiced in the Netherlands (Kessels, 1997).

THE FUNDAMENTAL ATTITUDE

As discussed before, the will to solve the problem together, to reflect together on the different opinions about the situation and to accept each other as equals, as well as being in a position to take decisions and accepting together responsibility for good progress in the dialogue comprise the elements of the fundamental attitude of dialogue.

The will to solve the problem manifests itself in a passionate and tenacious directedness to a good outcome. This directedness demands an alert though quiet attitude, which is essentially very serious, even though this does not exclude a lot of laughter. The directedness is focused on the final result. The way in which the good outcome is attained is explicitly unrelated to the directedness itself. The way in which the result is attained is intentionally left open to guarantee as much flexibility as possible.

The 'together' stems from the shared fate of the participants, their mutual dependency. The participants must actually experience the mutual dependency as such. The 'together' comes to the fore in the ways they relate to each other. These ways of relating are based on respect and interest for the other. There is an acute involvement in each other's ideas. The participants intensely focus on each other, without needlessly hurting or offending each other or without drifting apart otherwise. Still, it helps not to be hurt too easily. Furthermore, the participants see to it that the others don't lose or lack anything, especially also because this would be at the expense of the quality of the solutions and the time they will last. These ways of giving meaning to the idea of 'together' lead to more openness with each other, as well as to readiness to admit the others and what they represent. This openness and admitting the others are described in more detail later in this chapter.

Reflecting here means that the participants examine each other's assumptions, goals, values and ideas. Everything that arises they must then painstakingly assess, to find out which parts are of value, how they might improve these parts and make them more pleasant and smart. The careful assessment manifests itself also in the use of the interviewing techniques, which are described in Chapter 6. Examples are asking pointed questions, summarizing what the other says to test whether you have understood it and presenting tentative conclusions. This assessment, too, is a matter of being alert to mental blocks and counterproductive assumptions in our own thinking. The emphasis on reflection manifests itself also in a certain degree of thoughtfulness, in weighing and comparing things, as well as in silences to think and ponder. Another important part of this thoughtfulness is that we do not beforehand assume one idea to be true or false. However, we ought to judge each idea on its merits and possibilities of improvement. The focus is on optimal usability, while we pay a great deal of attention to clarity and conciseness.

Accepting each other as equal partners implies acknowledging the others as full persons and taking their interests seriously. When everybody is equal, nobody has a monopoly on wisdom. That means that everybody's ideas and assumptions can contribute to decision making and the final result, without a premature decision being taken. The fact that everybody may contribute everything increases the independence and diversity of the ideas that we can incorporate in the final result. In this way we can makes optimal use of the intelligence of all participants and come to much better results. In a somewhat different phrasing: we make best use of the collective intelligence (Surowiecki, 2005). As mentioned before, taking into account everybody's interests contributes to better, longer-lasting solutions.

Being in the position to take decisions implies that each participant either takes independent decisions or has been given the mandate to do so. So the participants must be free and authorized to present the final result as the new reality. They also must be free, and willing, to 'live' this reality. In the case of a mandate, we have to determine beforehand whether the representative at hand has indeed sufficient decision latitude to agree with the final result and can sell the outcome of the dialogue to the rank and file of their party.

Taking responsibility for what happens also manifests itself in the efforts of all involved to structure progress as well as possible and to actively guard this structure. When something goes wrong, or threatens to go wrong, everyone feels it as their personal duty to help to get things going again. Getting things going again can be, for example, a matter of proposing a procedure or a pause, presenting an interpretation or asking a question. Responsibility also implies that we accept responsibility for our own opinion, even when it deviates from that of the others. It means also that we dare to give unwelcome information, stand for what we are saying and do not hide behind others. The quality of the final result depends on the degree to which the different participants can think independently, do not all make the same mistakes and have divergent information at their disposal (Surowiecki, 2005).

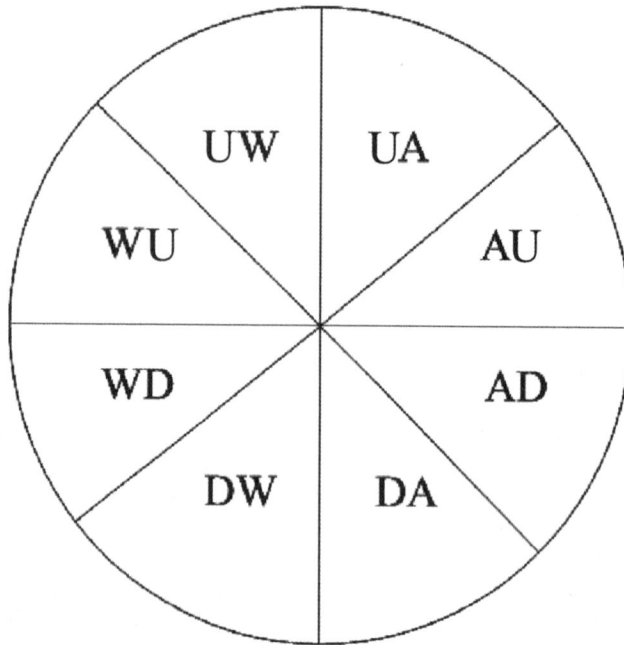

Figure 5.1 Leary's rose

While 'together', in terms of Leary's rose (see Figure 5.1 and Chapter 6), refers to 'with', taking responsibility can be typified primarily as 'up' in that terminology. The fundamental attitude in a dialogue is in principle that of the 'left upper' quadrant of Leary's rose. Dialogue thus is a matter of going to and fro between with–up (WU) and up–with (UW).

OTHER ATTITUDES

The fundamental attitude of dialogue, described above as Leary's left upper quadrant, is far from easy to maintain for the participants: maintaining it demands diligence and effort. Here we discuss the other possible attitudes, such as they can be described following the categories of Leary's rose. These other attitudes can each be regarded as a form of resistance to change (see Chapters 1 and 7); that is, exclusively within the context of a dialogue. This resistance is not about truth, but about what the others want, namely no change. Now the other attitudes.

First the attitude of the octant with-down (WD). This is an attitude of:

- being focused on getting appreciation
- guarding a nice climate
- soothing and covering up conflicts
- looking for the powerful and pleasing them
- doing things for the powerful
- lots of smiling

In a dialogue, someone with a with-down attitude does not feel directly responsible for solutions. If this person takes any responsibility at all, then this only happens for details, while the solutions must come from the powerful. We only, in Virginia Satir's terms (www.satirstances.com/placate.htm), placate the powerful: we make them feel good, help them and guard them. This pleasing must result in appreciation and a pleasant climate. From the point of view inherent in this attitude, we are inclined to divert attention from unpleasant things and prevent and smooth over differences of opinion. However, dialogue, by contrast, requires that the involved parties face the unpleasant sides of issues and expose differences of opinion before reconciling them.

The down–with (DW) octant implies:

- seeking protection and safety
- obeying, doing as we are told
- complying quickly with the powerful
- avoiding conflicts
- taking no initiatives

Essentially, people who assume this attitude do not take part in the dialogue. They just want to feel safe and protected. They leave the harsh outer world to those to whom they have delegated their destination and take shelter under their wings, a form of 'fleeing to'. Down–with is at odds with taking responsibility for the course of affairs, independent thinking and presenting their own ideas and unwelcome information. People in the down–with octant have by definition the same opinion as those from whom they expect the most safety; that is, the greatest threats.

'Up–against' (UA) is characterized by:

- defining the situation and how it should be (preaching)
- sticking firmly to that definition
- telling others what must happen (commanding and ordering)
- not tolerating opposition and playing down differences of opinion
- an unmoving face

This behavior is primarily displayed by people who perceive dialogue as a threat or an infringement on their power position. People in an 'up–against' position usually hold on to such a view in almost any situation where a change of the status quo is about to take place. They feel responsible for the status quo, to which they have aligned themselves, because the status quo offers them all kinds of outcomes. It is the attitude of an authority figure who wants to hold on to the past and feels threatened.

'Against–up' (AU) involves the following elements:

- getting angry and raising one's voice
- attacking the other person
- accusing and 'blaming' (www.satirstances.com/blame.htm)
- threatening
- showing contempt
- disqualifying the other person

Against–up refers to a more personal and openly aggressive response to someone who is experienced as infringing on our autonomy and personal functioning. A typical case of against–up reasoning is: 'You get me? Then I get you. And because you behave as you do, you are guilty of it all. You are bad and unreliable.' In short, anger and fighting as a primary stress response, when something threatens us from the outside. We typically display this attitude when we feel attacked.

'Against–down' (AD) comprises:

- sabotage
- feigning
- insinuating
- inciting others
- stalling
- disqualifying important moments

Against–down is a hostile reaction to an experienced infringement too, for example when someone feels forced to show openness. This against–down reaction is less primary in character than against–up. Somebody displaying this attitude has probably experienced infringements for a long time. That person does not see his situation as his own responsibility, but as caused by the actions of others. He lives the life of a guerrillero, alone or with some comrades. He lives in occupied territory, where the powerful are not to be trusted. Moreover, he has learned that displaying overt anger and aggression are dangerous.

Lastly, 'down–against' (DA) encompasses:

- lack of interest
- maintaining latitude
- not committing yourself
- keeping silent
- being late or not showing up at all
- being easily distracted

Down–against is a passive form of resistance, a response to a perceived lack of freedom. It is the conduct of a convict. People in a down–against position just try to evade the influence of the one in power, to maintain some freedom for themselves. People in this position don't feel responsible for the situation and are not really interested in more active participation. They do not actively participate at all, as they do not gain anything from it in any case. What they do want lies outside their horizon for the moment.

All these forms of resistance are a matter of a down and/or an against attitude, which of course is expressed in people's non-verbal behavior. In addition, these attitudes often are of a somewhat nervous nature, which also shows in their non-verbal behavior. I describe a number of these non-verbal behavioral elements in Chapter 8 and Addendum 1.

To complicate things further, often – but not continuously – we cover up these attitudes with a display of benevolence, paying lip service to the goals of dialogue. Disapproval and open criticism often are ventilated only in our own circle. This ventilating of criticism touches, for that matter, on another important point: this kind of resistance usually is not an individual but a collective affair. Those involved support each other and so reinforce each other's resistance: 'If all of us see it the same way, we can hardly be wrong!' This collective character can make the resistance surprisingly effective and well coordinated. As it is, people have proved able to coordinate their intentions when they realize that they want the same thing (Schelling, 1960).

Another point is that in principle all this behavior is situationally determined: these attitudes are responses to another party in a particular situation. As such, these attitudes are not personality traits, even though some people are more inclined to certain behavior than others are. Often the behavior in question is a response to a perceived threat, infringement or loss. It is important to realize that this behavior is not a constant, but a response stemming from a certain view on an event, which we can often exchange for another one.

In a dialogue we irrevocably touch on resistance from time to time. How do we cope with that? To start with, we should recognize resistance as such. That is why its different forms are elaborated in this section. Dealing with this kind of resistance consists each time of an invitation to the other to explain his attitude. Try to find out what has brought it about. What does he want? What doesn't he want? Which assumptions and goals drive him? What is really important and what is more of a side issue? What are the implications of his attitude? What is good about it? Is it possible to rephrase the attitude as a surplus or a distortion of an essentially good attitude? What can we do about someone's power position, their autonomy, his feeling of being suppressed and the lack of freedom he experiences? What must be done? The results of these questions should be taken seriously. The approach needed here consists each time of a mixture of inquiry, our repertoire of questioning techniques (see Chapter 6) and advocacy, clarifying our own position and the reasons we act as we do. In addition, we can use techniques such as 'really seeing' (see Chapter 6), evoking fantasies (see Chapter 6), being alert to non-verbal behavior (see Chapter 8) and wording (see Chapter 8).

In practice, coping with 'with–down' and 'down–with' often turns out to be extra difficult. Of course, we can ask questions about the attitude and clarify its implications as well. However, when the person in question goes along with that, this easily may turn out to be more of the same. Moreover, it is often not unpleasant, and actually quite tempting, when somebody agrees with us or tries to maintain a nice atmosphere. After all, it is a very socially desirable behavior, and can we blame somebody for being nice?

Coping with resistance usually implies that progress comes to a standstill for a moment. Raising the issue may start with a neutral phrase such as: 'I get the idea that something is the matter.' In addition, we can 'focus' on the person in question, following the techniques described in Chapter 6. When he denies that anything is the matter, while we are rather certain that there is something, we can say something like: 'I still get the idea that something is bothering you', perhaps adding our motives for thinking that. If this does not help either, we can propose a moment of awareness (see Chapter 6). Sometimes it is useful to propose a coffee or tea break. In other cases it turns out quite well to have a five-minute silence to think for a while; that is, when the group has some experience with dialogue and is open to such an approach. Lastly, it makes sense to return to the issue later when we together take stock of where we are, what has been accomplished and what still has to be done, episodes that are normal parts of a dialogue (see Chapter 6).

ASSUMPTIONS

As we have seen in Chapter 3, a reality is based on holding on to certain assumptions, while other assumptions – and another reality – in principle would have been possible as well. When a certain reality is assumed, however, it hides all other possible realities from view. By this suppression of all other possible realities, the actualized reality can present itself as an inevitable matter of self-evidence. This also provides the 'realized' reality with stability. So a given reality is the outcome of a self-fulfilling prophecy: by taking the underlying assumptions for true and believing in their truth, the resulting reality is actually 'realized'.

Inhabiting a certain reality goes together with certain feelings. These feelings vary from feeling fully absorbed by what we are doing, via feeling real contact, to feelings of pleasant quiet and safety. As a consequence of their everydayness and being taken for granted, we usually are hardly aware of these feelings. However, we do feel their absence, which thrusts itself on us when a reality does not work any more. We feel this absence either as the sensation that things are nor real or safe any longer or as the lack of all feeling. The feeling that things are not real or safe any more usually is unpleasant and consequently most people suppress it. The other outcome, the lack of all feeling, is – by definition – difficult to feel. However, in both cases it is possible to experience these states of mind by intentionally focusing your attention on them. Both the feeling that things are nor real or safe any more and the lack of all feeling can be described as stages of alienation. The second, feeling nothing at all, which I call secondary alienation, often succeeds the first, the feeling that something is not real or safe any more, which I call primary alienation (Schabracq & Cooper, 2003).

As primary alienation is accompanied by somewhat heightened arousal, primary alienation is, just like all other deviant activity states (Schabracq, 1991), highly contagious to the other people around: the sense of not being real and safe easily spreads. From an evolutionary perspective, this must have had an obvious survival value, as it put us in the right state to cope with impending danger. Secondary alienation can lead in the people around us to both primary and secondary alienation. In the first case we experience the absence of feeling in the other as strange and as a striking absence of human contact, the 'praecox feeling' discussed in Chapter 4. In the second case, we just match the absence of feeling. The latter especially happens as the absence of feeling is modeled to us by many other people around. We then enter into a similar state of secondary alienation, almost without noticing it, due to the essentially non-verbal nature of this form of contagion. Being taken over by secondary alienation manifests itself as a paralyzing influence that make us strangely drowsy, for example when we attend one of the highly ritualized meetings in a bureaucratic organization, such as a university or ministry department.

In spite of the self-evident nature of a reality and the tacit character of its assumptions, reality is in itself not unchangeable. Stronger yet, realities are never definitive but are subject to development. Sometimes, a reality in its present form does not fit any longer within its greater surroundings. Reasons to adjust a reality are for example:

• incompatibility with the realities of relevant others
• incompatibility with occurring facts
• a sense of alienation indicating that the reality does not work any more
• the outcomes of questioning our reality and its underlying assumptions by one or more of the techniques described in Chapter 7 and so on

Adjustments of our assumptions and the reality based on them are then an option. Essentially, this is a matter of intentional choice.

To come to a new reality with different situations, which is the purpose of a dialogue, we must get to know the others' assumptions. This knowledge must then lead to a clear picture of the mutual differences. Consequently, we have to take into regard both our own assumptions and those of the other. From there we develop together new assumptions about which we come to an agreement. We examine whether the new assumptions work in practice and when they do, we let go of the old assumptions and the power they have over us. This is a matter of much precise work and intense attention.

To start with, both our own and others' assumptions usually go their own tacit way. Also due to their pre-verbal origin, they escape for the greater part from inspection. This does not mean that they are completely inaccessible to our awareness, nor that we cannot put them into words to a certain extent, but it does mean that we must invest extra effort to bring them to the surface.

Tracking assumptions is foremost a matter of examining the 'why' and 'to what end' of our and the other's sayings, acts and attitudes. For this purpose, we can apply all the techniques intended to gather information about ourselves and others, described in Chapter 2. We can for example use the following approaches:

- Observing others' and our own attitudes (see Chapter 8).
- Observing others' and our own behavioral elements (see Chapter 8).
- Using the techniques of really seeing the other person or ourselves (in a mirror; see Chapters 6 and 8).
- Intentionally imitating or matching these attitudes and their elements to explore how they feel and to examine the situational and relational proposals they imply (see Chapter 8).
- Questioning the 'why' and 'to what end' of our acts and attitudes by applying the various questioning techniques, focusing, or using our imagination and asking for an image (see Chapter 6).

By applying these techniques, we want to uncover the implication of acts and attitudes: we want to know what proposal they make, where they lead and what their gains are. We can use the above-mentioned approaches in all kinds of combinations. What exactly we should do is mostly a matter of what works best for us in our particular situation.

OPENNESS

Allowing inspection of each other's assumptions demands a great degree of openness (Dixon, 1998) and honesty of all those involved. When this openness is mutual, it irrevocably leads to a form of intimacy (Senge *et al.*, 1994). We expose ourselves and so do the others. For many people, this is too close for comfort. Although some people have had bad experiences with openness and intimacy, that does not apply to everyone. Still, it can be an important stumbling block to successful dialogue. Several mechanisms play a role here. Though we can distinguish between them on paper, in practice they turn out to be inextricably connected and go beyond just being open.

The first point is that openness is closely related to power and power differences. When we can perceive somebody well, we can see what they are doing and planning to do. We can inspect their motives and if we want to harm them, we may abuse this knowledge. In this way, the other person is in our power, the special form of power expressed by the saying 'knowledge is power'. When the other is not able to perceive us so extensively, an essential difference in power comes into being, which puts him more or less in our hands.

An extreme example of unequal visibility is a panopticon, a circular prison in which each story consists of a ring of cells, of which the fronts consist of bars and there is an open space in the middle. From a room in the middle of that space, a guard can observe all these cells through small slits in his room, without being visible himself (Foucault, 1975). Other examples are the use of one-way mirrors, hidden cameras, monitoring equipment and dark glasses. So being exposed to other people's perceptions and the inherent openness are connected to power and the exercise of power, which makes openness in itself a tricky point.

Being watched is often described as unpleasant. Somebody who notices that he is being watched usually starts. Being unable to bear being looked at plays an important role in blushing, shyness, agoraphobia and other social phobias. Knowing that we are the object of another person's attention while being unable to escape that attention is described as an existential threat, a threat to our life (Sartre, 1943). This phenomenon manifests itself for example in a staring contest, gazing into each other's eyes as long as possible where looking away first is an act of submission, a mechanism that we share with other mammals (Chance & Larsen, 1976; Exline, 1971). Boxers do this, from very close range, just before a fight starts. In a watered-down form, this ritual occurs at the beginning of almost every human interaction, most of the time without our even noticing it. Who at the beginning of the encounter looks away first plays a relatively submissive role during the remainder of the situation (Strongman, 1970; Strongman & Champness, 1968). Looking away reminds us of the submission ritual of dogs who roll over on their backs, exposing their throats to the teeth of the other dog, as a form of openness as well. While the 'winning' dog usually finds this good enough and refrains from enthusiastically setting his teeth into that throat, we are less sure of such an attitude with humans. To conclude, the openness inherent in being looked at apparently implies a deeply rooted threat.

We learn very early in life not to stare at other people. Nor are we allowed to touch, address or sniff strangers. Therefore we are prone to experience the 'intrusive' gazes, smells and noises of others, as well as being touched, as forms of harassment or even infringement. The underlying principle is that we lead a rather 'narrow' life, characterized by a great deal of repetition, standard activities and a limited number of intimate and personal relationships (see Chapter 3). Obviously, the form of openness that dialogue demands from us is at odds with that discipline.

While the previous points were related to the threat implied by openness in general, there is also a specific problem with openness in organizations. Dialogue demands a comparable degree of openness from all involved. This implies an essentially balanced and symmetrical division of power between all participants, which is usually not the case in organizations, where typically a clear hierarchy of superiors and inferiors prevails.

In addition – and this is not any longer about openness in a strict sense – the opinions and assumptions of all participants must be treated as if they are of equal importance. Otherwise the dialogue cannot be successful. Moreover, all participants must subscribe to this principle of equal importance. This point also goes against the existing division of power in most organizations.

The openness inherent in dialogue can cause problems to employees of both higher and lower rank, at least when no provisions are taken in this respect. On the one hand, employees of higher rank often don't want to expose their ideas to the critical inspection of their inferiors, especially when they are not allowed to let these ideas prevail – as they are accustomed to do – over those of their inferiors. Having to expose their ideas to their inferiors implies an infringement on the superiors' power position, while the superiors just have to wait and see whether they can again restore that power later on. On the other side, many employees of lower rank do not like to give their hand away and are reluctant to criticize the ideas of their superiors. These employees simply are afraid they will be paid back for their sincerity by their superiors later on.

The following point concerns the general discipline of our attention (see Chapter 3). Here we only touch on the social side of that discipline. An example is that we learn already very early in life not to stare at other persons. Neither are we allowed to touch, address and sniff strangers. The other way round, we are prone to experience 'intrusive' gazes, smells and noises of others, as well as being touched, as forms of harassment, or even an infringement. The underlying principle is that you learn already early in life to lead the rather 'narrow' life, characterized by much repetition, standard activities and a limited number of intimate and personal relations, which had been described on Chapter 3. Obviously, the form of openness that dialogue demands from you is at odds with that discipline. For the rest, applying this discipline also is a matter of power, namely the power over designing and controlling our own life.

ADMITTING THE OTHER

The openness demanded by dialogue is not only threatening but can hurt as well, and bring suffering with it. We usually open up only to people with whom we maintain an intimate or personal relationship. These are usually people who are 'with' us, who are close to us, whom we may love and who agree with us. Openness in dialogue, however, is about people who are in the first instance against us, who are not close to us, whom we do not love at all and with whom we disagree. Openness here also means allowing ourselves to fully realize that the other is different and has different views on things. Openness means as well that we let that being different sink in fully, which is difficult and sometimes painful. To fully know the difference of someone else and to map it precisely, we have to be able to experience and bear it long enough. A clear view on and understanding of what is different are necessary for coming to a new reality later on. As it is, this new reality should preferably not be founded on the projection of our own assumptions and ignoring the reality of the other person (Dixon, 1998; Gadamer, 1960), but should combine elements of both realities without losing sight of their differences.

What is so painful about admitting the other person and his different ideas? We let something unknown penetrate into us, which we have rejected until now and the implications of which we do not know. The other's ideas threaten to become a part of us. In that we give up control over ourselves, especially because dialogue also implies that at the same time we suspend the self-evident effects of our own assumptions. The same goes for all that is attached to our assumptions, such as familiar behavior, thoughts and feelings, a repertoire that until now has always shepherded us in a self-evident way through everyday reality. We also suspend our assumptions in the understanding that this suspension might very well proceed into fully letting go. This letting go would imply abandoning something that is very much our own. Suspending our assumptions also is about a part of ourselves in which we have invested a lot of effort and trouble to appropriate it and enact it each time anew. A part of ourselves? To what degree are we actually our own ideas? This is a difficult question to answer. In this respect, it is instructive to do the exercise described in Chapter 8, in which we treat our own thoughts as temporary visitors.

So what is painful consists of a combination of insecurity, possible danger and the threat of further loss of certainty. All of this evokes shreds of memories of much earlier experiences. We are in danger, back in the world of our childhood fears and the less pleasant outskirts of dreamland. An example of this is elaborated in Chapter 7, which discusses radical changes in our life and the loss of the assumptions involved.

PROGRESS

Openness and admitting other people are hardly possible in times of intense emotions such as anger, fear, distress and so on. Nevertheless, these emotions are quite common in these circumstances. That is why in such cases it makes sense to start with discussing what has been going on and examining the emotions evoked, in order to calm these emotions down a little. Those involved then tell what has made this particular dialogue necessary: How has it come about, what has gone wrong and who and what have caused that? After that has been worked through, everybody relates what these events have meant for them personally. The emphasis here is on how the events felt, how these feelings have developed over time and what kind if influence these feelings have had on their further life. Apart from the fact that such a discussion of the emotions involved gives a first impression of the problem, it becomes clear in this way what the problem means, and has meant, at the experiential level. This approach has several positive effects.

To start with, by venting and naming the emotions involved, they become less all determining. Furthermore, we get a more realistic picture of each other's emotions. We learn to see the emotions for what they are: normal reactions to infringements, losses and threats. Also it is often instructive to find out that anger sometimes serves to cover up sadness or anxiety. Sincerely sharing all of this, including the personal vulnerability that it brings, creates a bond and boosts mutual trust.

The next step is about clarifying each other's views on the present state of affairs and their foundations. Ask the other person what he sees as the core of the problem at hand. What is important to the other person? Find out on what ideas these views are founded and what they imply. What possibilities for bringing about improvements does the other person see? What pitfalls does the other person expect and how does plan to get around them? In this stage, it is explicitly not the intention to overcome or otherwise annihilate these differences. On the contrary, this stage is especially concerned with clarifying and mapping the differences. Doing so is essential to the success of the dialogue. In William Blake's words, 'without contraries no progression' (cited in Berlin, 2000, p. 305).

A useful exercise here is making a point of suspending any form of judgment in a group meeting for a certain period. We can videotape these exchanges and discuss them afterwards. The goal of this videotaping is to demonstrate how difficult it is to suspend our judgments, as well as how deeply judging is rooted in our attitudes. In the end, judging means that we approach the world from our own assumptions as if those were the only ones possible. Moreover, by judging we allow ourselves to reject what the other does, as if it concerns a matter of good and evil. This kind of rejection is not wrong in itself, but it is good to be aware of the mechanism. It is also good to realize that judging gives you, as if on its own accord, a feeling of control: judging serves as an indirect but very effective magical spell to make our own assumptions inviolable.

A useful guideline when examining each other's assumptions is setting out to explore together our positive goals, as well as the elements and characteristics that we experience as unpleasant or dysfunctional. We then can examine these dysfunctional and unpleasant sides in more depth. There is a good chance that these sides are related to our 'allergies' (see Chapter 7), the characteristics we love to hate in other people. Identifying our allergies will give us clear pointers to the nature of our developmental tasks and challenges. Identifying our allergies also gives us indications for rephrasing these characteristics as a deformation of characteristics that are essentially good. We can use advocacy and inquiry techniques, especially the ones that work best for us, to learn more about these allergies, challenges, core competencies and personal pitfalls (see Chapter 7).

From time to time we come across stumbling blocks in this respect, both in ourselves and in others. Some issues are just not verbalized in discussions that can solve those issues, while those involved do discuss them with trusted other people. These are the so-called unspeakables (Argyris & Schon, 1978; see Chapter 1). Making them discussable is in itself not impossible, but it is a delicate matter that demands tact and social skill as well as mutual trust.

Sometimes, however, blocks are more deeply rooted. For instance, we cannot implement certain ways to solve frequently occurring problems in a particular organization when such an approach goes against the grain of that organization. In some government departments, for example, it is not done to directly approach someone who works either in an echelon several steps higher or a different department. So in certain organizations, it is impossible even to think of perfectly sound solutions for certain problems if these solutions imply that a personal failure at a considerably higher level must be specified. Needless to say, getting around or solving such blocks demands a great deal of circumspection and skill.

In this respect, it is essential from time to time to describe the state of affairs from the perspective of the other person. Make this into a standard approach! It is also a matter of skillfully and carefully applying the rules of feedback (see Chapter 6) and explaining each time why we are asking or saying something.

Furthermore, it is here of crucial importance to be willing to really see the other person with his good and strong points, his possibilities and the surplus or exaggeration of these (see Chapter 7), as well as in the incidental lacunas and distortions (see Chapter 6).

This is often a difficult stage. The underlying dividedness becomes more and more visible, which often leads to frustration. Opinions also get more and more extreme, usually because the perception of the other group is distorted. Back and forth, all kinds of stereotypes and prejudices come to the fore. These perceptual distortions, stereotypes and prejudices are mainly a matter of the dynamics of inter-group processes as described in social psychology (for example Gudykunst & Kim, 1992; Meertens, 1980). This stage of the dialogue can be quite unpleasant, and can go on for some time without any visible progress. During this stage, it is of utmost importance not to alienate ourselves from each other, to remain communicating, not to panic and not to fall into avoidance tactics. We must ask ourselves from what assumptions we are listening, what is going on and what can be learned from this. All of this asks for discipline, courage and trust (Senge *et al.*, 1994). Another important principle is from time to time to point out what we all have in common and what we all are aiming to achieve.

The next step is to work out how we can integrate our assumptions with those of the others in such a way that something new comes about, the new basis for a reality that is more rewarding to all parties than the present one. Being rewarding to all parties implies that we are looking for a reality in which the goals of all assumptions can be realized, so that no party experiences substantial disadvantages from it. Consequently, this approach does not entail a compromise but a win–win solution, one that allows all parties to realize their underlying intentions.

In practice, it appears that a win–win solution is often the consequence of a sharp as possible formulation of the different, apparently incompatible assumptions in the form of a dilemma (Hampden-Turner, 1994: Trompenaars & Hampden-Turner, 2002). Being able to come up with such a phrasing is indeed a crucial skill in this context. When everybody has all the available information and a good grasp on the dilemma, the next step is joint brainstorming about ways to solve the dilemma. We can apply here all the creativity techniques described in Chapter 6.

When we transcend the dilemma in a win–win solution – in Hegel's terms, integrating the antitheses into a synthesis – something magic comes about. By creating a new meaning, we change reality. We get new insights and create a new truth. This act of creation is an outstanding example of giving meaning. In this respect, Freire calls dialogue a creative process that creates meaning. 'Speaking a true word transforms reality,' he states (Freire, 1970, cited in Dixon, 1998). This act of creation amounts to our thinking of something that was not yet there and realizing or actualizing it in a material way as well. When we succeed, a very pleasant feeling ensues. I use the term 'realizing' as it means having or getting knowledge of, or insight into, something, as well as making something real or actual.

The next step consists of critically looking at preliminary solutions. Can it be done better? More pleasantly? In a smarter way? The results can be then tested with the help of criteria such as those formulated in Chapter 6. Lastly, we need to formulate agreements to which all parties are willing and able to adhere. Record the agreements very meticulously. The following step is that everybody records whether and how the new arrangement works, what incidentally can be done better, as well as how these improvements might look. If we have accomplished all that, we set a date for a new meeting in which we can discuss how things are working out in practice.

The effectiveness of the dialogue approach presupposes that all parties want to solve the problems in each of these steps and also believe that it can be done well, something that does not seem very self-evident beforehand. Successful accomplishment implies that all parties involved must know how a dilemma works. Moreover, the participants in the dialogue must feel challenged to proceed as discussed before, with the help of inquiry and advocacy, without becoming defensive and without drifting apart in unnecessary ways. Such an approach makes high demands on the participants' intellectual and emotional powers. For instance, the parties must be adept at logical reasoning, assessing the value of arguments and drawing conclusions. Moreover, they must be willing, if necessary, to change their views. Often it helps to engage a special discussion leader to facilitate the accomplishment of all challenges involved in the different steps. The role of such a discussion leader is elaborated later in this chapter.

From a completely different perspective, Altshuller, a Russian scientist who examined tens of thousands of patent applications, mentioned the above-described method of as sharply as possible formulating dilemmas as the most important element of the best methods for creating inventions (www.trizexperts.net). Goldratt, an author and organizational consultant who occupies himself with improving organizational logistics, speaks in this context of 'evaporating clouds' (Goldratt, 1990); that is, solving a dilemma by coming to a synthesis in which the paradoxes and contradictions at the level of everyday reality are overcome. In terms of game theory, win–win solutions involve each time creating mutual dependence and non-zero-sum solutions for the benefit of all players involved (Wright, 2001). The great gain of striving for win–win solutions is that optimal solutions are reached that can also count on the full support of all participants.

RESPECT AND SELF-RESPECT

The previous sections show that there are some quite painful and unpleasant sides to a dialogue that we cannot easily avoid. First, many people are only inclined to bear this displeasure when they consider the situation to be safe enough, and this perceived safety is foremost a matter of mutual trust. The availability of such trust is certainly not self-evident in the first place. After all, the parties do disagree and even oppose each other. That actually was the reason the dialogue was needed. Paradoxically, the same disagreement – when brought completely into the open – makes dialogue such a powerful tool.

How do we create mutual trust? How do we get people far enough that they open up to other people and their being different? What do we do to put them in perspective and abandon their own suppositions? How do people become willing to brainstorm about new possibilities and assume the eventual outcomes as a basis for their new reality? The answer is simple, though maybe not very encouraging. They must want to do that. Logical points of departure here are respect for ourselves and the other parties. Still not very encouraging, but let us examine these matters in any case.

What does respect for ourselves mean? If we equate self-respect with self-esteem, Nathaniel Branden (1987) gives an amazingly simple answer. He points out that we can reinforce our self-esteem by living precisely with as much awareness and responsibility as is demanded of us by the matters that arise in our path – note, not as much awareness and responsibility as possible, but as much awareness and responsibility as is demanded of us by the situation we are in. This awareness and responsibility are a matter of our conscience. We know what is expected of us in this respect, even if we do not meet these expectations. As the term 'conscience' already suggests, we are talking here about moral and ethical issues, matters of good and evil, no more and no less. Whether we come up with the right actions or not is our choice. When we act in the right way and meet the situational demands, we make the situational reality fully our own. Only in this way do we fully engage in our reality and fully experience it. That choice opens up a miraculously familiar world, in which we know very well what is right and what we should and shouldn't do. It is like coming home. At the same time, this implies a form of judging, though a form in which we are very aware of our judgment.

This discussion of self-esteem fits in with several other stories. What should we think of the following sentences of Saul Bellow, with which he closes *Mr Sammler's Planet*:

> He was aware what he must meet – and he did meet – through all the confusion and degraded clowning of this life we are speeding – he did meet the terms of his contract. The terms which, in his inmost heart, each man knows. As I know mine. As all know. For that is the truth of it – that we all know, God, that we know, we know, we know. (Bellow, 1971, p. 252)

Self-respect is entering into a contract to live with as much awareness and responsibility as our activities ask of us and each time to do what we, from our own assumptions, should do. When we respect somebody else, we are willing to see him as somebody who, from his own assumptions about how things are, wants the good and takes responsibility for it. In essence this is concerned with good will, Confucius's benevolence (1979), the will to create a new form of 'we'. With this we are back at the will to solve matters together, the first part of the fundamental attitude of dialogue.

When we want to approach good will at a more structural level, as a more or less stable attitude, we end up with concepts like conscience and honor. Both involve a fundamental attitude that we embrace intentionally. In both also, matters of good and evil are of prime importance. So we can take our conscience as the sense of good and evil that serves as a touchstone for the moral quality of actions, while we can take honor as its outcome: the reputation we gradually build up from our point of departure of wanting to do the right thing, even when that is not the easiest way to go. The moral sides of dialogue will come up later in this chapter more elaborately.

THE ROLE OF A DISCUSSION LEADER

We have discussed respect and self-respect, and even conscience and honor, but again: How do we get people far enough that they are willing to really apply these concepts? This time I pass over the simple answer – namely, that they simply should apply it – and attempt to give an answer that in many organizations is more useful. That answer implies that we delegate the care for what people should do to a professional, a discussion leader. A discussion leader is a kind of chairman who monitors and streamlines the proceedings. He spells out the proper fundamental attitude and takes care that the participants actually display it. Moreover, he states the goals of the dialogue, gets things going, sees to it that the proceedings go well and intervene when things threaten to go in the wrong direction.

Most importantly, the discussion leader should be a professional. What does this mean in this context? First, facilitating a dialogue must be something the discussion leader likes to do and can be fully absorbed in. Also, he should facilitate the dialogue appropriately: he must be able to do it well. Being willing and able to do a good job implies that the discussion leader must make a real connection with his task. Nevertheless, he can only do a good job when all parties allow him to take this role. Important qualities for the discussion leader are integrity, competence, previous successful experiences in dialogue facilitating and, based on the latter, some ascribed 'jurisdiction'. In practice, a discussion leader is somebody with extensive experience – and preferably also a relevant education – in dialogues and related forms of discussion. His background can vary, though, and can consist of negotiating, mediating, project management, management training, coaching and counseling.

Before the first session, the discussion leader makes sure that the participants have been sufficiently informed about the nature of dialogue. To achieve this objective, he provides them with a written text about the subject at hand and the ins and outs of dialogue.

In the first session, the discussion leader starts by asking whether everybody has read the text, which has been sent to them in advance, and whether there are any questions about it. Subsequently the discussion leader answers possible questions.

The next thing to do is establishing a 'safe place'. So the discussion leader separates the context in which the dialogue takes place from the normal, everyday environment of the participants; that is, the organization or organizations to which they belong. In this way, the discussion leader makes the immediate context of dialogue into a safe place, where all involved can feel safe and be open and honest, without needlessly being hindered by the existing inequality of power. To create a really safe place, the separation from the further environment must be clear and trustworthy to all participants. In practice, this boils down to agreeing some rules and principles. It also helps to let the dialogue take place in a somewhat secluded place, well removed from the organizational premises, preferable in a quiet resort situated in a beautiful landscape. Cell phones should be turned off.

The first step here is laying down rules that guarantee the perceived safety of all participants. One way of guaranteeing this safety consists of making clear that everybody has to indicate and guard, if needed, their own limits, even when this is at the expense of 'absolute' openness. Also, the discussion leader can propose to determine very precisely what can and cannot be communicated to the outside. Moreover, this is the right time and place to introduce the feedback rules (see Chapter 6). Subsequently the discussion leader explains the rules and principles ensuing from the fundamental attitude, as well as the importance of openness to the other people.

The way in which the discussion leader introduces rules and agreements has an obvious modeling function. This implies that he substantiates these rules and agreements with reasons and rationales and makes sure that possible objections are carefully examined and discussed. Therefore, it is important that the discussion leader continuously sticks to the rules and explicitly demonstrates the desired forms of openness and sincerity. To this end, he asks questions in such a way that he explains their own reasons, motives and goals for asking these questions. Put differently, he demonstrates all kinds of advocacy: he 'advertises' this own suppositions and goals. The discussion leader acts also as a role model for questioning, by asking about everybody's motives and interests. Relevant issues that are not clarified and secured undermine the future outcomes of the dialogue. In this way the discussion leader makes it clear that for everybody involved caring for the other parties is a matter of well-understood self-interest. To stress the importance of looking after the interests of all parties involved to an equal degree, the discussion leader also displays his concerns about this issue each time that is relevant, for example when a party's interest in keeping things as they are is at stake.

When all parties care about the interests of all other parties, the underlying common fate of all participants is taken seriously. In this way, a new form of 'we' is created. This new form of 'we' implies that each participant can have their own contribution and be respectful to each other, while at the same time everybody gets what they deserve and is not cheated out of anything. The discussion leader, of course, can play a determining role as well, again by setting the right example and asking the right questions.

The goal of the dialogue has been stated at the very beginning. The change agent or the manager responsible for the accomplishment of the goal formulates the goal and specifies the desired end result. Moreover, he substantiates the goal with its reasons and necessity. The formulation of the goal is open ended, in the sense that it only specifies what is desired, for example continuing together in such a way that all involved are satisfied and no one feels cheated or excluded. How this must happen and how exactly it is going to look like remain explicitly open. Generally speaking, the goal should be positively phrased and meet the criteria described in Chapter 6, at least to the degree that these criteria are compatible with the desired open end.

One reason for formulating a clear goal is that it enables the discussion leader to use the goal as a criterion for the relevance what is going on in the dialogue. Each time when the discussion gets off track, the discussion leader can ask questions such as:

- 'How does this relate to . . . (a description of the goal), the goal that we set ourselves?'
- And if it does not relate at all to that goal: 'OK, you said . . . (a very short summary, with a lowering tone of voice at the end, see . . .). Let's now go back to . . . (the subject just before the discussion was sidetracked).'
- When the discussion gets diverted again: 'This is the second time we have got off the track here. Tell me, why is that?'
- If necessary: 'What can we do about this?'

Formulating a clear goal also lays the foundation for moments of awareness (see Chapter 6) and reflecting together (see also Chapter 6) from time to time about questions such as:

- Where are we right now?
- How are we doing?
- What is not going well?
- How can this be done better?
- What are we doing right now?
- What has still to be done?

When the goal has been formulated, the discussion leader sketches briefly what dialogue is about. The discussion leader pays attention to points such as:

- fundamental attitude (see earlier in this chapter)
- different kinds of resistance and Leary's rose (see earlier in this chapter and Chapter 6)
- pitfalls, allergies and other distortions (see Chapter 7)
- formulating and solving dilemmas
- necessary skills and training
- transition process (see Chapter 7)
- possible agenda for progress

In short, the discussion leader finds out to what degree the participants have familiarized themselves with the material sent to them in advance and fills in any lacunas in their knowledge.

DIALOGUE AND ETHICS

The openness to be willing to look at other people's good and strong sides, their possibilities, their surpluses or exaggeration, as well as any lacunas and distortions of these good and strong qualities, can also be termed a form of love. Love of one's fellow people can then be conceived of as accepting others as they are, seeing their good characteristics, having compassion for their weaker sides and intending to assist them and make their life pleasurable. Thomas Aquinas, a thirteenth-century Italian philosopher and theologian sanctified in 1323, stated in this respect:

> the plurality and consequently the inequality among things provides the occasion for the performance of good acts. Charity is the more perfect when we love things different from ourselves. (Long, 2005, p. 60)

In that, we find ourselves in the middle of the domain of ethics and morality, and possibly even that of theology. As it is, charity is one of the three most important Christian principal virtues, according to the same Thomas Aquinas possibly the most important one.

The fact that we find ourselves in the domain of ethics and theology is really not so surprising. In Chapter 3 we discussed the relationship of ethics to customs and traditions. This ethical side of dialogue manifests itself also in the work of Paolo Freire, one of the so-called liberation theologians (Freire, 1970, in Dixon, 1998) and Martin Buber, a Jewish philosopher (Buber, 1957, 1966). Concerning the ethical sides of dialogue, charity is only the beginning. Other virtues play an important role in a successful dialogue as well.

Dialogue is also a matter of faith or belief, to be more precise the belief in the human ability to create and re-create our own world (Freire, 1970, in Dixon, 1998). This belief also refers to our assumptions: the belief that appropriate assumptions enable us to found a reality that we can inhabit and understand, a reality that manifests itself to us as if of its own accord (Heidegger, 1991; James, 1890/1950), a reality that we can share with others. Such a belief resounds for example also in Anselm of Canterbury's saying: 'I believe in order that I understand' (see Chapter 3). When all parties believe in such a way in common assumptions and the reality resulting from them, we have accomplished something: a seemingly solid reality in which we can comfortably live. As long as that is not the case, there remains work to be done. This reality is for that matter not the kind of reality that effortlessly encompasses the whole universe, but an irregularly formed space in which we live, which surrounds us and our relevant others, with a certain view on the past and projections to the future (Merleau-Ponty, 1945).

Then there is hope, namely that our project, the dialogue, will succeed; that there will be a solution that works for everyone. This entails the idea that the group and its individual members are smart enough to create their own solutions. This idea is actually well founded. First, it is a fact of experience that a conducive reality is definitely possible. After all, the previous reality served us for years too. Second, it can be defended that such assumptions always have, deep down, a positive goal. For example, an assumption's goal or function can be that we get somewhere, without getting in trouble. Moreover, our own assumptions have guided us through most of our life, and the same applies to the assumptions of other people. Consequently, we cannot exclude beforehand the fact that these positive goals can be united in a win–win solution, which in the end enriches all parties involved.

As stated before, the required openness, admitting the other person and letting go of a part of our assumptions and behavioral repertoire, are now and then painful and threatening. Moreover, dialogue demands that we willingly and knowingly enter a situation we do not fully control and of which we don't know the outcomes in advance. All of this asks for considerable courage.

To call out our own and others' assumptions, with their similarities and differences, without deterring or hurting anybody, demands a high degree of carefulness. This careful-ness involves both inquiry, asking questions without the other feeling observed, attacked or completely misunderstood, and advocacy, explaining our own ideas to invite the other to comment on these ideas and to point out possible lacunas, exaggerations and distortions in them (Dixon, 1998, p. 30). This is indeed a matter of great carefulness, in which the stem 'care' is telling. The term 'caution' applies here too, also in the sense of circum-spection, looking for possible risks and pitfalls, which may be inherent in the possible sensitivities of the other person. This carefulness and caution together can be described as prudence.

Another threat to dialogue consists of overstressing one or more virtues at the cost of the others. Such overstressing would endanger the whole ethical fabric (Berlin, 1998). For instance, too much carefulness interferes with courage, too much faith becomes fanaticism and interferes with carefulness, and so on. Overstressing one virtue constitutes a lack of moderation or temperance, the sin of *intemperantia*. Lack of moderation does not only jeopardize dialogue, but all forms of communication and action.

Lastly, in dialogue we should ensure that nobody is mistreated or cheated out of anything, as this always jeopardizes the end result. Essentially, we are talking here about justice, the right application of the whole ethical system. Justice results in rules about the exchange and division of property, hierarchical position, rights and attention, as well as in rules about the ranking and applicability of rules themselves (see also Storrs Hall, 2000). Socrates even called justice the only true virtue (Williams, 1985). An important point here is that the ethical system should be equally applied to everyone involved. As a result, no person or group of people should be preferentially or unfairly treated.

Perhaps not all readers have realized this, but what has been written in this section until now comprises a description of the seven principal Christian virtues, namely belief, hope, love, courage, prudence, moderation and justice. Does that mean that dialogue is a purely Christian affair? Absolutely not. To start with, these virtues are not exclusively Christian. Christianity shares these virtues for example with Islam and Judaism, while Paul derived the latter four – courage, prudence, moderation, justice – from Plato. Moreover, there are more virtues involved, such as sincerity and humility.

Still, the full applicability of the seven principal Christian virtues remains striking. Probably this applicability comes about because dialogue focuses on an area where ethics can be pre-eminently administered, namely circumstances in which the interaction of people is not structured and regulated in fixed ways. This lack of fixed structure and regulation is for example present when people do not know each other, have opposing interests and do not interact from an existing division of roles. Such situations are more prone to unrestrained aggression and conflicts. The principal Christian – or Islamic, or Jewish, or Greek – virtues can then be considered as a set of guidelines that have proven able to prevent and contain such conflicts. These virtues have proved themselves in this respect: they did the trick. Put differently, these virtues are reinforced by their outcomes: less manslaughter and greater wealth. As a result, these virtues simply make up a good recipe for what in game theory is called a 'non-zero-sum' outcome, an outcome of a game that provides gains to all participants (Wright, 2001). Another important point is that all participants in principle know these guidelines: they ring a bell because they have been a normal part of the participants' education.

Another good feature of dialogue is that it is a pre-eminent instrument for getting to know other assumptions, and for learning to appreciate these assumptions. That is why dialogue is also such an important tool in intercultural communication. Furthermore, Isaiah Berlin states – and I agree with him – that there is only a limited number of these assumptions or guidelines, without committing himself to a specific number. Learning to know assumptions is thus a matter of taking the position of the other party. The nature of these assumptions and acting on these assumptions are, according to Berlin (1998), part of the essence of what it means to be a human being.

Techniques, Personal Issues and Exercises

As stated in the introduction, this second part discusses personal issues that are relevant for your effectiveness as a change agent, techniques that you can apply to do a better job and exercises to help you to master the necessary skills to do a good job. Essentially, Part II gives the elements of a training program, which is intended for different groups of trainees.

First, there are the change agents. In the optimal situation they can engage a professional to facilitate their training sessions, but essentially they can do most of the training themselves, preferably in groups of four, which regularly and frequently – for example twice a week – come together. To be successful in developing and extending the existing assumptions prevailing in an organization, change agents must have a much deeper than average insight into their own assumptions. Change agents must also feel comfortable in advocating, discussing and suspending their own assumptions, as well as comparing these assumptions with those of other parties. Change agents, furthermore, need considerable experience in guiding other parties to do the same. Lastly, change agents must have experience in developing and extending their own assumptions. Only then they can hope to bring about similar feats in other people.

Secondly, the managers involved must be trained. They can be segmented in several layers if needed. The managers can be trained by the change agents or by the same external professional as trains the change agents. When the change agents do the training, it is to be recommended that they are supervised by the professional who has trained them. Managers must be proficient in all these skills as well, as they have to set an example to their employees and must be able to practice the art of dialogue themselves in their dealings with their people.

The third group of trainees consists of the employees on the shop floor who participate in the dialogue sessions. These employees are trained by the change agents. The training of these employees is no luxury. After all, they are the ones who have to change their whole working life and they need all the relevant skills they can lay their hands on.

In principle, all three groups get the same or a similar program, though there are some differences. The description of the exercises in Chapter 8 indicates for which group the exercises are primarily intended.

CHAPTER 6

Techniques and Tools

In this chapter a number of techniques are discussed that have proven to be helpful in organizational change. Subsequently, the followed issues are discussed:

- Asking questions, reflecting, and questioning techniques
- Matching
- Solution-oriented coaching
- Feedback rules
- Discussion of progress
- Moments of awareness
- Leary's rose
- Thinking of nothing in particular
- Focusing
- Giving ourselves assignments, setting personal goals
- Starting up 'slow brain processes'
- Affirmatives
- Really seeing somebody
- Imagination
- Delegating alternatives
- Helping creativity
- Goal-setting

ASKING QUESTIONS AND REFLECTING

Asking questions seems to be one of the easiest things to do, yet it is actually surprising how seldom questions are used well. Asking questions can mean asking other people questions as well as asking ourselves questions. The latter is a standard part of reflection. In addition, there is self-reflection; that is, asking ourselves questions about ourselves. This section examines all three kinds of questioning, as all three are crucial in dialogue and essential for leaders and change agents.

A question is here taken as a piece of equipment. A question enables us to focus our attention on something that doesn't demand our attention by itself, even on something that is at that moment still unknown to us. Questioning is playing with the searchlight of our mind. By asking a question, for the moment we suspend our existing knowledge and create a temporary mental void. This void provides room for something new, an answer, which can come to the fore now. This answer then can become a subject for further questions.

A question brings about a response that, at least in its effect, is related to the 'novelty response', a somewhat more sophisticated form of the orienting or novelty response (see Chapter 3). The relationship to the novelty response lies in the fact that both the novelty response and a question can bring about a sense of wonder or surprise, which is, according to Plato (http://classics.mit/edu/Plato/theatu.html) and Aristotle (1941), the starting point of all philosophy. When we are asked a question our activities come to a standstill: our speaking and thinking stop, our mind becomes empty and silent for a moment, and in this silent emptiness an answer can make its entry (cf. Verhoeven, 1967, p. 42).

There are questions of different kinds and measures. There are small questions, precision instruments for the square millimeter. There are also high-powered tools. With these questions we can undermine any established order or truth, shed light on unwelcome inevitabilities, as well as make pleasant illusions and castles in the air disappear. Injudicious use, of course, can cause significant damage: questioning *is* a very radical activity.

Questioning requires a strange kind of craftsmanship, a combination of much skill and admitting that we don't know something. Admitting that we don't know something is often felt to be risky. This feeling of risk is one reason we do not make optimal use of questioning. We must feel safe enough to expose that lack of knowledge. This feeling of safety implies that questioning presupposes some combination of trust, self-confidence and sometimes even courage; that is, we should at least not be ruled by anxiety or fear. A somewhat higher-powered position in which we feel completely comfortable may be helpful in this respect. Asking questions is a very effective leadership tool. 'What are you going to do about. . .? What do you need for that? What are the pitfalls? How do you going to deal with them? What would have been of help? How can things be done even better?' And so on. Questions are an excellent way to steer someone's behavior without giving any order or command. The point is that we are already the leader and the other person must do the job in any case. By asking questions we can steer the other to do a better job by directing their problem-solving qualities and creativity.

Another point is that a question presupposes another person with an own perspective who can throw light on the matter in question. Reflection then presupposes a self that consists of at least two sub-persons. The fact that reflection works rather well implies a convincing demonstration of the divided character of our self.

Asking ourselves questions gives rise to a form of internal dialogue, in which we take turns asking questions and giving answers. The strange thing about reflection is that we apparently can learn something 'new' from it. At the same time, however, we knew the answer already, even though we didn't know we knew the answer. Or more precisely: we knew the answer, but we didn't apply the information inherent in the answer to the situation in which we are using that information now. In the present situation, however, the answer can make a difference: the answer can lead to peace or turbulence, to really new ideas and even to spectacular innovations.

Essentially, self-reflection is a way to integrate ourselves. Self-reflection – that is, reflecting about ourselves or asking ourselves questions about ourselves – is concerned with connecting our different attitudes and positions with each other. We have assumed and developed these attitudes in the different situations to which these attitudes belong, or better: the different situations that these attitudes helped, and still help, to bring about. As these attitudes each occur in different situations, these different attitudes live separate lives and are not likely to 'meet' each other. What we do in self-reflection is bringing such a meeting about after all: we intentionally relate the different attitudes to each other. In this way, self-reflection helps us to integrate these different attitudes and to become more and more who we are. This is part of a creative process with an open end, whose success fully depends on two virtues: honesty and courage. Self-reflection is concerned with facing the truth such as it enfolds from the connection of two attitudes. The next step then consists of acting based on that truth. Both steps in principle imply that we are living in the here and now and add to our self-esteem (Branden, 1987). This integration can go on as long as we live, or at least as long we care and pay attention.

A last remark about questioning ourselves: when we ask ourselves a question, there is always more than one possible answer. Honor that and find different answers to your questions. It is a good Indian custom to give at least six answers (Stone, 1997), preferably even seven; that is, when the question allows this. Seven is namely the maximum number of items that most of us can comfortably keep in our short-term memory at the same time. Subsequently, put all these answers in a story that does justice to the richness of your reality.

Questioning Techniques

This section gives a short overview of common interview techniques. These techniques are for the most part applicable in interviews as well as in reflection. Even when one is an experienced interviewer, it can be quite enlightening to use these techniques on oneself to reflect.

Good interviewing most of the time involves that we begin with an *open question* – that is, a question that cannot be answered in a meaningful way by yes or no – and get deeper into the matter subsequently, for example with the help of probing (see below). Open questions often begin with:

- how
- what
- which
- in or to what degree
- why, and so on

A *closed question* is a question that can be answered in a meaningful way by yes or no. For example: 'Are you angry?', 'Do you understand what I say?', 'Do you have a moment?' and so on.

A *suggestive or leading question* is a question that indicates what answer the questioner expects or wants to hear. For example: 'Don't you want to say that...?', 'Don't you find also that...?', 'But aren't you of the opinion that...?'.

Suggestive questions are primarily intended to influence someone's answers. As such, they usually are undesirable when we are purely gathering information. In a way it can be defended that every question is to a degree suggestive, but here we only aim at 'too' suggestive questions.

Some questions can contain rather blatant *presuppositions*. Presuppositions are especially intended to let somebody commit themselves or to corner someone. For example: 'How many times a year do you beat up your partner?' Or, when nothing is actually sold yet: 'Are you paying cash or with a credit card?' This kind of question is usually undesirable in the case of pure information gathering.

The last question ('Are you paying cash or with a credit card?') is also a *double-barreled question*; that is, a question that is worded in terms of 'either... or ...' and thus suggests that there are only two possible answers. In the case of information gathering, a double-barreled question is not a good question, as it deprives the respondent of other answering possibilities.

Probing is a basic technique. Probing implies that we, based on the answer, are asking for explanation and clarification. Examples are:

- 'How do you mean that?', preceded or not by a short summary of the answer.
- Repeating a single word – here called X – from the answer: 'X?', possibly followed by: 'What do you mean by that?'
- 'You say that it is X. What exactly is so X about that?'
- 'And further?'
- 'And?'
- Phrases such as: 'Can you tell me more about that?', 'Please, elaborate that somewhat' or 'Can you explain that a little more?'

Paying attention, or active listening, is important for maintaining contact. This is concerned with 'rapport' or 'being with' somebody. In a talk with another person, paying attention implies, among other things, that we:

- Are sufficiently oriented toward the other person (not turned away, neither with our body, nor our face).
- Look sufficiently at the other person.
- Show understanding, for example by nodding now and then, when appropriate.
- Say 'Hmm' in agreement, but not too often and certainly not too mechanically.
- Show understanding by asking relevant questions and saying things that correspond with what the respondent is saying.
- Synchronize our behavior with that of the other person and now and then match the other person's behavior, which – when all is well – actually happens by itself.

In self-reflection, the bodily manifestations of paying attention are of course not applicable. Because self-reflection is less bound by the usual conversation rules, it is relatively easy to stray from its path. After all, there is nobody else besides ourselves to keep us on the right track. When we actually stray, we must go back to our last question, and from time to time we even have to start all over again. Though staying on track is initially a matter of some self-discipline, it will gradually become easier.

Paying attention is essentially a technique for *keeping the respondent involved*. Sometimes this may not be enough and we have to spell things out more. Examples of more explicitly keeping the respondent involved are:

- 'OK, I just want to examine... somewhat more.'
- 'We were talking about...'
- 'Let's go back a little, you said...'

We can preface the sentences above by a short conclusive summary – a single sentence – of the subject the respondent was talking about: 'You tell me that..., but now...' Keep in mind that a conclusive summary is characterized by lowering the pitch of the voice at the end of the summary.

This technique is of course also relevant in self-reflection. Here too, the respondent tends to become evasive and avoidant when certain subjects come up, and here too we should prevent ourselves from going astray.

Besides probing and paying attention, there are more techniques for thoroughly unraveling an issue.

Mirroring refers to representing in our own words – thus not literally repeating! – the answers of the other person with a questioning intonation; that is, with a rising voice at the end of the last sentence. This is a powerful technique, which shows understanding and acknowledgment. Mirroring is often appreciated by the respondent. A necessary condition for this is of course that we represent the respondent's answer properly and don't put words into their mouth. Examples are:

- 'So you mean that. . .?'
- 'Thus essentially you are saying that. . .?'

You may be surprised how instructive mirroring can be in the case of self-reflection. It is comparable to reading your own written text to somebody else, which makes you aware of a lot of errors, omissions and other shortcomings in that text. Or even better, having it read to you by someone else.

Summarizing implies that we formulate the essence of an answer. We can do this to examine whether we have properly understood the answer. A good summary evokes agreement and possibly a further explanation of a particular point. For example:

- 'All in all, you are saying. . .?'
- 'In short, you are saying. . .?'

We usually end this kind of summary with a rising voice, to give it a questioning quality.

A short summary can also be used to get somebody back to the original question. Toward the end of the summary, the voice then lowers a little, possibly followed by a 'but . . .':

- 'So you have had a good time there, (but) now I want to get back to our previous subject, namely. . .'

To understand somebody well and to explore a subject in more depth, we can *ask questions about the accompanying feeling*. For example:

- 'How was that for you?'
- 'How did that feel?'

Sometimes we can also word the accompanying feeling ourselves. For example:

- 'That must have been very sad, pleasant, challenging and so on.'
- 'Apparently that has – or hasn't – touched you very much.'

Of course, this technique can turn itself against us when we come up with the wrong feelings. Well applied, however, wording an accompanying feeling ourselves can work miracles. People tend to suppress certain feelings in order not to be overwhelmed by them. Later, when the event that evoked the emotion has been history for a long time, there is a good chance that the accompanying emotion still is suppressed. Questions about these feelings, intended to come to some acknowledgment of the accompanying feelings in the end, can still evoke strong emotions but can also lead to a great relief.

Though this may sound strange, this technique can also be very effective in self-reflection. For example, wording or questioning an accompanying feeling ourselves should be used as a standard intervention when we don't feel anything while it would really be quite normal to experience an intense feeling.

Either when somebody remains too vague or too abstract in their answers or when we really do not understand properly what the respondent means, we can ask them to *concretize* their answer by asking them to give an example.

- 'Can you give an(other) example of that?'
- 'When did this occur, for example?'

When the respondent gives an example, you can get a clear image of what the other person means, or is hiding, by exploring the example further with probing and other techniques. Asking for specific examples is also very effective in self-reflection. As you will have understood by now, you probably are no less evasive than the next guy.

The techniques to be discussed now are primarily intended to track underlying assumptions and goals. *Asking for assumptions and goals* often boils down to *asking why*. For example:

- 'What do you gain by that?'
- 'What does it do for you?'
- 'What is your motive?'
- 'Why?'
- 'To what end are you doing this?'
- 'What are you avoiding in this way?'
- 'What is important about that?'
- 'Why do(n't) you want that?'
- 'What makes you act here?'

It is good to realize that asking 'why' most of the time doesn't boil down to asking for causes. On the contrary, most often it involves asking for goals: things we want to attain or avoid.

Surfacing underlying assumptions often boils down to repeatedly asking why, sometimes even many times in a row. For example:

- 'Why do you laugh?'
- 'It's just funny.'
- 'Why is it funny?'
- 'The idea that in the end it is not my carelessness at all.'
- 'Why on earth would it have been a matter of your carelessness?'
- 'Well, I just thought it was a matter of my carelessness.'
- 'Why did you think that?'
- 'I'm often accused of carelessness.'

Of course, this can go on for a while, either resulting in a whole history of false accusations or wanting to be the cause of things and to be of influence, based on deeply rooted feelings of inferiority, caused by. . ., and so on.

Another point is that it is less than elegant to ask why each time. A better sequence would have been:

- 'You are laughing?'
- 'It's just funny.'
- 'What is so funny about it?'
- 'The idea that in the end it is not my carelessness at all.'
- 'Carelessness?'
- 'Well, I thought it was a matter of my carelessness.'
- 'How come?'

Though such an approach is often necessary to surface underlying assumptions – such as in the case of 'inquiry' (see Chapter 5), where it can be an important ingredient of a successful dialogue – it will not come as a surprise that the other party may experience this approach as aggressive. As it is, we do come close to the other person in this way. Consequently, we can apply this approach only in a climate of safety and mutual trust. Of course, such a climate cannot be taken for granted.

There are many different ways to create a climate of safety and mutual trust. Self-disclosure – that is, showing openness about ourselves – can help to set the tone. Explaining our reasons, motives and goals for our own questions and remarks helps too. This is called 'advocacy' and is also one of the crucial elements of dialogue (see Chapter 5). Being able to create a good atmosphere, a reputation of good intentions and the absence of malice are other ingredients. In addition, there is agreeing about certain rules. An example of such a rule would be that both parties are responsible for indicating and guarding their own limits. Another way to create such a climate is explicating the need of openness in a situation such as this one (see also Chapter 5).

An alternative technique to surface underlying assumptions and goals is *confronting*. Confronting implies that an answer is related to a datum external to that datum, which is incompatible with the answer. This also is often regarded as aggressive and demands a climate of safety and mutual trust as well.

Confronting can involve a previous answer, for example:

- 'You just said. . . Now you are saying. . . How do these two relate to each other?'

Confronting can also concern our own practical or theoretical knowledge:

- 'In general, it is the case that. . . How does that apply here?'

Or an incompatibility with the non-verbal behavior:

- 'Why are you laughing about this?'

Furthermore, we can consult our own feelings, however indeterminate they are:

- 'You say that in a very relaxed way. I would feel very bad if such a thing happened to me.'
- 'That gives me an indeterminate feeling. Can you tell me somewhat more about it?'

Still another option is examining what images the words of the other person evoke in our mind. If there is an image, we can simply tell them about it:

- 'What you say evokes in me an image of. . .'

Above the advice was given to give at least seven answers to a question and to make a story out of them that does justice to the richness of reality. One implication here is that it is a good habit to ask what other answers there still are.

MATCHING

In Chapter 3, it was discussed that paying attention to somebody goes together with taking the attitude of that person. There it was described how we, fully or partially, simulate or copy the other person's physical attitude, to be able to perceive the world from his perspective and to perceive ourselves from the other person's perspective as well. In this way we make, for the time being, a 'we' out of an 'I' and a 'you'. The 'we feeling' inherent in together making the same movements and assuming the same posture was discussed there also.

The psychotherapist Frieda Fromm-Reichman has made a technique out of this by deliberately adopting the – often weird – bodily attitudes of her catatonic patients. Catatonia implies that somebody assumes the same attitude for a long time and is known as a symptom of grave psychotic states. A little like the people who nowadays act as statues on busy shopping streets and squares, but without the make-up or the outfit, and unpaid. To Fromm-Reichman this appeared to be the only way to get a feeling of the mental state of these patients, as well as to examine whether in this way some contact was possible.

Imitating somebody enables us to feel to a degree how the other person feels and contributes to the intensity of the contact. It is, by the way, unclear whether the latter is a cause or an effect. Imitating somebody usually is, after all, the outcome of our focusing on another person. On the other hand, when we put in the effort to imitate somebody, we must be focused on that person as well and it is unclear whether the other person distinguishes between these two forms of imitation, equally because they do not deliberately pay attention to this difference. Moreover, dancing together or drilling military recruits can induce a 'we feeling' too.

We can imitate people in different ways. We can take over somebody's attitude or parts of it. This is what Scheflen (1964) called postural congruence, which in his opinion is a manifestation of connectedness as well. The same applies for movements and movement rhythm, phenomena that are known as mirroring and interaction synchrony (see for example Davis, 1982).

In everyday conversation, mirroring especially occurs at the beginning and toward the end of interactions, and at moments when the conversation halts briefly (Kendon, 1970; Schabracq, 1987). In itself this is only logical, for these are the moments when coordination is needed and then we are most focused on each other, while during the rest of the conversation we are primarily busy with formulating and understanding spoken text.

Mirroring for that matter can mean that we make really mirrored movements – for example moving our left hand when the other person moves his right hand – as well as that we do so symmetrically – both moving our left hand. Furthermore, it does not need to involve exactly the same movement. For example, while you take a sip of a drink, I can pass my hand through my hair.

Concerning interaction synchrony, this is so automatic a process that we can hardly switch it off when we are attending to somebody. Its total absence usually means that there is no contact: the other person does not listen and is elsewhere with his thoughts. This is something we can also feel. When this is a permanent matter, it is known as a symptom of schizophrenia, the so-called '*praecox Gefühl*' (see Chapter 4). Synchrony disturbances also occur in contacts with stuttering and spastic people.

Ginnie Laborde (1987) mentions, besides attitude and movements, three other 'channels' of matching. We can adopt somebody's words – a deliberate form of echolalia (Schabracq, 1991) – as well as somebody's breathing pattern and paralinguistic behavior, the way he talks. According to Laborde, these forms of matching all contribute to better empathy and contact. Concerning the way somebody talks, it is a simple act of experience that, when somebody talks very loud during a telephone conversation, this makes us talk louder as well, often in away that it is frowned on by the people in the room. The story about our breathing seems perhaps more problematic, because breathing is often hard to perceive, but there is empirical support for the phenomenon that the breathing patterns of people who focus on each other become more synchronous (Davis, 1982).

Lastly, we might mirror the other person's favorite representation system – visual, auditory or feeling – a form of matching that, for the same reasons, is recommended in the NLP (neuro-linguistic programming) literature (for example Seymour & O'Connor, 1994). This primarily boils down to adopting the wording of the other person's favorite representation system. With visually oriented people, this involves using words such as seeing, sight, view, light, color, mirror and so on; with auditory people words such as hearing, sounding and melody; and with feeling-oriented people words such as feeling, warmth and touch.

Here too, we must try out the different forms of mirroring and matching to examine what form of mirroring or matching works best for us.

SOLUTION-ORIENTED COACHING

In principle, each form of coaching wants to bring about a solution. Differently from other forms of coaching, however, solution-oriented coaching begins with the solution, at least with an imagination of a solution. In a guided fantasy, the client is invited to imagine how the world would look and feel like when the goal that he wants to attain, and for which he came into coaching, has actually been fully realized.

In a guided fantasy, clients then project themselves to a point in time when the goal is fully realized. The client imagines what that looks like, how it feels, what is being said and how sounds themselves. If desired, the taste and smell of success can be involved too, so that all five senses can contribute to the vividness of the fantasy. The client can in that fantasy also imagine what he has done yesterday, and what is going to do in a moment, as well as tomorrow and next week.

When the client has explored the fantasy in all its ramifications and with all its different elements and has familiarized himself with it, he is asked to look back in time from his fantasized future and reminds himself how the goal accomplishment was brought about. What has the client done to get there? How did he get moving? What has he done first, what then and what after that? What means has he used? Who has helped him? Who has opposed them? How have they dealt with that? What were in hindsight the biggest difficulties? And how has he overcome these?

If desired, the solution of the separate difficulties and the different stages of the goal attainment can also be approached through the same kind of fantasies. If needed, the fantasy about the future can also be repeated another time later in the coaching to examine whether things have changed in the meantime.

What is the advantage of such a beginning? Because clients start with a pleasant fantasy of success, the coaching receives a different emotional value, a more pleasant and lighter one than in a normal approach. Accomplishing the goal becomes a journey to a pleasant destination and gives energy. Moreover, clients can have the idea that it is they who determine what it is about. The fantasy is much more their own. Their creativity is already working. And very importantly, it is fun there.

By contrast, starting as usual with a problem activates – maybe not completely, but certainly partially – the whole range of resistance against change much earlier, with all the accompanying specters of fiascos and disastrous developments, as described in Chapter 7. It then is more difficult for the client to fully employ his problem-solving capacities and creativity.

Another advantage of this solution-oriented approach is that imagination is much richer in information than words. A strictly verbal approach most of the time is narrower and is more inclined to leave all kinds of elements and aspects out of consideration. More concrete, a fantasy usually stirs up unexpected aspects of the goal to be attained.

Are there also disadvantages in this approach? Not really. Sometimes the goal turns out to have unpleasant aspects. These really must be taken seriously and must be well explored. Apparently, the set goal is less simple than the client thought or pretended it to be. Maybe he is not voluntarily here, has his doubts or really wants something else. The image than has helped to find this out quickly and things have to be further examined.

Sometimes the client simply is unable to imagine the realization of the goal. In itself that is not a problem. Many people find it difficult to imagine things clearly. We then can let the client approach the goal in a more verbal way, by letting him describe it. If this also fails, something else is up. We then can ask ourselves whether the client really wants to accomplish the goal.

FEEDBACK RULES

Feedback makes another person aware of the effects of his behavior, preferably so that, if desirable, the other person gets the possibility to adjust that behavior. Essentially, feedback serves the other person. To be effective, feedback must adhere to the rules described below. It is our own responsibility to guard these rules.

- Feedback must be so concrete, simple, clear and unambiguous as possible. Prevent vagueness.
- Give your feedback as fast and directly as possible.
- Do not judge.
- In your feedback, stay close to your own perceptions and responses. Preferably speak in terms of I and me: 'I think, feel, experience that you. . .' Do not present your feedback as objective facts or truths. Do not use phrases such as: 'You are. . .', 'It is obvious that you. . .' Instead, say something like: 'When I see you behaving like. . ., I get the feeling that. . .'
- Make a clear distinction between what you directly experience or perceive and what you deduce from that (and how you deduced that). For example: 'I see that. . ., hear that. . ., perceive that. . ., feel that. . .' and so on versus: 'I gather that. . .' or 'Because you. . .,

I think that...' Realize that these terms also represent very different ways of mental functioning.
- Do not use feedback to get back at somebody.
- Word your feedback as constructively and positively as possible. For example: 'I find that you take an overly responsible position here' when you find somebody too domineering.
- Check whether the feedback is well understood.

DISCUSSION OF PROGRESS

Goals

- To find out how things are going, where you are now and whether you are still on track.
- To take stock of problems and things that are not clear and coming up with ways to solve these issues.
- If necessary, to adjust goals.
- To maintain the involvement of all participants.
- To get feedback from participants who leave.

Procedure

The discussions of progress preferably take place on a regular basis, for instance once a week, but can also be used when you notice some form of stagnation. Discussions of progress can be done with any number of people. You can even have one all by yourself.

A discussion of progress in a training program composed of the exercises described in this book, for example, may start with taking stock of the reactions to the different exercises of the last week. Then answer the following questions and comment on the answers:

- What did you like?
- What went well?
- What did not go well?
- What annoyed you?
- Was there any resistance or reluctance and how did that manifest itself?
- What can be done better?
- How can that be brought about?

Comments

- Discussions of progress are a regular item in dialogue sessions and action learning projects (Revans, 1998). However, we can apply discussions of progress much more widely, for example in training programs, all kinds of projects and all kinds of teamwork.
- We can use discussions of progress to address any problem in the progress of the program or project. In a dialogue context, this can for example be concerned with the results of the progress, but also with critique on the behavior or motivation of one of the participants.

MOMENTS OF AWARENESS (Adapted From Senge *et al.*, 1994)

Goal

• To develop a standard method for coming to yourself, for regaining your balance or getting in control again, at times of stress and at moments in which you don't know how to proceed.

Procedure

Follow the instructions. Pause and ask:

• What is happening now?
• What am I/are we doing here and now?
• What do I/we feel here and now?
• What do I/we think here and now?
• What do I want now?
• What do I/we want to accomplish here and now?
• How do I myself/we ourselves prevent what I/we want to happen from actually happening?
• Inhale deeply, exhale slowly and go on.

In the 'I variant' all participants do the exercise in silence, though one of the participants may state the instructions. In the 'we variant' the participants collectively discuss their answers. Try out both variants and examine the similarities and differences. Both variants can be combined as well, starting with the I variant and followed by the we variant.

Ideally the procedure specified in the instruction would kick in automatically each time you could really use a moment of awareness. To actually bring about this kicking in automatically at the right times, you can apply the method described later in this chapter for setting personal goals. Read the instructions several times and memorize them thoroughly. Set for yourself the goal that the method should step in automatically at moments when you want it to kick in. Then let the goal sink in.

Comments

• Applying moments of awareness usually is very rewarding. Applying them allows us to regroup, to regain control, and – often – to solve the problems at hand. We then can proceed after all. As such, a moment of awareness can make the difference between a successful and a failing dialogue session.
• Moments of awareness can also be applied much more widely, for example in all kinds of training programs and outcome-oriented meetings.

LEARY'S ROSE

Timothy Leary has been primarily known as a wild protagonist of LSD consumption. He went to jail, was liberated and smuggled out of the US to Algiers by the Weather Underground Organization. Before that, however, he was a lecturer at Harvard University, where he studied interpersonal behavior with the help of factor analysis. He came up with two factors, which turned out to be very useful in applied contexts.

The two factors that Leary distinguished were 'power' and 'affiliation'. The power dimension goes from absolute dominance (up) to absolute submission (down), the affiliation dimension from unconditional love (with) to unconditional hate (against). The two dimensions are represented by two orthogonal axes, which divide a circle through their four poles into four equal parts. Subsequently, Leary came up with a further subdivision into eight equal parts or octants. The resulting figure is called Leary's rose (Figure 6.1).

Each of these eight octants can be taken as a part of a relational or situational proposal to another person (see Chapter 3). In an organizational context, Leary's rose involves the following eight proposals:

- *Up–Against*. I am explicitly the boss, but in a businesslike, task-oriented way. I tell you how it is, I don't expect from you any own contribution in this respect, but I do expect that you obey me.
- *Against–Up*. I assume you are against me, but I am the boss and for that reason I force you to execute your tasks, I want you to execute them. When you don't, I punish you.

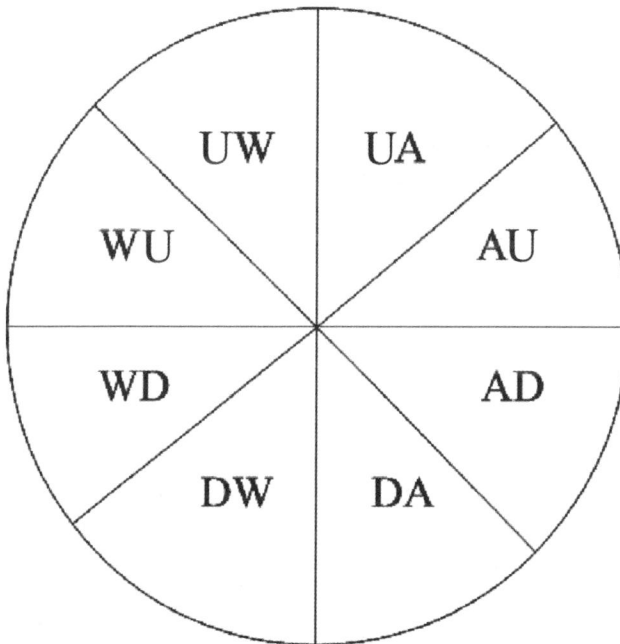

Figure 6.1 Leary's rose

- *Against–Down*. You think you are the boss, but when you expect it the least I'll try to take you down and sabotage your work.
- *Down–Against*. You are the boss, but don't expect any initiative from me. It just doesn't interest me enough.
- *Down–With*. You are the boss. Just tell me what I must do and then I will obediently execute it.
- *With–Down*. You are going to take care of me, because you are the boss and we are going to have a good time together.
- *With–Up*. I am the boss, but the main issue is that we have a pleasant time together. Leave that to me.
- *Up–With*. I am the boss, but in a humane, cooperative way, and I expect from you that you do your work well.

No relationship proposal is intrinsically good or bad. The ethical quality depends on the circumstances. Against–up can be acceptable to stop a suicide commando, while with–up usually is less handy in times of acute crisis.

As a relation proposal, an 'up position' tends to evoke a 'down position'. The other way around, a 'down position' tends to evoke an 'up position'. These relationships are called complementary. A 'with position', on the other hand, is intended to evoke a 'with position' in the other person as well, while an 'against position' elicits an 'against position'. These are the so-called symmetrical relations. Consequently, against–down elicits against–up, up–with evokes down–with, and so on.

When somebody makes a relationship proposal that you do not like, it usually is the most convenient option to take the position diagonally opposite to the one that the other suggests you take. When somebody takes, for example, an against–down position and 'invites' you in this way to take an against–up position, the most adroit thing to do is to take a with–down position. In this way, you propose that the other person take a with–up position and you may seduce them in this way to take more responsibility for the emotional climate.

Another issue concerns the circular form of Leary's rose, which is there for a reason. Fully against no longer is a matter of down or up. For example, a suicide bomber who blows himself up is free of the power dimension. Fully with takes out the up–down dimension as well: a secretary who manages to get her boss in bed effectively has switched off the division of power; that is, for the time being. Completely up, moreover, is power without regard to the affiliation dimension, and fully down is a form of passivity that is not for or against anyone either.

Each relationship proposal is predominantly a matter of non-verbal behavior and has its own non-verbal behavioral elements (see Chapter 8 and Addendum I). Non-verbal behavioral elements can be typified for the greater part as elements of one or two of these relationship proposals. In Addendum I Leary's rose is used to type behavioral elements. Is sticking out your chin down or up? Against or with? In what octant would you prefer to place it?

Leary's rose is also an important instrument for recognizing resistance during a dialogue (see Chapter 5). In principle, dialogue involves alternating between with–up and up–with. All four kinds of against behavior stand here – keep in mind: *here*! – for resistance against change, while down–with and with–down here indicate that one is for the moment not really busy with dialogue.

THINKING OF NOTHING IN PARTICULAR

An old man with a fishing rod wrapped up warmly on a small folding chair protected from the rain by a huge umbrella at the waterside. A woman knitting at her dinner table. A teenage boy sitting on his moped chewing gum in front of a cafeteria in a small, desolate shopping area. A jogger in the park. A meditating monk in his cell. What do they have in common? They are all thinking of nothing in particular.

Goal

• To introduce a number of ways to attain a state of mental quiet, or 'thinking of nothing in particular', and give you the possibility to find out what technique works best for you.

Introduction

There are many techniques to free us from our everyday worries and provide us with some moments of mental quiet. This mental quiet is characterized by what I have called 'thinking of nothing in particular', which I use as a kind of generic name for all these states of mental quiet. These techniques transform a situation into a moment of quiet and recovery.

The common features of these techniques are:

• They stop our usual lines of thought.
• We cannot do anything wrong in it.
• We do not need to worry about a thing.

These states of quiet vary in depth: from simple musing and reflecting to being completely away from the world.

We can use these techniques in many places, for example at work, during breaks and waiting periods, but also at home or in transit. We can use them also in various combinations. The important point therefore is: determine what you like best and what works for you.

Preparation

A good preparation for the following techniques is stretching completely as if you are about to go to bed: stretch and feel fully comfortable, as a cat does.

Techniques

First, a simple but effective technique. Close your eyes, take one or two deep breaths and exhale quite slowly. Repeat this and empty your mind completely. Pay special attention to exhaling slowly and as completely as possible. Bear in mind that breathing frequently and deeply in succession, without properly exhaling, can lead to dizziness and sometimes even fainting, a phenomenon called hyperventilation.

Another technique: Focus with your eyes open on a single point in front of you. For example, focus on a point on the wall, a candle flame, the central point of a basic, symmetrical geometric shape and so on. Try the same with your eyes closed on a point somewhere before you.

A third possibility: Listen with your eyes closed to music and dream away. Use headphones if you want.

A fourth option: Repeat for some time a so-called mantra, a single word preferably of one syllable, either silently or aloud. Appropriate words are love, nice, fine, hope and so on. This is a simple but effective technique for cleansing all thoughts from your mind.

Fifth, imagine the nicest smile possible – your own, that of a loved one, the smile of a favorite painting, statue or movie star – and send it to a place in your body where you feel tension or pain.

Sixth, use a muscular relaxation exercise. The exercise described below you can apply yourself without any risk – the worst that can happen to you is that you fall asleep – though you should not do this exercise when you are plagued by injuries or other complaints concerning your muscles or bones.

If you want, you can record the instructions yourself on an audiotape, CD or DVD. Of course, you can also use headphones.

Instructions

- Sit down on a chair with armrests.
- Stretch fully, like a cat would do.
- Sit in a relaxed way, though straight, your back against the back of the chair, your arms on the armrests.
- Close your eyes.
- Take one deep breath and exhale slowly, as completely as possible.

The exercises then consist of each time stretching each of the following groups of muscles separately during about six seconds – not *too* forcefully, of course, you don't want to get muscle cramp – but still so that you feel the tension well. Then let go of all tension from the muscles in question for half a minute. Focus for another half minute on the deepening relaxation of these body parts. Feel the relaxation and the warmth. Feel how heavy these body parts become.

Each time I'll mention first the muscles one by one, without you doing a thing yet, so that you know what is expected from you. Then I mention them again, while you now tense each of them the moment I mention them.

Successively, this is concerned with the following groups of muscles, which you each tense for about six seconds.

- *Arms*: clench your fists, tense your underarms and biceps.
- *Face*: frown, close your eyes tightly, turn your nose up, clench your jaw, bare your teeth.

- *Neck*: push your chin against your chest and keep your head in that position by putting your hand behind your head to provide counter-pressure. Now push your head backwards. Your shoulders are not involved.
- *Upper half of the trunk*: pull back your shoulders, your elbows against your trunk, so that your back comes loose from the back of your chair; ensure that your hands stay relaxed.
- *Lower half of the trunk*: strain your belly and bottom muscles at the same time, as well as your sphincter, as if you are holding your water.
- *Legs*: stretch your legs in front of you, your feet flexed upwards as if you are pointing with your big toes at your nose.

Sequel

You are very relaxed now. To relax even more deeply, you can imagine that you are walking down a flight of stairs of five steps. Each step down relaxes you more. I now count slowly to five... One: you feel yourself relaxing even more... And two: and more and more... Three, even deeper... Four, still deeper and deeper... And five, now you are totally relaxed... Enjoy your relaxation, as much as you want... Know that, when you come back to your normal state of consciousness, you will feel completely rejuvenated and energized. However, that is not your concern now... Just let yourself sink into this marvelous relaxation... Enjoy it to the full.... There is nothing you have to do... Just enjoy your relaxation...

If you wish you can enjoy some fantasy during this relaxation. For instance, lying in an easy chair in the shade of a giant umbrella on a beautiful tropical beach, a nice cool drink on the little table next to you, the sound of the waves breaking, the smells of the ocean and now and then a whiff of the exotic palm tree garden behind you.

Or swimming in the clearest of waters, the brilliant sun on the water, on the drips on your eyelashes, the coolness of the water on your skin and feeling how you become totally clean. And so on.

When you want to go back to your everyday state, just imagine going up the five steps again and come more and more back with every step into your normal state of consciousness. Count back from five to one, and at once open your eyes. Clench your fists and look around you. Everything is still precisely as you left it. Stretch again, and feel how rejuvenated and energetic you feel.

- How does it feel to do these relaxation exercises?
- Which of these relaxation exercises is the most effective for you?

When you have become fully familiar with the relaxation exercise, you may skip the tensing part. Just breathe in deeply one time, then out, and relax successively each of the muscle groups. Once you can control this technique, the next step consists of practicing doing this without shutting your eyes. This allows you to evoke some thinking of nothing in particular in all kinds of situations without anyone noticing it, for instance during a meeting.

Still another way to 'empty' your mind is engaging in all kinds of sports that involve endurance. Examples are running, swimming, bicycling and all other forms of lengthy rhythmic movement such as dancing, which in time lead to thinking of nothing in particular. However, it does not have to be that drastic. Leisurely walking or bicycling is also good for musing and daydreaming. As well as each of these forms of movement being an effective method of reaching a state of thinking of nothing in particular, they also contribute to your physical fitness.

- How does each of these methods work for you?
- Which is the least appropriate one and why?
- Which one do you find the easiest and which the most pleasant?
- What makes it pleasant?
- What possibilities do you see to make these techniques more effective for you?
- Where and when can you apply these techniques best?

Comments

- What can we do with all these methods to be able to think of nothing in particular? To start with, we can practice them at fixed times of the day. We can practice thinking of nothing in particular also during the breaks and waiting periods mentioned before. This is simply pleasurable, but it can also help us to center our thoughts, concentrate better at work, prevent and counteract stress and sleep better. All in all, we can use mental quiet purposely to refresh ourselves and to feel more energetic and centered.
- All of this makes bringing about mental quiet an important tool in a dialogue session, both as a part of preparation as well as to cool down if things become too heated.
- In addition, we can use mental quiet in a more focused way to calm down and make contact with ourselves, when that is needed. In this way, we can better control interfering thoughts and emotions such as anxiety and tension. We then can think more clearly about our next moves. To this end, we must sometimes retreat from the situation at hand. At other times, however, we can use the relaxation techniques to calm down on the spot. Apart from this, we can use this approach to ask ourselves questions and give ourselves tasks (later in this chapter).

FOCUSING

Goal

- To get experience with focusing to determine whether this is something for you.

Introduction

Focusing is a technique to get answers by examining vague, indeterminate feelings. These feelings can emerge by themselves, but can also be evoked by asking ourselves a question. Feelings are part of emotions, and emotions essentially imply an evaluation of the situation in which we are present. Emotions also involve a readiness for a certain line of action

(Frijda, 1986). That is why examining our feelings can give us all kinds of information about our attitude and position in the world at the moment.

There are different indications that we should resort to focusing.

First, it is the proper technique when you have an indeterminate feeling that something is not right, is strange or odd. This involves questions such as: 'What is the matter?', 'What is this about?' and 'What is happening here?'

Another indication is the striking absence of any feeling where you would expect a clear and intense feeling. An example is thinking back indifferently to an event that must have been intensely traumatic.

Still another indication is when you are faced with a difficult choice or don't know what to do next. Also there are more practical questions that refer to choices or seeking for a more desirable alternative. Focusing then can give answers to questions such as: 'What should I do?', 'What do I want?' and 'What is now the most important to me?'. The good thing about focusing is that it can provide valuable as well as fully unexpected answers (Gendlin, 1981, 1986).

Instructions

The technique begins with concisely formulating a question. For example: 'What do I want from this organization?' Write the question down and read it over a couple of times. This enables you to evoke the question effortlessly in a light state of thinking of nothing in particular. Then empty your mind, without getting too far 'away', and ask yourself the question you have memorized. Imagine that you put your question some meters in front of you, for example on a chair, as if it concerned an object. Stay explicitly 'outside' the question: do not go into the details and intricacies of it nor into the emotions attached to it.

For example, focusing does *not* involve thinking: 'What about a higher salary? A better room?' and so on. Though such further questions in themselves are quite harmless, they are just not part of the technique.

When you notice that you still are going *into* the problem, start all over again. Again, just let go of your thoughts. If solutions are going to come, they will come completely by themselves. They will develop calmly and silently, and when it is their time they will present themselves in some way.

Then focus on your body, somewhere in the middle, and examine how it feels. Note the feelings and sensations of your various body parts. This may take some time. Just relax and quietly examine whether you feel something. When a sensation comes to the fore, just focus your attention on it quietly for some time.

What does the feeling make you think of? What comes to your mind? What does it remind you of? An image, a memory, a thought? Is there some shift in your feelings? Does the new feeling give you new energy? Stay with that new feeling and ask it questions. How is it related to you? Is it about your past? Or about your future?

Often these ideas and images – and that is what is so curious about this method – relate to the original question. Maybe not at first, but then often at a later stage.

When something emerges that throws a new light on your question, that information often goes together with a peculiar feeling of certainty about its relevance and validity: a feeling of self-evidence. This is a little like suddenly remembering where you put an object that you had not been able to find for a long time.

If you somehow lose the new feeling, you can go back to the initial feeling, the feeling before the shift. Then try to find your way back from there to the new feeling.

When a shift in feeling takes place, this is also expressed in your attitude and behavior. Just let that happen fully. Exaggerate it a bit. Play with it. You even may walk over to a mirror, to see what it looks like.

So it might happen that the question 'What do I miss in my job?' evokes a particular feeling in your chest, which makes you breathe in deeply, to evoke then a memory of your childhood: that first time that you went bicycling with the children next door, without your parents, on a warm summer evening, outdoors, the smell of hay, a beautiful world of unlimited challenges. That marvelous feeling of the freedom and adventure of that occasion. Could it be that you want more freedom and adventure in your organization and that you have hopes that steps in that direction can be taken?

Often it is pleasant to hold on to the feeling and the accompanying ideas and images for a moment, to breathe in deeply once and breathe out very slowly. After this, you can examine each insight separately, looking at it from all perspectives. Of course, you can make notes.

Try focusing on a suitable problem, following the instructions given above.

Comment

• If focusing works for you, you have found a way of functioning that helps to give meaning to your life, to integrate yourself in a way that you feel more 'whole' and function in a more focused way, without being needlessly diverted by intrusive thoughts and feelings.

Focusing on Separate Body Parts

Another version of focusing consists of successively focusing on the bodily sensations in a number of specific body parts and the accompanying images and ideas. Consecutively, this involves our neck and shoulders, throat, chest and stomach (Hendricks, 1998). For the remainder, the technique is the same as described in the previous section.

Procedure

The various body parts each play a different role here.

Shoulders and neck. Focus for some time on the back of your head, your shoulders and your neck.

• What do you feel when you focus on the back of your head, neck and shoulders?

Loosen up your shoulders, relax and take a deep breath.

• What images and ideas make an appearance?

Here, you are mainly tracing 'forgotten' memories of intrusions. These may be intrusions on your wishes, needs, personal space, interests, (ownership) rights, integrity or bodily immunity. Each of these can be an issue about which you were – or should have been – angry. However, many people prefer not to express their anger and not even to feel it.

Throat. Focus on your throat.

• What do you feel in your throat?

Relax your throat and take a deep breath.

• What comes to your mind?

Concerning our throat, this involves primarily tracking down 'forgotten' instances of loss – something which, or somebody who, is not there any more for us – and the accompanying grief. This may evoke a feeling as if there is a ball in our throat, which makes it difficult for us to swallow. Here too, focus on these feelings and once or twice breathe in deeply and breathe out fully and slowly.

Chest. Focus on your chest.

• What do you feel in your chest?
• Do you recognize what comes to your mind?
• And what happens when you connect what you want most right now to what you feel?

Relax your chest and take a deep breath.
    Focusing on our chest is foremost a matter of identifying our hidden unfulfilled desires, the matters 'for which our heart longs'. Focusing on our chest and a deep breath can also contribute to reinforcing the goals that we have set for ourselves, at least when these goals are compatible with what we really want. Doing this intentionally can help us to hold on to our goals.

Stomach. Again, the same procedure, only now it involves our 'forgotten' fears.

• What do you feel in your stomach?
• Of what or whom are you afraid?

Relax your stomach and take a deep breath.

Comments

• This technique is especially appropriate for re-examining and solving unfinished problems. As described in Chapter 7, old problems that are never solved still tend to demand energy, even when we hardly pay any attention to them at a conscious level any more. By focusing on the separate body parts mentioned above, with the intention of making us aware of old problems again, we can sometimes trace these problems, even though we thought that we had completely forgotten about them. Then we can 'solve' them after all. We can bring about such solutions because now these problems tend to be much less threatening than when they came into being. To the extent that we succeed in solving such problems after all, they stop bothering us. As a result, we have more energy at our disposal, which allows us to go full speed ahead. To solve such old problems, we do not need to ask ourselves a specific question, as long as we keep in mind that this is about identifying unfinished business from the past. Focusing consecutively on the body parts mentioned from a moderate state of thinking of nothing in particular is already sufficient.

- 'Working through' these body parts at the end of the day, before going to bed, is also a good way to identify and get rid of the smaller frustrations and displeasures of the day.
- 'Working through' these body parts is also a good way to end a dialogue session.

GIVING OURSELVES ASSIGNMENTS, SETTING PERSONAL GOALS

Setting a goal for ourselves in a state of thinking of nothing in particular is a technique to enable us to achieve the intended goal in a relatively effortless way. It is a form of self-suggestion, which makes the goal seem to realize itself. This technique allows us to reach the goal without being distracted and without having to force ourselves, in short without being bothered by any unnecessary resistance or strain (Baudouin, 1924; Stokvis, 1947).

Procedure

In the light of this method's effectiveness, it is important to be very precise in formulating the goal. To be as precise as possible, use the procedure for testing goals described later in this chapter. Do all these tests and adjust your goals according to the test outcomes.

Formulate the goal to be as short and concise as possible, preferably in only a few words. Write it down, read it a couple of times over and learn it by heart.

Use your favorite technique to bring about mental quiet and go into a state of thinking of nothing in particular – the deeper, the better. When this is achieved, evoke your goal. Think of it for a moment without losing yourself in its ramifications and implications, exactly as in the case of focusing (see later in this chapter), and then let the goal dissolve and disappear in your mental quiet, in the pleasant understanding that everything will take care of itself from now on. There is nothing left to be bothered about: just surrender again to your pleasant state of mental quiet.

A variant is imagining how you attach your goal to a balloon. Let the balloon go and watch how it takes off and gradually becomes a little dot in the sky, to disappear altogether from your view in the end. You just enjoy the cloudless, blue sky.

Examples of Goals

- I want to be in the most productive state of mind to make this dialogue session a success.
- I want to feel good doing my job in this organization.
- I want to be able to focus completely on. . . (a task).
- I want to learn all that is to be learned about. . . (a project or course).
- I want to remember everything about. . .
- I want to notice everything related to. . .
- I want to have all my abilities at my disposal concerning. . .

We can use the same technique to question ourselves. This will be described in the next exercise.

Comments

- In more extended projects, we can repeat this procedure periodically – each day, each week, each month – to keep it alive and fresh. As such, it can be a useful part of the preparation for a dialogue session.
- In order to make setting personal goals more effective, we can combine it with focusing on our chest and once or twice breathing deeply.

STARTING UP 'SLOW BRAIN PROCESSES'

A 'slow brain process' is a kind of searching process in our brain, which happens in an automatic way. It consists of generating all kinds of possible solutions, each a little different from the previous one, which are pitched against what would constitute a feasible answer. When a solution is rejected, the next process cycle starts and so on, until an answer appears to be feasible. When such a feasible answer is identified, it pops up 'by itself' into our awareness (Claxton, 1997). The answer then can be further tested in 'reality' and the slow brain process stops.

Goals

- To practice starting up and dealing with 'slow brain processes'.
- To get answers to the question you asked yourself.

Procedure

Essentially the procedure is the same as giving yourself an assignment (see the previous exercise), only this time you formulate a concise question instead of a task or goal. This exercise you do on your own.

You can ask yourself all kinds of questions, for example:

- 'How would I like my organization to change?'
- 'What would be rewarding about that?'

Go through the procedure in the previous exercise and let your question disappear into your mental quiet, your thinking of nothing in particular, fully knowing that you now have started up a slow brain process to come to satisfying answers. Now go for a walk, or a run if you prefer. Let the question surface from time to time when you are walking (or running). Find out whether you already have an answer. If not, let the question go again. There is nothing to worry about, answers will come. Sometimes an answer comes immediately, sometimes it comes (much) later, and often a lot of additional answers make their appearance one by one. Don't stop too soon.

How did this feel?

Comment

- Starting up a slow brain process is a basic technique, which can be used each time you are faced by a difficult choice or problem. As such, starting up a slow brain process can be of help to leaders, change agents and participants in any task-oriented project, including dialogue.

AFFIRMATIVES

An affirmative here stands for a short positive assertion about or for ourselves, which we repeat to ourselves many times a day, many days in a row. Essentially, an affirmative is a phrasing of an assumption or goal. This phrasing goes beyond what we, purely rationally speaking, can account for, as all assumptions do and essentially all goals as well. However, this assertion works as a self-fulfilling prophecy: the affirmative tends to make itself true; that is, when we set ourselves to believe in it. As such, an affirmative operates as a surprisingly effective charm, invocation or prayer.

Formulating an affirmative in the right way is a painstaking job. For example, an affirmative must be:

- Very precise: it should exactly mirror what you want to accomplish, as this focuses you and helps you to recognize the outcome when it presents itself.
- As short and concise as possible: it must be easy to repeat fully, time after time, without letting out one of its parts.
- Fully meaningful: it should make absolute sense.
- Stated in a positive way (see later in this chapter for the reasoning behind this rule).
- Stated in the present tense.

The last rule is not absolutely necessary, but it helps you not to postpone assuming the right attitude to undertake real action.

For example: 'What I need for... I am finding.' Alternatives are 'I am convinced that I find what I need for...' and 'I fully trust in finding what I need for...' At first, this may sound like a nonsensical declaration. However, the statement starts to make sense when I believe in it. When I deeply believe that I am finding something, I am much more likely to look for it, which makes it more plausible that I will find it. Sometimes this is a matter of searching intensively and sometimes what I need is just staring me in the face. Recognizing it is then the only thing required of me. Such recognition, however, is often far from self-evident.

The assumption, in order to do its work, must have really sunk in deeply. What techniques will help us to accomplish this sinking in? As mentioned before, there is the sheer repetition of the affirmative time after time, preferably also when we are most susceptible and impressionable, for example lying in bed just before going to sleep or in the shower. Another technique is to let the affirmative sink in in the same way as we did with the assignments to ourselves; that is, using self-suggestion: Don't we fool ourselves in this way? Yes and no. Yes, but who cares? And no, not when it works. And believe me, our brain doesn't mind.

If you are still skeptical, think about the opposite possibility. When we make it a habit to say to ourselves that we are not finding what we want to find, we will not search or look for it either. Even when it stares us in the face, we will probably not recognize it as such. Some people do act this way and successfully so.

- Which self-fulfilling negative ideas run now and then through your head?

So go after what you want, but keep in mind: as this is a rather effective formula, be extremely careful in formulating what you ask. You wouldn't be the first sorcerer's apprentice who found themselves in an awkward spot.
  A few examples of affirmatives:

- Chances to get out of here are coming.
- I am intelligent enough to cope with... well.
- I can see the good in any other person.
- I am attracting whomever I need for...
- I recognize a solution for..., the moment it presents itself.
- I am creative and resourceful enough to solve my problems.
- I am capable of living the life I want to live.

Goal

- To practice formulating and applying affirmatives and to find out whether that works for you.

Procedure

What is at the moment your biggest problem, need or challenge? What do you need to bring about an improvement in that? Choose or make your own affirmative. Adjust your affirmative by applying the five rules described earlier in this section. Do all of this as well as possible and then practice this affirmative for the next days. Monitor how it feels and what the outcomes are. Make notes.

Comment

- Obviously, affirmatives can be of great importance when we go through a change or transition. As such, they are useful in any cultural change and in any dialogue.

REALLY SEEING SOMEBODY

When we assist, teach or advise somebody, this implies that we look at another person in a certain way and can see him in a certain way. What all that implies, it is hard to describe. It involves, among other things, the issues specified in the instructions.

Goal

- To practice really seeing someone else.

Procedure

You can do this exercise on your own or in pairs. In the first case, sit in front of a mirror or video camera. In the second case, select somebody with whom you are working on an important project and with whom you disagree on one or more issues.

The one leading the exercise keeps an eye on the time and reads the instructions aloud, point by point. There is silence during the exercise. Take three minutes per point.

Then write down for three minutes how it felt, as well as what you saw and experienced.

In total, this takes 9×6 minutes = 54 minutes, followed by a discussion (if you are alone, this discussion becomes time for reflection) of 15 to 25 minutes led by the one who read the instruction.

If you do the exercise in foursomes, it is a good idea to repeat the exercise once more, after a pause but now with other pairs and with another one leading the exercise. What is the same? What is different?

Instructions

Follow each of the assignments one by one.

- Look at the other person and see their good points. What do you see?
- What possibilities do you see in the other person? And what good intentions?
- See what is essential, unique, different and typical in the other person, without judging or evaluating. Just see it. Put it into words.
- See the other person in a higher-order context, something of which you are both a part, this process of cultural change for example. How does that feel?
- Consider how, in spite of the intimacy of this exercise and being part of the same higher-order context, there is also a clear distance, a separation between you: you are you, while the other person is the other person.
- Imagine that you are there for the other person, undivided and with all you have. How does that feel? Feel your responsibility for the other person.
- See possible problems and things about the other person that you find unpleasant or unattractive as a distortion or a too much of a positive characteristic or attitude. How do the other person's possible good intentions go wrong? What kinds of things do you see?
- What solutions do you see for the other person? What would be a good form for that? What is appropriate?
- What role is there for you? What does the situation ask of you? What does it allow you to do?

Comments

- This exercise addresses a way of information processing that in our culture is used relatively infrequently and is undervalued.
- You can always use really looking in discussions. In addition to leading to better discussions and relationships, it can also be a pleasant way of being and acting. When you

really look, you are fully in the here and now and the world is more challenging and exciting.
- This exercise is applicable in every situation where communication, or the lack of it, is important.
- Of course, the environment should be such that this kind of exercise is accepted.

Sequel

If you have not done this exercise on your own, it is recommended to do the same exercise alone in front of a mirror: really see yourself. Go through all the steps of the exercise with your mirror image.

Make it a point to look at others in a more aware way for the next few weeks, a little as you have done that in this exercise, but of course not each time with the same intensity. Do this with people you know as well as some you do not know. Really looking also can be a way to turn watching television into a more valuable activity.

- What are their good points and good intentions?
- How could they improve these good points and be more effective by these improvements?
- What effect does this way of looking have on you?
- What effect does it have on the others you look at?

It is also instructive at people in other ways. For example, you can look at other people from the following perspectives:

- What are they bringing?
- What are they taking?
- What can you give them?
- What can they give you?

A final exercise concerns people against whom you feel a clear antipathy. If you have to meet with one of your 'token enemies', use the following approach.

- Be friendly.
- Find out how the most annoying traits of the other person can be seen as a surplus or a distortion of an essentially good trait.
- Send acceptance over.
- See how the other responds and turn the antipathy around.

IMAGINATION (Glouberman, 1989)

Goals

- To practice with imagination.
- To get new ideas and a better understanding of the issue at hand.

Procedure

You can do this exercise on your own, in pairs or in a small group. When you are not doing the exercise on your own, one of you introduces the exercise, gives the instructions each time, but also takes part. The one who gives the instructions is the only one to talk. For the remainder, the exercise is done in silence. Afterwards everybody relates their experiences and everything is discussed. When you do it on your own, you cannot of course discuss the outcomes. Instead, you can do some more reflection. In all cases, take enough time and do make notes.

Sit down, in a relaxed way but upright. Close your eyes. Stretch. Take one deep breath. Just relax. Think of nothing in particular. Then go through the following steps.

Evoke an Image

Say to yourself: 'I want to evoke an image that is closely related to... (your problem, question, area of interest), an image that is relevant and important to me. And I know that I must use the first image that emerges.'

Study the Image

What image is evoked? What strikes you? How does it relate to the wider situation? Look at it from all sides. What colors does it have? What mood does it trigger? What sounds and smells belong to it? And what feelings? What is the most characteristic feeling?

Become the Image

Take the identity of the image: become the image. How does that feel? What is most characteristic of that? How does the world look from this perspective? What is most pleasant about it? And what is most unpleasant?

How Does the Image Relate to Your Past?

To what degree does the image represent something new? What does the change consist of? What is your opinion about that?

What Promises Does the Image Hold?

What does the image imply? What is the logical next step? How do you continue?

Summing Up

What has the image brought you? What new ideas, feelings and insights has all this brought to you? What can you do with it? What are you going to do with it?

Comments

- This exercise focuses on a way of information processing that is also relatively seldom used in our culture or is delegated to writers and artists.
- Evoking an image is always useful in the case of personal choices, problems concerning your life and making plans; in short, when you want to know more about an issue that directly concerns you.
- This technique is also useful in contexts such as developing a common vision (visioning), dialogue, brainstorming and team building.
- In difficult discussions and in a dialogue, evoking an image can be of decisive influence, certainly at difficult moments when everything seems to be at an impasse. Apart from the fact that you can learn a great deal from it yourself, you can also simply announce: 'The following image came to me.' Then describe the image and find out whether this image means anything to the other person or people. Don't do this with people who find this odd, but then again don't be too afraid in this respect either. Sometimes this use of imagination results in a breakthrough.

DELEGATING ALTERNATIVES (Adapted From Senge *et al.*, 1994)

Goal

- To practice a method of clarifying and solving dilemmas in a group.

Procedure

Here too, your ideal organization can be used as an example.

Preparation

Determine two alternatives for your ideal organization, preferably two equally attractive ones, but your most attractive one and the runner-up will do as well. If you have not made up your mind yet in this respect, think of another real dilemma or choice (actual, real and still unsolved) with two alternatives: either–or. Take five minutes for this.

Step 1

This exercise is done in groups of four: one change agent, a problem owner and two 'actors'. The problem owner describes his dilemma, chooses which actor he wants to give which alternative and gives for each alternative the related motives and objectives. The actors who work with the alternatives particularly focus on the underlying feeling that their alternative evokes and identify as much as possible with their role, non-verbally as well. They are helped in this by the problem owner: 'So?' 'No, a little more like this. Yes, like that.' The problem owner also places them so much 'in the room' that their mutual relationship is represented as well as possible.

Step 2

The problem owner steps back and gives the actors who are playing the two alternatives all the space they need to enter into a discussion with each other.

Then those representing the two alternatives start to discuss the dilemma, each from its own position, as thoroughly as possible. They also try to clarify each other's and their own underlying ideas, and try to come to a win–win solution.

The change agent from time to time asks the two alternatives how they feel, what they really want to do and why they want to do that. If nothing happens, he can place them in a different way in the room and change their non-verbal behavior somewhat, to ask them then how that is for them and how that feels.

The problem owner keeps quiet and sticks to listening.

Step 3

When the discussion of the alternatives is complete, all three tell how it was and how it felt. The change agent is the discussion leader. Usually the problem owner gets a better understanding of the dilemma and its assumptions and underlying thoughts. All of this can result in a definitive choice, but also in an integration of both alternatives in a richer win–win solution.

Together these three steps take about 20 minutes to half an hour.

After Step 3 the players change roles, until everybody has taken turns as problem owner and change agent (four rounds, therefore).

Discussion

The underlying thoughts are revisited once more and there is a discussion of how people are apparently able to take part in each other's thoughts, assumptions and motives.

Comments

- This exercise demonstrates how we all, apparently effortlessly, can step into each other's patterns, as well as how we equally simply apply to or project such patterns on other people. As such, this exercise is a good preparation for dialogue.
- The exercise is a good way to make the different voices in your head manifest.
- The exercise is also good for empathy and demonstrates the role that matching can play.

HELPING CREATIVITY

When we are looking for creative ideas and new angles, all kinds of techniques to get us out of our normal assumptions, underlying ideas and ways of thinking can play a useful part (most of these techniques are also discussed in von Oech, 1983; and De Bruyn, De Bruyn & De Gier, 2000). The point here is to generate ideas and solutions in response to our question, without being blocked by shame or self-criticism. In the next two stages, these ideas are checked for soundness and usefulness. This approach has been called the Disney approach (Seymour & O'Connor, 1994).

To optimize our own creativity on a certain point, it is primarily important to formulate what we want as carefully and as concisely as possible. Then we let it sink in, in the way described earlier in this chapter. We can use the same approach to concentrate better and not be diverted.

Goals

- To practice different creativity techniques.
- To determine which techniques suit you best.
- To get some new ideas.

Procedure

Read the introduction. The brainstorming techniques you can apply in small groups, though in principle you can do them on your own as well.

The one who leads the exercise tells about the object of the brainstorming, the problem to be solved, puts into words what that problem means to him personally and invites the others to state this as well. Then he introduces the first technique. Everybody applies the technique to the problem for a couple of minutes, then relates what this yields and makes short notes on this. When everybody has finished making notes, the next technique is introduced and so on.

Imaginary Counselors

When we get stuck somewhere, it is a good idea to imagine how other people would approach the problem and what they would advise us if we asked them for help. These other people don't need to be geniuses, though that of course might help. The important point here is that they think differently than we do. Stupid counselors can be helpful too, to the degree that they would give advice that we must not follow, but that can warn us about pitfalls and errors in thinking.

Think in this respect consecutively about:

- somebody you know who is very clever
- somebody you know who knows everything about the area to which your question refers
- somebody you admire, a personal hero
- somebody who always makes you laugh
- somebody who knows your weak aspects very well

Breaking Rules, Suspending Assumptions

When we are trying to devise creative solutions, our assumptions, convictions and rules often hinder us. We can solve the problem by acting as if these are not applicable for the moment. For example, what kinds of answers would come up if we:

- were completely ruthless?
- broke every rule in the book?
- wanted to bring about a total disaster?

- had much more time?
- had much less time?
- had much more money?
- had much less money?
- could count on everybody's cooperation?
- could count on very favorable circumstances?

Changing Perspectives

Here too it is about freeing our creativity by departing from different assumptions. This time we do that by taking the side of other parties and examining what new insights those new perspectives provide. When we have a problem, the question would be: How would we proceed if we were:

- our own father?
- our own mother?
- our teacher?
- our competitor?
- our boss?
- our colleagues?

We also can approach this as if our personality had gone through a series of major trans-formations. So we can approach the problem as if we consecutively were:

- very perfectionist
- very sensitive to the needs of others
- very freedom loving
- very goal oriented
- very socially skillful
- very creative
- very esthetically oriented
- very theoretically oriented
- very practically oriented
- very careful
- oriented to excitement and new things
- very power oriented
- primarily oriented to creating a pleasant atmosphere

Using Transitions

Transitions imply among other things that we must abandon fixed ways of doing: we must adapt to another reality, for which we don't have clear, ready-made approaches. In this way, transitions offer possibilities for creativity. For example, imagine how we would approach our assignment if we:

- had to do it in a totally different country
- were deprived of all contact with our close friends

- had just retired
- had just been left by our partner, or – if we do not have a partner – now actually had a partner
- had become blind or deaf
- had just had our third child

Left–Right Method

Write down a question. Then answer it yourself by writing down that answer with your other hand, the one with which you usually do not write. Do not worry about the quality of the handwriting. Subsequently ask further questions with your writing hand – 'What about that?', 'What do you mean?' – and give yourself answers with your non-writing hand, and so on. Other questions might be:

- How could this be done better?
- How could this be made more pleasant?
- How could we learn more from it?

Comments

- These techniques are applicable in organizations, but also in our private lives, each time problems occur in determining 'what' – goals – and 'how' – strategy, approach and tactics.

GOAL SETTING

This section describes a number of criteria for formulating a goal or objective in such a way that it becomes more worthwhile and more easily achievable, in such a way also that we do not give ourselves excuses to abandon the goal's realization. The criteria have been formulated as questions, with which we can interrogate our goal. Each question can lead to answers that are a reason to adjust our goal.

The first point is whether the objective fits in with us: with our basic motives, with what else we want from life, with what kind of person we are, with what we have found important until now.

- 'Does the goal sufficiently fit in with who we are? And if not, how could we adjust the goal in such a way that it does fit?'

What the people who are important to us feel about our objective is, of course, an influential factor too. Do they get along with our objective? What does the goal have to offer them? What does it cost them? These considerations are not only a matter of pondering, but also of actual conversations, in which we properly present our objective to them. Apart from changing the goal, this also might lead to somewhat adjusting our relationship with them.

- 'Does the goal sufficiently fit in with what the people who are most important in our life want? What must happen to realize such a fit?'

Goals can be set too high as well as too low. In the first case, they are not realistic and are impossible to achieve. In the second case, their outcomes are too small and they are not particularly motivating. For example, losing 20 grams of body weight over a week can hardly be called a motivating goal. Both cases provide easy excuses to abandon the goal altogether. Therefore the following questions apply:

- 'To what degree have we set our goal too high? What adjustments are needed?'
- 'To what degree have we set our goal too low? What adjustments are needed?'

In practice, it does not work out well when we describe our goals in terms of what we do not want, or put differently: in terms of what we want to prevent, decrease, reduce, counteract or avoid. For that reason, state your goals in positive terms, not in negative terms. There are two reasons for this. A negation of an activity only gives information about what we are not going to do and no clues about what we actually *are* going to do: 'I am not going to swim' leaves totally open what I *do* plan to do. This makes such a negation too unspecific to be part of an objective. The other reason is that words such as 'no' and 'not' do not work well in this context. 'Do not think of a house' and 'no red' make you think of a house and red. In a similar way, an unskilled skater is irresistibly attracted to the only hole in an otherwise unblemished ice rink, while a steep abyss has a strong draw for people with acrophobia, fear of heights. Therefore, always describe goals in terms of what you do want to accomplish. For example, goal setting should not be concerned with reducing limits but with extending freedom; not with fighting illnesses but with promoting health; and so on.

- 'To what degree have we formulated our goal in a way that it is against something? If needed, rephrase the goal in positive words.'

When setting a goal, do it so that you make yourself not dependent on other people or circumstances, on which you cannot count and which you essentially cannot influence. In that case, it becomes impossible to take responsibility for accomplishing your goal. So we must devise ways to be less dependent on uncontrollable people and circumstances. To what degree can we influence those other people after all? To what degree can we adjust our objective? In this way we prevent building in excuses for letting go of our goals.

- 'To what degree does reaching our goal depend on other people whom we cannot influence? What can we do about this?'
- 'To what degree does reaching our goal depends on circumstances that we cannot control. What can we do about it?'

To accomplish a goal, we must also know *when* we have accomplished that goal. This means that we need specific and concrete criteria from which we can 'read' whether, or to what degree, the goal has been attained. In that way we take away the possibility of hiding behind the vagueness of the objective when its accomplishment has failed.

- 'To what degree does our goal encompass concrete criteria to measure whether, or to what degree, we have reached our goal? What concrete results are we trying to achieve? If necessary, reformulate the goal so that it does encompass such criteria.'

Another issue is the point in time at which we want to have accomplished our goal. By taking in a time scale that sets deadlines for the goal and sub-goals, it becomes impossible, in the case of failure, to excuse ourselves by referring to a possible future in which everything will come together after all.

- 'To what degree does our goal encompass a time scale with sub-goals and deadlines? If necessary, reformulate the goal so that it does encompass a time scale with sub-goals and deadlines.'

Another important criterion for goals is whether they have undesired side effects. For example, quite a number of big dams have been built to generate electricity without anyone paying attention to their possible environmental effects, which afterwards turned out to be disastrous. Examine what kinds of undesired side effects your goals might have. To this end, it is useful to look at the case from the perspectives of the other parties who are – directly or indirectly – involved: what might they be worried about in this respect? Actually ask them this.

- 'What undesired side effects can successful goal attainment bring? What adjustments does that require?'

To make our goals our own and to make them into a guideline for our future actions, it is furthermore important to word our goals as concisely and as simply as possible. This enables us to let the goals sink in by self-suggestion, so that they will do their job as if by themselves (see earlier in this chapter).

- 'How do we phrase our goal as concisely and simply as possible?'

Lastly, we subject our objective to a last, radical test. Imagine that a miracle has happened and suddenly our goal has already been accomplished. All our wishes are fulfilled and the state of affairs is exactly as we have described it in our specified and adjusted objective. Imagine that as vividly as possible.

- 'Suppose a miracle has happened and suddenly our goal has already been achieved. How does that feel? What indications does that give us about the desirability to go on? What adjustments are needed?'

Goals

- To practice clarifying and accentuating a goal and making it more accessible.
- To have a more realistic, clear and accessible image of your goal.

Procedure

Read the introduction. You can do this exercise on your own, but also in pairs and small groups. In pairs and small groups, one of the participants introduces the exercise and gives the instructions, but participates in it themselves as well. Essentially it is a pen-and-paper exercise that is discussed afterwards, or reflected on in the case of doing it on your own.

First, the participants write down a description of, for example, a change they want to accomplish in the organization. When everybody is ready with that, the one who is leading the exercise reads the first question aloud. When everybody has finished, the next question is read, and so on. Afterwards, both the new insights and the method are discussed. The questions are as follows:

- 'Does the goal sufficiently fit in with who you are? If not, how could you adjust the goal in such a way that it does fit?'
- 'Does the goal sufficiently fit in with what the people who are most important in your life want? What must happen to realize such a fit?'
- 'To what degree have you set your goal too high? What adjustments are needed?'
- 'To what degree have you set your goal too low? What adjustments are needed?'
- 'To what degree have you formulated your goal in a way that is against something? Rephrase your goal, if needed, in positive words after all.'
- 'To what degree does reaching your goal depend on others whom you cannot influence? What can you do about that?'
- 'To what degree does reaching your goal depend on circumstances that you cannot control? What can you do about that?'
- 'To what degree does your goal encompass concrete criteria to measure whether, or to what degree, you have reached your goal? What concrete results are you trying to achieve? If necessary, reformulate your goal so that it does encompass such criteria.'
- 'To what degree does your goal encompass a time scale with sub-goals and deadlines for your goal and sub-goals? If necessary, reformulate your goal so that it does encompass a time scale with sub-goals and deadlines.'
- 'What undesired side effects can successful goal attainment bring? What adjustments does that require?'
- 'How do you phrase your goal as concisely and simply as possible?'
- 'Suppose a miracle happens and suddenly your goal has already been achieved. How does that feel? What indications does that give you about the desirability to go on? What adjustments are needed?'

Comments

- This testing of goals on a series of criteria such as the above-mentioned ones is usual in many organizations. The returns are obvious: manageable goals that are not easily abandoned because they turn out to be unreachable or offer too many loopholes.
- Often a somewhat shorter series of criteria is used, the so-called SMART criteria: **s**pecific, **m**easurable, **a**cceptable, **r**esult oriented and **t**ime bound.

CHAPTER 7

Personal Issues

Nasrudin walks into a shop.
'What can I do for you?' asks the shopkeeper.
'Did you see me walking into your shop just now?' Nasrudin asks.
'Of course.'
'And you have not ever seen me before?'
'No, never.'
'How, then, did you know that it was me?'

(based on Sjah, 1969)

Changing culture involves changing people; that is, changing and developing their assumptions and goals. This implies that we must be able to elucidate the assumptions and goals underlying the intended change or development, which, in its turn, demands also that we know our own assumptions and goals. Only when we have acquired sufficient insight into our own assumptions and goals can we properly explain and advocate the assumptions and goals underlying the intended change, and only then can we help others in developing and changing their assumptions and goals in the intended direction. Consequently, we have to find out more about our own assumptions and goals; in other words, we first must examine who we are ourselves.

This chapter gives an overview of issues that are important to examine when we want to find out who we are and how we have become who we are. The chapter is concerned with our goals and assumptions, as well as with how certain events have influenced us. In short, this chapter is about the issues we want to examine by reflection and introspection. This examination is a matter of asking ourselves the right questions and applying the other techniques described in Chapter 6.

The resulting insights and knowledge will also give us a better understanding of our own strong and weak points in changing a particular organizational culture. Moreover, the resulting insights and knowledge will result in ideas about how we want to develop ourselves with respect to these issues. Though perhaps a superfluous remark, it is important to realize that the same issues are highly relevant for the other people with whom we want to change the organizational culture. In this sense, we are our own exercise ground for the insights, knowledge and techniques that we will then be able to apply together with them later on.

The following issues are discussed:

- Unfinished business
- Our own mortality
- Resistance to change

- Early youth
- Leitmotifs
- Points of resemblance with your kin
- Assignments by your parents
- Transitions

UNFINISHED BUSINESS

Not everything in life runs smoothly. Things happen to us that we do not want to happen. This can be an illness, an accident or a colleague intruding on our turf. Moreover, from time to time we must do things that we cannot, should not or do not want to do. These things may be simply too difficult or extensive, may go against all we stand for or are unable to retain our attention. There are countless examples of this at home, at work, on the street, everywhere. In all these cases, we essentially to some degree lose control over our own life. Our first response is usually an emotional, primitive, animal response: anger, fear, disgust, anxiety and other similar emotions. If possible, we try to restore the original state or find a safe haven, while sometimes we just keep quiet, hoping that the disturbance will pass by itself (Schabracq, 2003a).

However, often we cannot do much about this kind of problem. Our only option then consists of ignoring it and working around it in order to minimize the inconvenience, without any certainty that things will turn out for the better. Sometimes, we even skip the emotional stage and reconcile ourselves to the inevitable from the beginning, especially if the people around us are modeling such an attitude.

In these cases we play down our own feelings, or more or less suppress them. As a result, we barely feel that something is not as it should be. We do not feel much at all. We also don't go into the feelings of others. We just don't sympathize with them and do not get caught up any more in what moves them. We withdraw and if others still approach us, we rather rudely fence them off in an impersonal way. This state of mind is what I call secondary alienation or, for short, alienation (Schabracq & Cooper, 2003). Our reality has shrunk, has become less colorful, less adventurous, and has lost much of its meaning and direction. We do not enjoy things as much any more. Also, the idea of being a creative, autonomous person, who determines his own course, slips away without our noticing it. We start to behave like a robot or a puppet. A sleepwalker? Yes, but in a very small room. Sometimes it is as if someone else has taken us over, someone who shows characteristics we always used to detest the most in others. This is the world of Ecclesiastes:

> All doing is so full of effort, that nobody can express it; the eye never sees itself sated, and the ear never hears itself sated. What is it that has happened? Just the same as what happens after this. What is it that one has done? Just the same as what one will do after this again; and nothing new happens there under the sun.

(Ecclesiastes, 1: 8–9)

The essence of alienation is that we do not use our attention any longer to 'live' in the world, to experience it fully. The fact that we do not pay proper attention any more to what presents itself to us negatively affects our self-esteem (Branden, 1987). Though the state sketched here is a serious one, it is essentially a normal way to deal with an abnormal situation that we cannot control. This way of living not only has a high incidence, but is highly contagious as well. There are many ways to get into such a state of alienation. A few variants follow.

Some people have been trained from early in life to suppress certain specific feelings, such as anger, sorrow or anxiety. Instead of switching off all feelings, we can also split ourselves and store a feeling in a part of ourselves for which we do not take responsibility. By doing that, we alienate a part of ourselves. We are not afraid, sad or angry, but the suppressed feeling takes its toll: we may then be taken over by panic, depression or a tantrum, something that seems to come from the outside and to which we are defenseless (Perls, Hefferline & Goodman, 1951).

One step further, alienation evolves into all kinds of functional complaints. These are bodily complaints that disable us from doing certain activities, especially those activities that evoke the feeling we do not want to feel. It is as if our body throws itself in the breach for us: I really want to do it, but I am not able to do it any more. The complaints just take us out of the situation. RSI (repetitive strain injury) or mouse arm, for example, can take us out of the situation of working with a computer, when we really feel used or manipulated by our boss or job description, but don't see any way to ventilate our indignation or powerless anger about this. As the term indignation already suggests, functional complaints often are a matter of our conscience: we do not allow ourselves to ventilate these feelings because we are too loyal to the organization and ventilating these feelings would not feel right. A similar mechanism plays a role in other pain complaints and in sudden intense fatigue, which make certain activities impossible. In the latter case, it is remarkable how a single remark, that maybe there is such a mechanism at work, can evoke an unexpectedly fierce and energetic response in the fatigued person. This is not to say that the pain or fatigue is not real or that it will go away by itself. On the contrary, the complaints usually stay as long as the cause stays. When our conscience does not allow us to admit that the complaint is 'really' a matter of suppressed feelings, the complaint may even bother us for considerably longer.

In both cases, when alienated feelings take us over and when there are functional complaints, we don't pay attention to what is really going on. Typically, we don't even take note of the source of the problem. Moreover, feelings of alienation and functional complaints both soothe a guilty conscience, to the outer world but also to ourselves.

Sometimes also all kinds of adaptations, which involve us habitually suppressing certain feelings and lines of behavior, are so rewarded that these feelings and lines of behavior more or less wither away without our noticing it (Bolen, 1989). Luxury, comfort, power, money, belonging, prestige, status, quiet, a risk-free existence – these all are very powerful rewards. This may happen to a child in a family, but also to an adult who lets himself be socialized in a company. Such a form of socialization can also lead to alienation, listless living without real high and low points. Here too, we forgo the possibility of taking responsibility for what is going on and fully living and experiencing our reality, and here too we jeopardize our self-esteem (Branden, 1987).

Then there are the institutions that take over our whole life, such as sects, cloisters, barracks, prisons, retirement homes and hospitals. This taking over our life occurs also – to a lesser degree – at work. There we quickly learn to comply with the rules, make ourselves dependent on those who are in power and see the world through their eyes, since such an adaptation offers the best possibilities to lead a bearable life. Our own personality then gradually dissolves without our noticing it, mostly because we are not allowed to take care of ourselves. Others take care of us. Maybe the quality of such a life is hardly adequate, but other options seem absent. This going along with the rules and giving up our personality are called institutionalization. Again, we are alienated from ourselves. When others get into trouble because of the fact that they are not able, or do not want, to adapt, that is not our problem. So prisoners display an impassive face, the so-called dog face, nuns say without much emotion that a runaway nun obviously did not feel really called to the vocation, patients ignore a frequently complaining fellow patient, and psychiatric patients – and their keepers – remain fully unmoved by the bizarre behavior of other patients (Goffman, 1968). Being transferred suddenly from such an institution and having to take care of ourselves again is far from simple and, consequently, some people find it impossible to return to the free world.

The gist of this description of institutionalization and similar phenomena is that related adaptations can play a role in 'normal' organizations as well, though most of the time we are confronted there with less severe versions of such adaptations. However, as a change agent we always have to be alert to such adaptations and also find ways to deal with them, as in most cases they are clearly dysfunctional.

A remarkable, related phenomenon in cloisters is that of 'acedia', the ghost of the afternoon (Pranger, 2002). Acedia is taken to be a state of apathy prompted by the devil, in which everything is useless and futile, and terms such as God and the hereafter have been robbed of all meaning. The most popular explanation is that acedia is caused by too fanatically and one-sidedly throwing oneself on the prescribed exercises and the resulting negligence of the rest. As a state of apathy, deprived of meaningfulness, acedia comes close to secondary alienation. The imbalance stemming from focusing attention only on one small part of life while ignoring and suppressing the rest, which is reported to cause acedia, is also clearly related to the ignoring of vital parts of life conducive to secondary alienation. Karl Marx connected alienation with the dulling, monotonous and endlessly repeating character of certain simple production tasks, as did many after him (Hackman & Oldham, 1980; Karasek & Theorell, 1990; Ollman, 1971). There is a system in it!

There are many other ways to lead an alienated life. Addiction to alcohol or to other drugs that influence our feelings is a good example. A phobia – that is, systematically avoiding a significant part of our life – is another possibility, as is a compulsory neurosis, filling our life up with endlessly repeating certain actions or thoughts and shutting out other options. Thus, alienation can be brought about in many ways, occurs frequently, is essentially an unpleasant state and is hard to give up. Moreover, it is unhealthy. It affects our vitality, by affecting our energy level as well as our immune system. The important point here, however, is the general principle: alienation occurs when we prefer not to feel or experience certain things, because way back we concluded that our life would be less terrible this way. Alienation only disappears if we go back to the event in question, face it and experience after all what we shunned and still avoid. Whether we face that event or not is a matter of choice. Not facing the event, however, can effectively block any change. Going back to painful original events in an organization thus can be necessary to get sufficient support and energy for a fundamental change in that organization.

In this respect, a 'growing' past usually implies dragging along an increasing amount of alienated material, while it would be more convenient and pleasant to travel more lightly. Apart from clearly painful events, alienation entails also business, relationships and projects that are not properly finished or tied up. This unfinished business keeps on taking energy from us, even when we barely think of it.

Apart from a useless loss of energy, cleaning up unfinished business also leads to a more centered and 'undivided' existence. We obstruct ourselves less: there are fewer 'partial people' who disagree about everything. The partial people are the thoughts or nagging voices that make themselves heard as 'Yes but...', 'That will never work' and 'That will only result in...' Cleaning up does not imply eliminating these thoughts or voices altogether. Eliminating them for good would even be far from wise. These thoughts do not exist without a reason. We need them, because they are also part of our reflection and asking ourselves questions. Banning these thoughts for good would imply that we rob ourselves of the possibility of reflection as well and put ourselves in an even deeper state of alienation.

Instead of banning these nagging thoughts, we can use them by letting them cooperate constructively. These thoughts can help us, for example, to achieve better solutions. We can also invite these thoughts to reconcile themselves with the decisions taken and choices made. Then, if we feel like it, we can consult them deliberately. Moreover, we might agree with them that they only raise their nagging little voices when they can be really useful, for example to give constructive advice or useful warnings.

Taking care of our unfinished business, of course, does not imply that we can change the past. What we can do, however, is face what we have avoided and allow ourselves to experience the accompanying feelings after all. We can learn from these experiences and give them the place they deserve. This is exactly what we are going to do now. First, we examine our unfinished business with people and institutions that have treated us wrongly. Here this primarily concerns our work life.

Think about those broken promises, the lack of recognition and the other people who took the credit for your efforts. The times when you have been used, the bad faith and its consequences. What was prevented from happening as a consequence, though you wanted it so badly to happen? Of course, this is about your own contribution to that event too, for nobody is completely innocent. Moreover, in a way you allowed people to misuse you. How could you have been so blind, so stupid? Think of all the fruitless brooding, the plans about how you would get even with them, what you would say, thoughts that have kept you shut up in an angry, dejected mood. Thoughts also that made it impossible to do anything worthwhile for a long time.

Do you still get angry about that particular situation? Or is there only a dull resignation, as well as reluctance to stir things up again? If so, realize that in both cases that situation still has you firmly in its grasp. Even when you cannot change the past, you can see to it that it no longer affects you and you can learn something from it. You can free yourself from the conclusions that you drew then and that are still blocking your way. Resentment and avoidance are simply not the best solutions. The other person is not bothered by it, while you are spoiling your own life. It is better to pay a visit to each event that still gives you trouble. Start with the worst one:

- What happened?
- What were the consequences?
- How bad was it?
- How did you respond?
- What did you feel?

Use your different senses to recall this as clearly as possible. What did it look like? How did it sound? How did it feel? Was there a specific smell? Go on until you are completely in the situation again: yes, that's the way it was. Now, take some distance from it. Step out of it. Look at the situation as if you were an outsider, but one who has gone through all of it from close by, knows everything about it and observes it keenly. Now answer the next questions:

- To what degree was what happened to you directed against you personally?
- How could this have happened?
- Would it have happened to any other person in your place as well?
- What did you do, and fail to do, which made this possible?
- Did the other person think that you yourself had given reason for it?
- What can be learned from this?
- What are you going to do differently from now on?
- What has happened that would not have happened if this event had not taken place?
- What did you gain from that?
- If this had not happened, what would have happened and what would you probably have spared yourself by this?
- Did the person who did this to you have any alternative line of action?
- And if so, does this make the other person into somebody with whom you would change positions?
- Would it not be better to have some compassion for such a person?
- Is it possible for you to forgive the other person, in order to go on and not look back?

Go through your whole list. Education does not come cheap, as Keith Richard said when his manager took off with his millions. You have already paid the price; you had better take the lessons to heart.

The world is organized in such a way that there are only very few people who never do something bad to somebody else. However, we usually do not pay much attention to the injustice we have done to other people. What's done is done. But still, open accounts cost us a strange kind of compound interest. This interest is composed of the costs of alienation, diminished self-esteem and the opportunity to learn that we deny ourselves. The alienation also becomes manifest when we meet the other person and do not talk about it. The alienation does not only make the relationship less meaningful – if anything is left of it – there is also a silent reproach in ourselves.

Here's another list, this time one of people you have abused, treated unfairly, deceived or abandoned, and what exactly you have done to them. For each person, there are the following questions:

- What exactly did or didn't you do?
- Could you have acted otherwise?
- How?
- Why haven't you done that?
- How does that feel?
- How would you do differently now?
- If the other person is still alive, what do you want to say to them about this?
- Do you want to apologize?
- What more can you do to make up for your actions?

The fact that we apologize does not necessarily mean that the other person forgives us. It does mean, however, that we have done the best we can. We have been honest, have faced our own actions and no longer need to avoid the thoughts and feelings involved.

At the same time, we can never avoid all guilt. Sometimes we have to make decisions that badly hurt individual people. This applies to an extreme degree to somebody who decides to sacrifice some people in order to save others. To a lesser degree, however, it also applies to the simpler choice between alternatives in which people have invested much effort and time. As long as we have chosen an option that appeared the best at that moment – that is, as far as we could know then – we are ethically speaking in the clear, even if in hindsight we were wrong. Being wrong remains our responsibility – and maybe we have to answer for that – but we have not done anything bad.

OUR OWN MORTALITY

> I asked a child that walked with a candle: 'From where does that light come?'
> Immediately, the child blew out the candle.
> 'Tell me where it is gone – then I will tell you where it came from.'
>
> (Hasan of Basra, from Sjah, 1969)

Accepting that sooner or later we will die is an important developmental task. When we succeed at this task it allows us to relate our own death to our everyday life. By accomplishing that, we have taken an important step toward a life that is less dominated by alienation and anxiety, maybe the most important step. Taking the realization of our own mortality as our point of departure in the way we experience our life is what Heidegger calls *sein zum Tode*, being toward death, relating ourselves to our death in a conscious way. Living as if any moment can be the last is, according to Heidegger (1962), the only possibility for living authentically, for living a real life.

Near-death experiences are instructive here. Many people who have experienced a near-death experience not only say that death is no longer threatening to them, but also that they experience the time that apparently still has been allotted to them with more gratitude, attention and pleasure.

Cicero indicated in his *De Senectudine* ('About old age', 1909–14) that the realization of our own mortality is a reason to live with more wisdom, attention and courage. When it has got through to us that we are going to die, the finiteness of our time and the once-only quality of each moment get through to us as well. It then becomes more urgent to fully experience each moment and to handle the remaining time more precisely and attentively. Consequently, we spend less time on what does not interest us and occupy ourselves more with what really moves us, our own motives. In addition, a genuine realization that we must die anyhow makes all those little fears that steer our decisions in everyday life less meaningful and compelling. These fears can keep us away from changes in the direction that is most essential and meaningful to us. Not letting ourselves be ruled by these fears gives us a pleasant feeling of liberation and excitement, the feeling that we are living to the max, in full command of all our abilities and possibilities.

More possibilities to extend our life will probably arise and already some life processes can be kept going for some time with the help of all kinds of machines, but that is not essential. There does come a moment that the conditions that are necessary to sustain our life are no longer met. Sometimes this comes as a liberation, sometimes not at all. In both cases, it is absurd to let our life be embittered because of its finiteness. Hopefully, we don't do that either with a good meal, a beautiful day or making love.

Another point is that we associate death with suffering and pain. Yes, possibly, but isn't it just death that implies the end of the suffering?

Also, there are the intense feelings of loss and mourning related to death. But whose feelings are these? In any case they are not the feelings of the deceased.

Then there is still the saying *partir c'est mourir un peu*, leaving is dying a little. This suggests that dying is an awful lot of leaving. It is as long as we are still living, but here too actual death is the end of this. Again, this is a matter of thinking from the perspective of the survivors, which actually is the only perspective we can share.

Ultimately accepting our own mortality implies that we can see death as the end or goal of our life, the destination we are heading for, without knowing when precisely we will arrive. Though we exert ourselves to postpone the arrival at that destination, death is still unavoidable. Is that the deeper meaning of the saying that the journey is of more value than the destination? And didn't that saying imply also an exhortation to live more intensely and to pay more attention to the here-and-now?

The issue here is that our tendency to ban our mortality from our consciousness goes hand in hand with clinging to the mock safety of an alienated life, governed by all kinds of cowardly objections and fears.

I am not suggesting that we should literally organize our own near-death experience by fooling around on the roof of a skyscraper or on a small railway platform where a fast train is due any moment. Cleaners and engine drivers already have enough on their minds. However, the sentences about near-death experiences are the introduction to a thought experiment. All you need is a pen and paper and a place where you are not disturbed.

First, no longer avoid the matter but face it straightforwardly. Relate your own death to your life! The questions intended to bring this about follow two lines of thought: that of your own death and the death of somebody else.

- How do you imagine your own death?
- What are you afraid of?
- What is the worst thing that may happen?
- What horror stories occur to you?
- Who told you these stories?
- What purpose did these stories serve?

- Have you been present at the death bed of someone else?
- What happened, particularly for the person who died?

- What part of this do you want for yourself too?
- What do you want to do differently yourself?

- How do you want to die?
- What can you do to achieve that?

Imagine this as vividly as possible.

When you have answered these questions honestly, you have made substantial progress. Maybe it is a good idea to put aside the book for a while now and to do something else. Just look around you. Has anything changed? The questions and your answers will go through your head somewhat more and you will notice that you feel better and better.

The next exercise is of a different nature. It is a fantasy. In this fantasy, you have no size and weight. You are gliding above the world. Feel how very light you are. Nobody can see you. It is very pleasant – all the intense quiet, all the light. Enjoy the flying. Feel that marvelous lightness, the quiet. Then look down, and see what is happening there: There is some kind of performance going on, rows of people in chairs looking at a stage. Have a closer look. You know the person who is telling the story very well. Now you are watching still more closely, you notice that in fact you know almost everybody there. There is a coffin on the stage. A funeral? You look at everything, unmoved, very calm and serene. Of course, it is your own funeral. No fear, you just watch calmly, objectively. You are completely free of any judgment or interest.

- Who is sincerely sad and who has a really difficult time?
- For whom is it only a matter of obligatory attendance?
- Who is there from your work? How do they behave?
- Who are the speakers?
- What do they say?
- Do you recognize yourself in their words?
- Who is looking at his watch?
- How does all of this relate to how you allotted your time during the past few years?

Take a deep breath. Look around you for a while. The good news is that you are still around. What does this experience imply for your priorities in the near future? What changes come to your mind? What do you want to write down?

The next exercise you can do at any time or place. Observe closely an environment that is very familiar to you as if you are there for the last time and bid it farewell. Involve all your senses at once. What do you see? What do you hear? How does it feel? How does it smell? What kind of taste is there in your mouth? What is different from usual?

You can do the same with somebody you love. Or with familiar acts. A little bit like near-death experience, but a safe one.

"And docter?"
"I'll not beat around the bush. May be You only have two more months to live"
"But docter, from what?"

RESISTANCE TO CHANGE

In every life things happen that are very unpleasant. We can become ill, waste chances, fail in front of a huge audience or have an accident. Our loved one can leave us for another person; we can be fired and become unemployed. Our parents die, a friend passes away and we ourselves are facing a serious depression.

Other things are less easy to point out, develop more gradually, have more of a stealthy nature but are also really very sad. We are not ill, but we do not feel well either. We don't waste chances, but we do not do anything really well either. We never fail publicly, but only because there is no audience. We do not have an accident, but are we so happy? Our loved one is still around, but we talk less to each other than we used to and if she left us it would not be the end of the world. And so on: work that could be more pleasant, parents with whom we might have better contact, friends we hardly see any more and the idea that if we died now, we would not have made the most of our life.

- To what degree do you admit to yourself that some things can be improved?
- Are you completely honest in this respect?
- When you realized that you could do better on one of those points, what did you think?
- What did you tell yourself then?

Such questions evoke all kinds of answers and most of these imply that we are not planning to do much about it. A corny joke about this is that civil servants rise to their creative peaks when they make up reasons not to do something. The joke is primarily corny because the same principle applies to almost everybody.

An important category of such answers consists of arguments that the present situation may not be ideal, but that it is good enough. Good-enough solutions frequently occur elsewhere in nature (see the story of the duck and the cormorant in Chapter 1).

However, good-enough solutions are sometimes good enough indeed, especially when they are consequences of a deliberate choice. We can choose a car that performs badly because we find it so beautiful, a poorly paid job because it offers us much freedom, an incompetent lover because he is so rich and generous. It also can be that we really don't care. We don't need a beautiful house; we are never in it, after all. We look terrible, but we don't go out anyway. We would like to think that this 'functionally' applies to all good-enough solutions, but unfortunately that is not the case.

Go back to the list of imperfections again. Wouldn't we really prefer to feel better? Wouldn't it be pleasant to be a social success now and then, when we feel like it? How would it feel to be really happy, enjoy the company of our lover, have a job that is a real treat and live to the full?

Often, however, this triggers thoughts such as that would be all very nice indeed, but that is not how things are arranged; we should remain realistic; our path is just not strewn with roses; there are no peaks without valleys. Moreover, having it all would be damned egocentric and egoistic as well.

To start with the last concern: who would suffer as a result of our being happier? Who would gain something by that, for that matter? And further: of course our life cannot be composed of mere peak experiences and happiness, but it could be better, at least a little better, somewhat more adventurous, somewhat less dull. Apparently, something is pulling us back. There is some reluctance to bring about a change for the better. What underlies this reluctance?

Why don't we put in more effort to get a more pleasant and more meaningful life than the one we are living now? To answer this question, it is worth having a look at the positive outcomes that our present way of living apparently offers us. This refers to the positive outcomes of the collection of good-enough solutions with which we have reconciled ourselves. What could these outcomes be?

First, it is a matter of avoiding risks. We know what we have; we do not know what the future will bring us. Think of everything that could go wrong: the same list of imperfections again. After all, it is very possible to waste chances, fail in front of everybody important, get injured, find out that our relationship with our lover is based on a misunderstanding, be reduced to beggary because we quit our present job, have an accident and lose our friends. And yes, then a deep depression becomes a feasible option.

Thinking about the consequences of a radical change provides sufficient material to easily fill several evening-long disaster movies, especially when we wake up at night. However, how realistic all those doom-laden thoughts are remains to be seen. Their main purpose probably is preventing us from changing something or preventing us from doing something. This mechanism can be clarified somewhat by the following story about Nasrudin, the legendary character from many eastern stories.

> A neighbor wants to borrow Nasrudin's clothesline.
> 'I am sorry,' says Nasrudin, 'but I'm drying my flour on it.'
> 'Your flour? On a clothesline? How can that be?'
> 'You don't understand that? As it is, it is not so complicated at all when you don't want to lend out your clothesline.

> (based on Sjah, 1969)

Those scenarios may be not very realistic, but we can learn about their lack of validity only by making some attempt. To start with, we can thoroughly examine the change we want to make. Do nothing yet, but just let your thoughts wander over the different possibilities. If we don't explore the different possibilities, these ghostly disasters keep us grounded. Lying flatly on the ground is an excellent way not to fall.

As it is, we can better forgo some risks, as long as we are not suicidal. Russian roulette, welding without goggles, smoking too much, unprotected sex with a hersin prostitute, picking a fight with a street gang – these all are matters of very unfavorable ratios between possible costs and gains. Here, however, we are not talking at all about such risks. Here there is a world to win and the risk that everything turns out badly is relatively small.

Avoiding the risks related to change is really a strange form of cowardice. In everyday life we take all kinds of risks without giving them a thought. How about learning to walk? How about driving a car, bicycling in heavy traffic, eating in a restaurant, being at home alone and knowing that the chance of surviving a heart attack is much higher when we are found in the street? How about consulting a general practitioner or specialist who can make the most ghastly errors?

Compared to familiar everyday life, we evidently let ourselves be led by completely different fantasies in the case of change. Apparently, we are willing to accept these disaster scenarios as reasonable reflections of reality. At the same time we don't take fantasies of happiness and success into consideration. We don't even start with them.

What kind of strange anxiety is this? An anxiety that keeps you away from a fuller life, which would be more worthwhile. Maybe we should ask ourselves: where does this anxiety come from? Are we sure that this is really our own anxiety? Who may have suggested it to us? Who wants – or wanted – to keep us away from everything that might go wrong? Or right, for that matter? Or who wants or wanted to keep us in their immediate vicinity? Whatever the answers to these questions, realize that it is now actually your own anxiety and that you can decide how determining you allow it to be. In any case, know also that this kind of anxiety is not in itself the best possible adviser.

Risks are obviously a huge factor in resistance to change, but that is not all. Our peace of mind is also an issue. There is the comfort stemming from inhabiting a familiar reality, as well as the sense of control resulting from it. We have built our own niche, a reality that is completely ours. Also, it took a lot of work to make and keep it so ordinary and orderly. Maybe this could also be a matter of the material comfort this niche offers us, or the status that we derive from it, our prestige, our power position. This niche, our own reality, is the area in which we feel comfortable: it represents our comfort zone. When we approach its borders and threaten to step outside them, all kinds of alarm bells go off: 'You are approaching the end of pleasure. Stop. If you still go on, we cannot guarantee you anything any more.' Most of the time we don't look for these limits at all. Still we are aware of these possible dangers. It is also considerably more comfortable not to put in that extra effort. Indeed, don't we do more than enough already? How could we make time for such a change?

OK, if our days are so filled and we are deeply satisfied with that, of course we must not wrack our brains over other possibilities. Moreover, success is explicitly not guaranteed. The only certainty is that not much will change if we do nothing. Maybe it is actually good to ask ourselves to what ends are we putting in all our effort. Is it really so worthwhile? And one other thing: What are we so busy with? What tires us so much? Something of great value must be involved! And also, if we are so pressed for time, we should think about how we can do something about that.

After avoiding risks and striving for peace of mind, a third point concerns the reactions of the people who are close to us. How would they receive attempts from our side to initiate changes? Would they welcome our efforts with applause, or would our efforts evoke a lot of 'yes buts'? How would our partner respond? And our friends? And all the others? What exactly are we afraid of in this respect? What is the worst possible response? How likely is it? And what precisely is so bad about it? This third point is probably the most realistic one. When we actually carry through drastic changes, we may indeed expect some serious disapproval from the people around us. At the end of the day, we are also part of their life and they probably don't want to change any more than we do.

As it is, the way we run our present everyday life gives us a strong experience of control. We know exactly what to do and what not to do. We know the signs of potential threats and dangers and what to do to avoid or counter them. Our familiar way of living also enables us to keep our mind free for what we really find important. Moreover, as we have seen, it enables us to avoid risks and provides us with peace of mind and acceptance by others. According to Philip McGrath (1999), better known as Doctor Phil, these outcomes form together a cocktail that is more addictive than heroin. Considering the form that many lives take, he might well be right about this. We administer ourselves a huge number of doses each day while we do not even notice that we are doing it.

The present state of affairs thus indeed provides powerful rewards and gains, which possibly hover on the borders of addiction. Perhaps it has also become clear that it is important to thoroughly examine our own life every now and then.

In the end, we are responsible for our own life, our own experiences. That is not to say that we are guilty when things don't go well. It does imply, however, that we are responsible for making our life as valuable as we can. Making our life valuable primarily is a matter of reflection, observing ourselves and questioning ourselves.

- Am I really living authentically?
- Am I really satisfied and happy?

- To what degree am I settling for good-enough solutions?
- How strictly do I confine myself to my comfort zone?
- What do I systematically avoid?
- What am I able and willing to do that I do not do?

Answering these questions in a productive way demands honesty and tenacity. As it is, we are very good at keeping feelings and problems away from ourselves. Besides that, we probably have a strange manic side to us by which we obscure our own vulnerability: 'That will not happen to me' or 'It will not happen in my lifetime'. We may be right, but that life time does happen to be finite.

When there are problems, but also when things can be improved, we have to decide what we are going to do about them. We can choose to ignore things and we can choose to do our best. In any case, we can solve problems only when we acknowledge them. A truism, but this time a very true one indeed.

These reflections become acute in times of cultural change. Do we want to face our problems? Are we willing to take risks? Do we want to give up our peace of mind for a while? Can we find it in ourselves to go our own way, without needlessly being dependent on the judgments of the people close to us? In short, can we find the courage to leave our comfort zone in order to make things better?

EARLY YOUTH

By developing in a certain way, we exclude all other possibilities (compare Chapter 1). This particular development is the consequence of the choices we have made along the way and the alternatives we have blocked by making these specific choices. As it is, most of these choices are implicit and tacit in nature, and so are their results. However, these choices are very important, as they result in our fixed, habitual ways of dealing with familiar situations. As we don't question our habits, nor our choices for that matter, our own habitual behavior is self-evident, normal and familiar to us and we are the last ones to see our own peculiarities. This section intends to make us somewhat more aware of the nature of our habitual behavior, its inherent goals and the assumptions underlying it. To this end it contains questions that relate to the mostly tacit choices we made in our early youth.

The questions are grouped in little clusters, each of which deals with a particular issue. Such a cluster is really answered only when you know what influence the point in question has had on you, and when you know whether and how you want to change the result of that influence. To this end, each time go back as the adult you are now to the child you were then. Find out – from the adult perspective – what you would have liked better then, as if this were possible. Don't be disturbed by the impossibility of it all. The exercise is only a matter of 'as if'. Feel free. It does imply, however, that you must go back to the original event to experience it again, with all the accompanying feelings. If you do not allow yourself to experience these feelings, you run the risk of getting stuck in alienation, which may cost you energy without your noticing it.

First, go back to the family you came from. Essentially, the family in which you grew up is your great model for how to live your life and – primarily – how to relate to others. Here you got your first experiences and developed your first strategies.

Take a deep breath and feel how things were then. The house in which you lived, the different rooms, the kitchen, the bathroom, the furniture, the floor covering, the room in which you slept. The voices, the radio and television programs, the sounds from outside. The smell of the food, the taste of your favorite sweets. The clothes you wore, the clothes of the other people.

- Who is present there?
- Who is not present, or is not present most of the time?
- How do they relate to each other? What is the division of roles?
- What does the division of power look like? What hierarchy does that result in? What is your position?
- Are you welcome?
- Do the people around you give you the idea that you are good enough just as you are?
- How does each of them relate to you?
- How do you relate to each of them?
- What kinds of conflicts occur?
- How are these conflicts dealt with?
- What in your behavior have you taken on from each of the people close to you?
- Who do you resemble most? In what ways?

These questions are intended to surface your most basic ways of relating to other people. Did you succeed in that respect? If not, go back once more to the questions above, but now knowing that this really is about your most basic ways to relate to other people. Make precise notes. Take a short break and then continue with the following questions.

- When you now go back as an adult to how things were then, what would you have liked to have done differently?
- What would you have preferred?
- How was that as a child then?
- How did you cope with that?
- What advice would you, as the adult you are now, give the child you were then to do differently?

This cluster of questions is intended to show that you have now developed more options for dealing with such situations. Read your notes once more to find out which specific options this relates to. This is also a good opportunity to determine what you are still lacking in skills for coping more successfully with such situations. Quiet maybe? Or flair, spunk, conviction, power of expression? What are these skills exactly and can you attain them?

If you would behave differently now than when you were a child, it implies that the effects your family had on you do not need to be so influential on your present life any more. If you had entered your family's situation knowing what you know now, you would have come to another solution after all. So knowing what you know now, it makes no sense to let your current behavior be determined completely by your childhood solutions. This is very important, especially because it applies to many situations. You know far more now. Use what you have learned! Let this sink in fully.

Back again to your childhood. Based on your experiences then, you have shown the same conduct and behavior in many other situations. That has become an automatic habit. When you always behave the same way, you know exactly what you can expect from other people as well. This works as a self-fulfilling prophecy. The fact that this way of acting actually helps you through certain situations implies an extra reinforcement of that way of acting, for better or for worse.

This applies, for example, to people who almost always behave in a passive way. Though initially a good solution in all those situations with that bossy older sister or brother, it gradually may become a fixed way of behaving with other people as well. It often – though not always – still works, because some others like to take decisions and automatically arrange everything for you.

The same applies to taking responsibility: if you do this and you do that, I will... The same goes for getting angry, walking away, dreaming and so on. By behaving in such ways, you evoke reactions that you know through and through, reactions to which you can respond blindly and which from time to time offer real rewards as well. By doing so, you have it your own way. That just seems normal, while thinking things over again and again and coming up with new solutions seems needlessly complicated and tiring.

The reverse is that without wasting a single thought on it, you limit yourself to only one option, which is not always the best option and sometimes is even downright wrong. Besides, it is not even your own option. You have just mindlessly picked it up from your environment. However, since then you have learned all kinds of things that provide you with other options, which are sometimes much more appropriate. Blindly holding on to your fixed ways of doing things then turns against you.

In summary: take into account that you still often do things that are less than adequate, only because you acquired that conduct at a time when you had less understanding of such things than you have now. The next questions are intended to explore to what degree you indeed limit your own options in such a way.

- To what degree do you still behave toward others in the same way as you did in the family in which you grew up?
- To what degree people nowadays do the same to you as the members of the family you came from?
- How does this manifest itself when relating to:
  - your boss?
  - your colleagues?
  - people in everyday life whom you do not know specifically?
- To what degree does each of these people resemble in their behavior a former family member?
- And the other way around, how do your ways of acting toward your or other people's children resemble how your parents treated you?
- Can it be that you select certain people toward whom you can behave in a certain way?
- Or do you challenge people to treat you in a particular way by how you behave?
- How do you do this precisely?
- What do you want to change in this respect?
- What can you do about that?

If you indeed have the idea that you select and treat people in such a way, you must realize that this behavior pattern has become a part of you and, moreover, that this has been the basis of the relationship you have with these people now. Radically changing the pattern – if you were able to do so at all – might strike the roots of your relationship. However, you *can* play around a little with other options and watch closely what happens. This of course does not apply to new people you meet; here you are much freer. Also, you had better be very careful over formulating what you have learned now. By the way, you will be surprised by the stubbornness with which you hold on to your old ways of relating with others.

This is a whole lot of information at once and it is advisable to return to these questions a couple of times in the coming days and weeks. Really mastering this section will give you a much richer behavioral repertoire and will make you much more effective as a change agent.

LEITMOTIFS

Everybody has their favorite ways of dealing with life. Usually we are quite good at these, depending on our specific talents. Some people are good at taking the lead, others are good at creating a pleasant climate, and still others like to help other people. In this respect, Ofman (1995) speaks of 'core qualities'. I speak here of a 'leitmotif' or 'main motive'.

A way to determine our leitmotif simply consists of asking people who are dear to us what they find our most irritating trait. Usually this is a dysfunctional exaggeration of our leitmotif, an enlargement that the people who are dear to us cannot bear. This especially comes up when we are tired or under pressure. Ofman calls this our 'pitfall'. For the abovementioned leitmotifs, this could be tyrannical conduct, avoiding conflict at any price, or spoiling someone. By communicating in terms of pitfalls it becomes considerably simpler to give positive feedback. In this way, we can for example tell somebody who displays overly dominant behavior that they show an awful lot of responsibility, while we then still can tell them that we find it overbearing.

Another way to determine our leitmotif stems from the fact that we often react against behavior that is opposite to our own preferred behavior. For instance, somebody who almost always acts in a responsible way often dislikes people who let things slide, subtle people have an aversion to rude and uncivil people, and diligent people don't appreciate lazy people. Ofman calls such conduct our 'allergy'. Each time this is about behavior that we do not allow ourselves to display and we try to suppress; that is, a part of ourselves that Jung (1970) called our shadow side. This side often comes up when we make sufficient progress in a stress process (Schabracq, 2003a). Very active people then may become passivity personified, while very quiet, composed people suddenly begin to act agitatedly, to the surprise of their direct acquaintances: 'He certainly is not herself lately.'

The good thing about a shadow side, or allergy, is that it always implies indications for our personal developmental task of the moment, the direction in which we can further develop ourselves. Ofman calls this our 'challenge'. The risk of one fixed way of doing things is that we develop ourselves too one-sidedly. As a result, we cannot cope with situations that demand another approach. Moreover, under pressure we risk lapsing into the behavioral patterns of our pitfall and allergy. Al Siebert (1996) advocates developing a so-called bipolar personality. This implies that we should develop the behavior opposite to the way in which we automatically tend to act. So a very introverted person should also learn to be more extraverted, though in a well-adjusted way. Siebert demonstrates that people who succeed in this are better at surviving all kinds of perilous situations. All in all, this is a matter of identifying our allergy, exploring the positive side of that behavior and then starting to try it out and exercise it. Our developmental task can also be described as the inversion of our pitfall, but in positive terms. The pitfall of being overly dominant, for example, can be translated into the developmental task of 'being able to let go' and 'being able to surrender'.

It is very useful each time we find somebody hateful and irritating to ask ourselves whether this perhaps is a matter of an allergy of ours. What actually is so irritating about the other person, why is that so irritating and how does this relate to our leitmotifs? Besides this being very instructive – it puts us on the right track for developmental tasks – we also become angry less easily and less often, which makes us more pleasurable to be with.

We should also not neglect our leitmotifs. Become acquainted with your leitmotif and make a point of taking enough time to realize what it is, of course without neglecting your developmental tasks. Only when you live from your leitmotif can you live fully and with self-respect, utilize all your energy and give yourself entirely. And only then can you be optimally meaningful for the people around you and contribute to the world. Being optimally meaningful for the people around you and contributing to the world are big words, but living from your leitmotif really is about giving what you want and are able to give so that you make a real contribution to the world. Consistently neglecting your leitmotif, by contrast, leads in the long run to a colorless and alienated life. Consequently, it is crucial to explore your leitmotif to be maximally effective in everything you undertake. From a change agent's perspective, it is important to thoroughly examine your own leitmotif as well as those of the other participants in the change process.

In this book following your leitmotif is primarily a matter of work, career and study, but essentially living according your leitmotif pertains to each important choice or decision in your life. What consequences are there each time for your leitmotif and developmental task? This is the acid test. For now, it has the following implications for your life. First, get rid of the tasks that do not allow you to follow your leitmotif and developmental task. Then, acquire more tasks in which you can make the most of your leitmotif and developmental task. However, in practice both assignments are sometimes difficult to achieve. When these difficulties are too big, try to change your existing tasks in such a way that they offer more room for the realization of your leitmotif and developmental task. Staying with your leitmotif and your developmental task – and taking some rest from time to time in order to unwind – can lead to the most effective and pleasant forms of working possible. Such a way of working is also a good medicine for stress, for that matter.

Both our pitfall and our allergy are based on assumptions that are in many situations counterproductive. Surfacing these assumptions is a matter of asking the right questions or applying the other techniques described in Chapter 6. Addendum 3 contains a whole list of examples of such assumptions.

POINTS OF RESEMBLANCE WITH YOUR RELATIVES

In Chapter 3 and earlier in this chapter it became clear that we have adopted most of our attitudes from our parents and other relatives, and that these attitudes gradually develop into whole systems of acting, thinking and feeling that are similar to those of the members of our family. We are usually unaware of this resemblance for different reasons. First, we are inclined to think that we have effectively stood our distance from our parents during our puberty. Second, we tend to think that our education and the independent life we lead now have had a decisive impact. Still, we have unknowingly developed all kinds of basic convictions, values and opinions that match those of our relatives rather well.

These are not only the personal views and opinions of our parents, but the ideas that stem from their – and our – societal and cultural background. For example, there are the influences of their:

- philosophy of life and (the remains of) religion
- socio-economic status
- work and profession
- place of residence
- political background

This for instance concerns ideas about:

- good and evil
- coping with emotions
- handling power
- work
- relationships and love
- education
- gender roles
- money and so on

We are prone to see the differences between us and our relatives. As it is, something different is more likely to catch the eye, almost by definition, particularly when it is about a change we have fought for. At the same time, what we share with our relatives is so present everywhere that it tends to become invisible to us. We have lived for quite a time very close to each other, have inhabited a common niche in a common culture, and for a long time they were the only ones to turn to for most of our learning. An unprejudiced outsider, preferably one from a different (sub)culture, who took the trouble to get to know us and our family might point out to us a surprisingly large number of deeply rooted similarities.

Realizing how we are determined by our background is important for several reasons. Maybe we want to change a little, maybe not, but it is good to be able to put our own views and opinions into perspective, as well as to understand what they are. Moreover, by looking at our views and opinions in this way, we get a better understanding of how the opinions of other people have arisen. All these three skills are especially important in the context of dialogue. Essentially, there are two ways to look at the resemblances and differences with our parents and other relatives: we can observe the resemblances and differences themselves on the one hand, and the influences that brought them about on the other.

ASSIGNMENTS FROM YOUR PARENTS

The previous section may give the impression that the transfer of views and opinions from parents to their children is always a matter of a kind of tacit reproduction. This is of course not the whole story. Parents want all kinds of things as well and they have dreams. This can concern ideals, their own business, a career or a certain kind of life. Some parents achieve their wishes and dreams. Most of them do so only partially, and still others fail on all fronts.

Many parents expect their children to do the same as they have done themselves. What turned out to be good – or good enough – for them should be so for their children as well. Of course, this does not apply to all parents. There are also parents who don't want to impose such assignments on their children and who only want their children to live a good life and become happy in their own way. Nevertheless, the first group does exist. There are for example children who are supposed to take over the family business, follow the same career and commit themselves to the same kind of partner. Some parents are quite compelling in this respect. For example, a visit from a son or daughter to their own comfortable office interspersed with remarks such as 'Yes, one day all of this will be yours' can be rather forceful. Other families produce generations of doctors or lawyers, as well as life partners of doctors or lawyers. This is not only a matter of all kinds of prestigious positions and professions. A parent may also transfer pride in a certain kind of craftsmanship. Or less pleasant, a bitter father who says to his son: 'This is the factory. You'd better start getting used to it.' Again, not all parents are so compelling by any means, even if they maybe would like the idea of their children walking in their shoes. But whose parents can be characterized as change agents?

Other parents would have preferred to lead a different life than the one that has unfolded for them. Some have not got – or grasped – the opportunity to get the education they wanted and consequently have not become what they wanted to become. They lacked the right talent, a certain body build, the financial possibilities, the stamina or the courage. Others landed in a marriage with a partner who fenced them in, got stuck in a work situation they didn't really like, suffered from poor health or became disabled. Many of these parents want their children to do a better job and to get where they themselves couldn't. These parents are inclined to treat their children as substitutes for themselves, which can also lead to compelling assignments.

Lastly, there are people whose life has really failed, for whatever reason. In addition to the fact that they seldom make model parents, with all the undesirable consequences of that, this can give rise to assignments that can have very undesirable if not downright poisonous effects: 'Nothing will become of you', 'Don't count on doing any better than me' or even 'Don't you dare do better than me'. These assignments can have a poisonous effect because children tend to be very loyal to their parents. If we have received such assignments, we should obviously get rid of them as soon as possible. In practice, getting rid of them often turns out to be very hard. Such curses may even be passed on from generation to generation.

What about the assignments of parents who want their children to live the same or a better life? In themselves such assignments are compatible with a productive and successful life; that is, if the assignment is compatible with our own motives and talents. If that is not the case and we heroically stick to our assignments, as a loyal child should, we find ourselves running out of energy sooner or later. We then fall into a boring and meaningless life, or we sabotage our own projects in a way that appears to be unexplainable to all involved. In this case it is not unlikely that the parents have also devoted themselves against their will to realizing a counterproductive assignment from their own parents.

So it is important to examine your motives well. To what degree are you busy achieving other people's goals? To what degree does that go against what you really want? Sometimes, what you and your parents want can coincide perfectly. Sometimes also, you must negotiate and rearrange things, in such a way that all parties are satisfied and a real win–win solution is reached. And not so often, you should say goodbye to your assignment and follow your own main motive. You then have to deal with the disappointment, pressure and blackmail of your parents, for real or only through condemnatory voices in your head. However, executing the assignment at any cost will make all parties unhappy in the end. You cannot live your parents' lives for them. Moreover, will they be any happier if they have the misfortune of their child to answer for?

TRANSITIONS

While the section on resistance to change was mostly about voluntary changes of a modest nature, this section examines radical changes that happen to us and from which we cannot get away, the so-called transitions. There are transitions of all kinds and sizes. Birth, our own, of brothers and sisters, of our children and grandchildren. Going to school for the first time, going to another school, our first job, our retirement. Moving to another house, going to live independently, alone or with a partner, marriage. Losing relatives and friends, divorce, losing our job, accidents, illnesses, winning first prize in a lottery. Some transitions are regarded as pleasant, others are not. The changes inherent in reorganizations and interventions in an organizational culture imply for almost all involved a real transition, which is often not experienced as pleasant.

The defining characteristic of transitions is that they demand a really different adaptation from us, a different way of living. This means that we have to let go of certain assumptions that underlie who we are, our identity, in order to connect ourselves to other, new assumptions. In this way, a transition involves letting go, leaving and saying goodbye. Again, bidding farewell is dying a little and leads to mourning for what we leave behind.

Of course, there are great differences among transitions, but there are resemblances as well. Transitions begin with the disturbance or untenability of the way of life we have led until now. Our comfort zone breaks down. This goes together with a loss, which we have to work through first before we can come to a successful new adaptation, a new comfort zone. We can distinguish several stages in transitions. The idea that all transitions proceed in the same way has been subject to criticism; rightly so, for no transition is exactly the same. Not everybody goes through all stages and there are differences between different kinds of transitions. Sometimes a stage is skipped and more often than not we temporarily shoot back to a former stage, sometime even many times in succession.

Nevertheless, a description of a typical sequence of the different stages (see Figure 7.1) makes sense. As it is, many transitions imply a real loss, the loss of an adaptation in life, in which those involved have invested a lot of time and effort and which offered them what they expected of it. Many people prefer not to feel the feelings that such a loss evokes. Consequently, this loss cannot be worked through emotionally. Not working through such a loss means that those involved do not overcome their resentment or passivity. In such a state of resentment or passivity it is it hard or even impossible to mobilize sufficient energy to achieve a new adaptation. The main risk here is getting stuck in this state, which then can result in a lengthy depression. The description of the stages of a 'typical' transition in Figure 7.1 allows us to point them out to people who are tempted to skip crucial stages. Also, it gives them the option to interpret their feelings and give meaning to them. Coming to terms with these emotions then enables them to see these emotions for what they are: just normal.

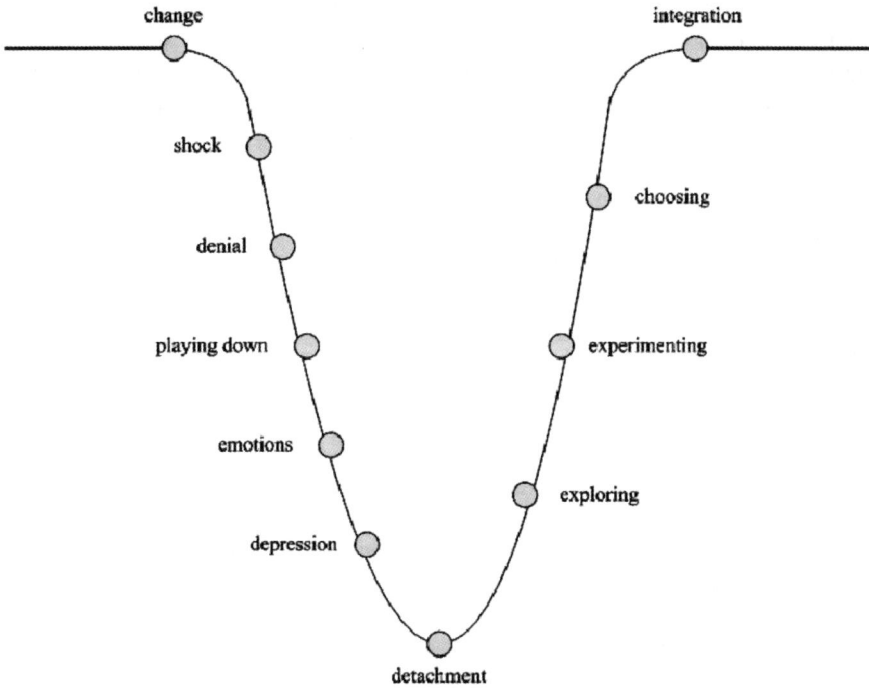

Figure 7.1   The transition curve

They are not 'mad' and there is really no need to avoid these emotions. These understandings give then the right basis for working through the emotions evoked by the transition.

That is why I describe a 'typical' sequence of the different stages. In principle, this concerns a not so cheerful transition in which working emotionally through the loss is the first matter of importance. That kind of transition often occurs in the context of an organizational change. And again, it is not unusual to skip stages or to shoot back to a former stage.

The first stage of a transition is often *shock*. For a while, we don't know what is happening or has happened. We feel nothing, as if we were sedated. Also it is just as if it is not true. Everything seems unreal, as if we are dreaming, as if we are not our normal self. In short, this is about a feeling of primary alienation.

The first stage often turns seamlessly into the second one, *denial*. The most extreme form of denial, assuming that in a while everything will be as it was before, may still be part of the former stage of shock. However, then there follow forms such as 'This just cannot be true', 'This is impossible', 'They cannot do this', 'This will just pass' and 'In the end, everything will turn out well'.

Denial then can turn into the next stage, *playing down* the seriousness of what is happening: 'So what?', 'What else is new?', 'What's the difference?', 'It is not that important' and 'Just a matter of. . .' A popular form of playing down is comparing the event with something much more serious: 'You know what is really bad?', 'The tsunami, that was really bad'.

However, gradually it becomes clear that this will not just pass and also that it is very important. Now all kinds of *emotions* make their appearance. This may be anxiety. What will become of us? Disaster scenarios emerge, so realistic that they keep us awake at night. It may also concern grief. Sometimes our eyes get moist and we feel like crying about what we have lost. Other emotions are indignation and anger. One thing we know for sure: this is not fair. We just don't deserve this. This indignation and anger often lead to an attitude of frustration, resistance and suspicion. We are against what happened, against everything and everyone responsible for it, but also against those who in reprehensible ways survived the event, as well as against ourselves because we didn't see it coming, or because we did see it coming but didn't take any action to prevent it and let ourselves be led like a lamb to the slaughter.

But what good does it do to be anxious, sad or angry? Gradually the emotions fade, though they may also flare up from time to time, to make way for *depression* and dejection. Apathy kicks in. Nothing interests us any more. Food and drink seem to have lost their taste. The world has become dreary and bleak. The world has changed and this will not turn out right.

This depression, however, goes away as well and is exchanged for *detachment*. We feel lighter now, but for the rest it is as if our feelings have disappeared all together. As if all feeling has been used up and there is nothing left any more. A form of resignation takes possession of us. This is the absolute low. The crisis has been reached. The good news is that once we have arrived here, we have really worked through the loss of our former way of life. Essentially, we have now given up the assumptions on which our former existence was based. We have let them go. This creates a void that offers room for something new: there is a vacancy for new assumptions.

The next stage is *exploring*. Initially, this is a matter of asking ourselves questions. 'What do we want to do now? What have we wanted to do all along? What are we good at? What possibilities are there? We can review different options in our thoughts and inform ourselves about them.

The following stage consists of *experimenting*, working out one option. What do we need for that? Who should we get to know for this?'

When the experimenting is successful, we may *choose* to stich to that option: we choose what we actually want to do. This involves making a plan, setting goals and sub-goals, making a time schedule and collecting the resources and the proper help. We really get going. If we do succeed, we can go on to the next stage.

When we have really shaped a successful solution, *integration* is the last stage. We develop this solution into a self-evident and manageable adaptation, a new comfort zone. This is about going into the details, as well as about developing efficient routines. As Figure 7.1 shows, this new adaptation lies at a somewhat higher level than the original. It means that we have grown. To use Nietzsche's (1909) words: 'That which does not kill me makes me stronger.' We have done what we needed to and from now on we know more about how it has to be done. We have developed ourselves. We have learned, and we know now that we do not need to be so anxious. The next transition will be somewhat easier for us. As it is, we are, almost by definition, good enough for our own life. The troubles we experience are, in the end, our troubles and they are there to make us stronger. In this respect, Frankl (1978) says that when an architect want to strengthen a dilapidated stone arch, he will increase the weight that rests on that arch, so that the separate parts of the arch are pressed against each other more strongly.

In transitions that are very positive – finishing your studies, marriage, a first child, a new job, winning the lottery, an early pension – the feeling of loss often does not get enough attention. Maybe this is obvious, but after the first elation it often leads to a somewhat unreal, disappointed feeling. Then too, it is important not to avoid this feeling. That is why winning a big prize in a lottery is nowadays accompanied by some guidance from a professional who knows something about such transitions.

- What are the most important transitions that you have experienced in your own life?
- To what degree do you recognize the stages described and the emotions mentioned here?
- How exactly did it happen for you?

CHAPTER 8

Exercises

This chapter describes a number of exercises. Doing these exercises helps you to develop a number of mostly social skills. Though these skills are valuable to anyone who wants to make the most of their life, they are crucial for change agents, as well as to anyone who wants to be a productive participant in a dialogue.

Most of the exercises are written for four people, some for two and some for only one. If that is the only option, most of the exercises can be executed alone as well. Sometimes this may involve the use of a mirror or video set (that is, a camera, a recorder and a monitor). The use of a video set allows us, for instance, to do all the micro-teaching exercises alone, even though it may feel awkward to change roles between interviewer and respondent. However, if we can handle the awkwardness this very well may be the perfect reflection exercise, as it allows us to watch our performance from all four perspectives (the perspectives of the interviewer, the respondent and the two process observers, who each have their own observation tasks; see later in this chapter for a more elaborate description of these perspectives).

Some of the skills involved in the exercises serve more or less the same purpose and can be used as alternative approaches in the same kind of context. Try all of them, examine what their differences and similarities are and find out which ones you like best. Develop in this way your own overall approach, the one that suits you best.

Doing the exercises demands an attitude characterized by the following points:

- The willingness and the opportunity to actually do the exercises with sufficient effort and attention.
- The willingness to reflect on our own acting, particularly when it involves going to a certain depth.

See to it that you have a place were you can work without being interrupted.

The following involvement is expected of you to attain the most effect:

- Practicing.
- Experiencing with sufficient awareness.
- Giving and getting feedback.
- Considering and asking yourself questions (reflecting), mental quiet and its applications, using your fantasy and giving meaning to your experience.
- Examining how you can apply all this and what more you still need.
- Writing a report on each exercise.

A continuously recurring theme in the exercises is looking for the layers below the actions, feelings and thoughts, especially the layer of assumptions, objectives, values and ethics.

Reflection – an exercise in itself – is an important and indispensable part of the exercises in general. Writing thorough reports about each exercise has proved to be a good form for achieving such reflection. The more time and attention we spend reflecting, the more we learn. Making a report about an exercise is a matter of answering the following questions.

- How did it go?
- How did it feel?
- Did you experience any resistance (uneasiness, being giggly, having trouble starting, being overly critical of the exercise)? If so, how did you cope with the resistance?
- What did you learn from the exercise?
- What was difficult about it and why?
- How does the exercise relate to:
  - what you knew already?
  - your learning goals?
  - your development as a change agent?
- How are you going to use the new insights and skills?
- Does it make sense to repeat the exercise?
- What more do you want to learn about the skills and further content of this exercise?
- How can you extend and improve the exercise to that end?

Writing a report on an exercise has several functions:

- Writing a report naturally leads to reflection about your experiences. This leads to more insight and a further structuring of those experiences.
- Writing a report prevents you prematurely forgetting what you have experienced.
- Re-reading previous reports now and then can be very clarifying, because it helps you to relate different experiences to each other.

As for the origin of these exercises, some are derived from the sources indicated, though most of them are adapted somewhat. Some other exercises are borrowed from the set of exercises of the former 'Gesprekspracticum' (an experientially oriented training program in social skills from the Psychology Department of the University of Amsterdam), where I used to work some 25 years ago. The origin of these exercises is veiled in cloud, such as is usual in social skill courses and literature. Still other exercises I devised myself.

FIRST IMPRESSION FEEDBACK

Goals

- To get to know each other as a first step in training programs and forms of dialogue.
- To gain some experience in giving and receiving feedback.
- To gain some experience in using the feedback rules (see Chapter 6); that is, rules for making feedback as effective as possible.
- To experience the differences between statements about direct experience and statements about derivations of direct experience. An example of a statement about direct experience is: 'When you do . . . , I get the feeling that . . .' The point of departure here consists of our own attitudes, feelings, ideas, goals and so on, and we explicitly communicate that point of departure. Derivations of direct experience, on the other hand, can be interpretations

such as 'You are ...' or 'It is ...' and judgments such as 'You should ...' or 'You are wrong/right about ...' In general, statements about direct experiences are more preferred in a dialogue setting than statements about their derivations. Statements about direct experiences also come rather close to advocacy (see Chapter 5).

• To demonstrate the mechanics of first impression formation and self-fulfilling prophecies. This refers to the following sequence. The first impression we form of somebody involves some evaluation of that person. This impression is based on all kinds of perceivable characteristics (sex, age, body build, face, facial expression, clothes, hairdo, make-up, degree of taking care of these) that help us to categorize that person. Once this categorization has taken place, we behave toward the person accordingly, evoking in this way complementary behavior from that person. This complementary behavior by definition fits our categorization and we feel we were right from the beginning. In this way, our guess about the other person has become a self-fulfilling prophecy.

• To demonstrate the effects of your appearance and what you can do with it.

• To demonstrate the differences between the impression you think you make and the impression you do make on others. For example, you may think you look sophisticated, while somebody else sees you as conventional or even dreary. This is, for that matter, not concerned with a right or a wrong impression, but just with different perceptions.

• To provide the opportunity to formulate, state and possibly adjust your learning goals: what you want to learn from the program.

• To examine the assumptions of the participants; that is, surfacing from which assumptions you acted when you presented ourselves as you did.

Procedure

Read the instructions and introduce the feedback rules (see Chapter 6).

Step 1

Write for 15 to 20 minutes about yourself. Use sound bites. Describe, as shortly and precisely as possible:

• who you are (personal data, work, hobbies)
• what you have done in your work
• how you think other people see you
• how you would like to be seen by other people
• your learning goals

Then the group members describe each other. If the group is too big, it is convenient – considering the available time – to divide the group in two or more sub-groups of about four. Each sub-group member writes down descriptions of the other members of their sub-group. Pay attention in your description to:

• the other's appearance and what strikes you in that
• the general impression the other makes on you
• what you can say about the kind of person the other is
• your reasons and considerations for this
• what this says about your own suppositions in this respect

This description forms your feedback for the other people.

Step 2

Feedback is given person by person, with the whole group present. All the members of the sub-group give their feedback and the other group members also get the opportunity to say what was is most striking about this person to them. This takes 10 to 15 minutes per person. The person receiving the feedback, the recipient, does not respond immediately but makes notes. When all the group members have given their feedback, the recipient says what he has written down about himself and responds to the feedback. This response can, for example, involve recognizing or not recognizing feedback, as well as asking for or giving explanations. The recipient makes more notes. The recipient can stop the feedback procedure at any time if the feedback becomes too overwhelming.

The person who facilitates the exercise monitors proper use of the feedback rules and asks questions if needed. The facilitator's questioning aims at clarification of what is being said, probing for further information and surfacing underlying assumptions and goals.

Step 3

Elaborate your notes and reflections in your program diary. Do this at the end of the exercise and later that day. Pay specific attention to the goals of the exercise and examine for each of the goals to what degree they have been attained.

Comments

- First impression feedback is a good 'getting to know each other' exercise to:
  - start a more elaborate dialogue or training program
  - demonstrate the personal character of the program
  - demonstrate that the program will be exciting but safe
  - clarify and improve mutual relationships
  - set a first step toward further teambuilding
- First impression feedback can involve an initial exploration of explicating suppositions. It is enlightening to see how people get totally different first impressions and that this is strongly related to their own assumptions. The facilitator – or participant, for that matter – then can surface these assumptions, demonstrate how different assumptions can lead to different perceptions and show how these different assumptions can be the starting point of all kinds of self-fulfilling prophecies.
- Formulating your own learning goals is intended to bring about a more focused and involved attitude and also can be used later to evaluate the program. Sometimes the feedback given in this exercise already leads to an initial adjustment of the learning goals. Adjustments of the learning goals during the program are quite usual.
- Feedback exercises also can be used at the end of a (part of a) program as well. A feedback exercise at the end of the program can then be concerned with what everyone has learned about the other people, their strong and weak points and the progress they have made, as well as with further advice. Feedback exercises can also be used in existing groups or teams, to explicate mutual relationships, clarify mutual expectations and improve team functioning.

NON-VERBAL BEHAVIORAL ELEMENTS

Goal

- To become aware of the meanings of non-verbal behavior and its overwhelming impact.
- To examine the assumptions underlying non-verbal behavior.
- To sensitize you to Leary's up–down and with–against dimensions in non-verbal behavior (see Chapter 6).
- To sensitize you to your own and others' non-verbal behavior and the entrances it offers for learning more about underlying assumptions and goals.
- To sensitize you to inconsistencies and dividedness in behavior and to examine the underlying conflicting assumptions or goals. As it is, individuals are supposed to be acting from consistent sets of assumptions and goals at all times. It is no coincidence that the Latin word *individuum* means undivided.
- To get to know others and yourself better.

Procedure

This exercise can be done with any number of people, preferably with the help of a big enough mirror or a video set. You can do it alone as well, though a mirror or video set is absolutely necessary then.

The exercise takes approximately five minutes per element. The best way to do it is to work through no more than one numbered group at a time. In this way you divide the exercise into 12 subsections, which you can intersperse between the other exercises.

Each time one of the group members demonstrates the elements (agree each time beforehand who will do that). The others imitate:

- first normally
- then in an exaggerated way

Try out some variations of each element. Take sufficient time for each behavioral element: do not stop until you feel that there is nothing more to learn about it.

Questions to answer:

- What does it look like?
- How does it feel?
- What does it mean? What does it express?
- To what degree does it reflect dominance or submission (up or down), affiliation or aversion (with or against); more specifically, in what octant in Leary's rose does the element belong (with–up, up–with, up–against and so on, see Figure 6.1).
- What situational proposal does the behavioral element imply; that is, what complementary behavior does the element evoke from other people?
- To what degree is this element typically male or female? Does the element have different meanings in men and women?
- Is this a habitual element for you? If so, when do you display it?
- Do you know somebody who does this frequently? Maybe a well-known person (television, film, public life)?

- What other behavioral elements usually go with this element?
- What are the underlying ideas of this element?
- What is the relevance when people at your work are doing this?

Write down everything that is of importance for each element.

If you have no mirror, repeat the exercise at home in front of a mirror.

Elements

In Addendum I some (possible) meanings are given against which you can check your own answers. However, I advise you strongly to try out the elements first yourself to accomplish the maximum learning effect. The meanings given in Addendum I are not meant as the last word on the subject: other meanings are possible as well.

I

- Raise your head a little (movement) so that your upper eyelids become or are visible and hold it that way for some time (posture), chin up.
- Hold your head backwards, as if you are examining the ceiling.
- Hold your head to one side (left or right).
- Shake your head when talking, slowly and more quickly.
- Nod; try out different variants of nodding.
- Let your head hang down; do that in several degrees.

II

- Laugh, smile, and grin; try out the different variants. How can you tell if a smile is 'real'?
- Bare your teeth.
- Press your lips together.
- Purse your lips, pout them.
- Run your tongue over your lips, quickly and slowly.
- Draw the corners of your mouth down and up.
- Swallow; repeat that a number of times.

III

- Gaze direction in general.
- Gaze upwards.
- Gaze downwards.
- Shift your gaze quickly and frequently.
- Shut your eyes.
- Look with screwed-up eyes.

IV

- Shut and open your eyes slowly, while looking at somebody.
- Blink frequently.
- Don't blink at all.
- Raise your eyebrows.
- Raise one eyebrow.
- Quickly raise your eyebrows just for a moment ('eyebrow flash').

V

- Hunch your shoulders (one and both).
- Draw your shoulders backwards (note the difference between men and women in this respect).
- Orient your trunk as much as possible toward the other person (direct shoulder orientation).
- Orient your trunk away from the other person at different degrees, so that in the end you have turned your back on that person.
- Turn your trunk back and forth.

VI

- Keep your upper arms away from your body.
- Clench your elbows to your trunk.
- Put your hand(s) on your hip(s).
- Put both hands behind your head, your elbows sticking out.
- Put one hand behind your head or your neck, your elbow not sticking out.
- Fold your arms (first as a movement, then as a posture).
- Unfold your arms.
- Make your hands invisible, for example by hiding them behind your back, under the table or in your pockets. Where is your hand right now?

VII

- Run your forefinger or the side of your hand under your nose.
- Keep your forefinger alongside your nose.
- Hold your nose with your thumb and forefinger.
- Sniff.
- Wrinkle your nose, as if you smell something dirty.

VIII

- Touch your face.
- Hold, caress or rub your face.

- Scratch your face.
- Do the same, but now with different body parts.
- Explore the differences between touching yourself with your left and right hand.

IX

- Make some speech-supporting gestures, of different sizes, with different energy (for example to emphasize, negate, ask for extra or less attention, warn, approve, disapprove, reject and accept).
- Make some gestures that illustrate or imitate a meaning or content (for example to order a beer or another round at the bar, to ask for the bill, to describe a woman's body and so on). Here too, use different sizes and different energy levels.
- Put the palm of your hand next to your head.
- Hold up your hand or forefinger.
- Clench your fist(s).
- Point with your forefinger.
- Start a gesture strongly and then let your hand flop down.

X

- Hold your breath.
- Sigh.
- Pant.
- Inhale deeply.
- Breathe quickly.

XI

- Sit inclined forward.
- Sprawl in your chair.
- Sit with your legs folded under you.
- Sit on your hands.
- Sit very straight.
- Sit on the edge of your chair.
- Fidget in your chair.

XII

- Sit reclined with your feet on a desk or table.
- Sit with your legs crossed, so that the ankle of one leg rests on the knee or upper leg of the other one.
- Sit with your legs wide apart.
- Sit with your legs pressed against each other.
- Make kicking movements while seated.

- Fidget with your feet while seated.
- Flex your foot upwards.

Comments

- Intentionally attending to another person's non-verbal behavioral elements contributes to being more aware of that other person, the social interaction and the relationship. Consequently, minding the other's non-verbal behavior can improve rapport, provided that the verbal content is not so complicated that it demands all our attention, which occurs only rarely.
- Intentionally taking account of non-verbal behavior is useful in all cases in which inter-personal sensitivity is important and communication has to be of a high quality.
- The resulting skills play an important role in developing inquiry, advocacy and dialogue skills (see Chapter 5).
- The skills of labeling the behavioral elements in terms of Leary's up–down and with–against dimensions (see Chapter 6) are especially important, because they enable you to recognize the different form of resistance in a dialogue session (see Chapter 5).
- These exercises make clear that everything one does or does not do has a communicative function.
- This exercise can turn watching television into a more active, rewarding and useful pastime by using it to raise your sensitivity to the non-verbal aspects of communication.
- A word of warning: occupying ourselves 12 times consecutively with non-verbal behavior in this way demands discipline. Some people quickly get the idea that they already know it all. Others feel different kinds of resistance. Still, it is of great importance to keep on doing these exercises conscientiously. It really is a very quick and effective way to sensitize you to others' attitudes, intentions, resistances and underlying ideas.
- A different point is that it usually is not wise to refer directly the other's non-verbal behavior. Just ask 'What's going on?' or something like that. If such a general question gets you nowhere, you can then say something like 'I get the feeling that . . .' and then you mention what you think that is going on. Again, don't verbalize what you saw. Many people tend to feel intruded on. As a result they may get defensive and may even deny having displayed the particular behavior at all.
- The non-verbal side of communication is much wider than only the messages inherent in visible behavior. There is the impression made by our body build and facial features. There is also the whole domain of the voice and of speaking, which gives the observant listener a very precise account of somebody's age, sex, emotional state, personality, health, socio-cultural background and sincerity. Then there are involuntary responses, such as skin color, temporary red and white spots on the skin, fleeting changes in facial expression and pupil dilatation, which can inform us about somebody's emotional responses and health. Furthermore there are clothing, hairdo, make-up, perfume, shoes and all kinds of artifacts such as watches, bags, jewelry and spectacles, which are all bought and worn for the sake of giving a certain impression, even though the one who is using them is not always aware of that. Lastly, there is the way we take care of ourselves and our outfits, the incongruities in these outfits, our weight and the activities we undertake. Most of these features give indications of our attitudes, assumptions and goals, and a good change agent must learn to read these items. However, it would take too much space and time to go into more detail on all of these facets here.

EXPLORING YOUR OWN ATTITUDES

As stated before, the term 'attitude' refers in this book both to a bodily posture and the accompanying mindset.

Goal

- To gain a better knowledge of your own attitudes and by that a better understanding of your situational proposals.
- By implication, to gain a better understanding of the situational proposals of other people.
- To acquire more self-knowledge.
- To have a better understanding of situations.
- To detect and try out better alternatives.
- To gain more control over your attitudes and by that over the situations in which you participate.

Procedure

Read Chapter 3. Do this exercise on your own. It requires a big mirror, as well as privacy and quiet. If you do not have such a mirror, find one elsewhere. As an alternative you can use a video set.

Assume an attitude, standing or sitting, which is characteristic and normal for you, in front of the mirror. It is useful to have a particular significant situation in your mind's eye and to assume the attitude you assumed there. Then observe what situational proposal you make with that posture.

- What strikes you most?
- How energetic does it look?
- Are you 'with' or 'against'? What makes it so?
- Are you 'down' or 'up'? What makes it so?
- What complementary behavior of the other person does your situational proposal invite?
- How 'undivided' does it look?
- If there is dividedness, of what does it consist?
- Do you like what you are seeing?
- What underlying assumptions about yourself, the situation and the relationship does your mirror image express?
- Do you have any idea how long you have doing this and from whom the situation proposal originates?

Test a couple of small variations and look what changes (in energy level, 'with–against', 'down–up', complementary behavior evoked by it, dividedness and attractiveness) are associated with them. Which do you like best? Practice these in everyday reality and find out what responses you trigger with these 'new' attitudes. Make notes.

Do this with all your characteristic attitudes, but take enough time: spend one whole session on each attitude and at least one week on testing out its different variants.

Comments

- Usually, you are not aware of what situation proposal you are making. Often this is so automatic that it is hardly possible to say anything sensible about it. Still, this behavior is decisive for the design of your life. By assuming different attitudes in front of a mirror it becomes possible to see them with 'new' eyes and to monitor them in real-life situations. You will probably be surprised about the situational proposals you are making in this way. The exercise can help you understand why you find yourself time after time in particular situations and relationships, while it also can help you to try out 'new' proposals to make your situations and relationships more productive.
- You often incorporate such attitudes and their underlying assumptions early in life, for example from a parent, brother or sister. Often you adopt these attitudes without noticing it. Can you determine the origin of your attitudes?
- You can use this exercise each time you want to know more about why a certain encounter or meeting went as it did. What have you done? What could you have done differently?
- This exercise can in principle be applied each time more precise and better communication and more self-knowledge are at stake.
- Knowing more about your own habitual attitudes and being able to display them at will make you a more effective leader (see Chapter 3) and change agent. The same applies to being more aware of the situational proposals of other people. Knowing your own situational proposals and consciously recognizing those of other people are crucial skills in dialogue sessions.
- The same exercise can also be done to examine the impact and situational proposals of different forms of clothing, hairdo, make-up and so on.

NON-VERBAL SELF-DISQUALIFICATION

Disqualification is here used in the sense of not taking somebody seriously in an interaction. By not treating him as a full person who is entitled to normal civility and respect, for instance by ridiculing or ignoring him, we don't take his message seriously either (Watzlawick, Beavin & Hackson, 1968). Self-disqualification then is not taking yourself and your own messages seriously. Self-disqualification negatively affects the impact of your attitude as a situational proposal: it makes you less influential. As a result, somebody who uses a great deal of self-qualification is usually not an effective leader, and most of the time not an effective change agent either. Self-disqualification is also incompatible with the with–up and up–with attitudes of dialogue (see Chapter 5).

Goal

- To discover how you non-verbally disqualify yourself from time to time.
- To learn to recognize non-verbal self-disqualification in others.
- To learn about your own and other people's underlying reasons for self-disqualification.
- To learn about the effects of self-disqualification.

Procedure

This exercise can be done in small groups or pairs. Doing it on your own is possible as well, provided that you do it in front of a mirror or a video set. Talk to each other for about five minutes about what you really think your ideal organization should look like. Talk in such a way, however, that you intentionally weaken and play down each sentence by non-verbal means (that is, by posture, movement, facial expression and so on), as well as by the way you are talking (loudness, emphasis, speed, silences and so on). Pay attention that you only disqualify in a non-verbal way, not with the content of your words.

Afterwards discuss for 15 minutes the following issues:

- What behavioral elements and manners of speaking do you employ to disqualify what you are saying?
- What is the actual message when you speak like that?
- When do you do this?
- Why – that is, to what end – do you do that?
- What are the most frequently occurring effects?
- What are the underlying thoughts?

Comments

- Most people are very skilled at disqualifying their own goals from time to time. It is not only important to become more sensitive to your own self-disqualifications, but in dialogue it is also indispensable to recognize other people's self-disqualifications and to explore these further: why do people use self-disqualification; what does self-disqualification bring them; what does it cost them?
- Self-disqualification is not by definition always undesirable: sometimes you intentionally want to diminish the impact of what you are doing, for example to prevent resistance. Of course, whether you intentionally use self-disqualification or not is contextually determined again.
- The same exercise can – and should – be done focusing on the verbal side of communication. Then it is for instance about phrasing, wording and the use of diminutives, and their underlying assumptions and effects.

LOOKING IN THE MIRROR

Goal

- To learn to know yourself better.
- To accept who you are and how you look.
- To build up a better sense of self-esteem.

To the degree that you achieve these goals, you can do a better job in dialogue sessions, as the skills implicated by the goals make it easier to take up an up–with or with–up position. The same applies of course to being a better leader and change agent.

Procedure

Do this exercise on your own. It consists of five parts. First read the procedure for each part.

Part 1

The first part essentially consists of looking at your own face in the mirror for five full minutes. This is rather lengthy. Use a kitchen timer to mark the five minutes. During these five minutes you ask yourself the following questions:

- What strikes you most in your mirror image?
- How does that feel? Carry on, even if you don't like it.
- What kind of person do you see in the mirror?
- What mood comes across from your mirror image?
- To what degree do you make an undivided impression?
- On what is your possible dividedness based? Which are the underlying considerations?
- What do you like about what you are seeing?
- What is pleasant about that?
- What don't you like about what you are seeing?
- What is unpleasant about that?

Answer the questions also in writing.

Part 2

Go back to the mirror and look again for five minutes (use a kitchen timer) at your own face, this time explicitly willing to accept yourself as you are. You also can say to yourself, silently or aloud, just what you want:

- 'Whatever is wrong or imperfect about me, I fully accept myself, and without any reserve.'

Answer the same questions as in Part 1.

Part 3

Do the same again, but now as if you are your own loving parent. See what is good about you, what you are able to do and how you still can develop yourself. Look at yourself with love and compassion. Answer the same questions again.

Part 4

Make it a habit to watch yourself in the mirror for a few minutes each day with love and compassion, as well as with full acceptance.

Part 5

Do the same with other people for the next few days: look at them with love, compassion and acceptance. How is that for you? How does it influence your mood? How does it affect the way you relate to the other person? What effects do you notice in the other person?

Comments

- Many people are not at all happy with what they see in the mirror. This can be a matter of (parts of) the face itself (nose, mouth, eyes, chin and so on), but also the facial expression or traces of fatigue or aging. Often it is not easy to remain looking at what you do not like. Keep it up anyhow. It helps!
- Concerning the remainder of the exercise, it is nice to discover that you can do this just like that. And mind you: this is a basic skill. When you from time to time look at yourself with compassion, love and acceptance, your self-esteem benefits. Gradually, it then becomes easier to pay the right attention to what you are doing and what comes your way, as well as to take responsibility for that. This enables you to live more fully in the here-and-now.
- Looking at others in this way can strongly improve your mood. It can also work as a self-fulfilling prophecy, in the sense that those people behave better toward you. This also is a basic skill, which can be crucial in a dialogue session.
- This exercise is in principle applicable everywhere in organizations where abilities for development, learning and creativity have to be mobilized.

YOU-WE-IT (Based on Stevens, 1973)

Goal

- To sensitize you to the use of different personal pronouns and their meaning and implications.
- To sensitize you to how the use of different personal pronouns and their meaning and implications can make you more effective in communication, both in listening and speaking. Being able to surface the assumptions underlying the use of different pronouns can be crucial in dialogue. This is also important because the use of personal pronouns can be a cultural matter as well: some cultures display a clear preference for certain personal pronouns and the assumptions underlying this use of these pronouns. In general, being more sensitive to the use of different personal pronouns is an important asset for both change agents and leaders.

Procedure

This exercise can be done in small groups or pairs. Doing it on your own is possible as well, provided that you use some audio recording device. The procedure consists of having five conversations each of three minutes, in which every sentence must contain a certain personal noun or its conjugations. The subject of the discussions can be an issue that is important for cultural change. Each conversation is followed by a discussion of two minutes. How does it feel? What meanings and implications does each of these pronouns have? In Addendum II some (possible) meanings are given to check your own answers against.

The person who introduces and leads the exercise – and participates as well – also keeps an eye on the time.

- Use in the first conversation the personal pronoun 'you'.
- In the second conversation 'we' and 'us'.
- In the third conversation 'it'.
- In the fourth conversation 'one'.
- In the fifth conversation 'I' and 'me'.

At the end of the fifth discussion, there is a 15-minute general discussion of the differences in meaning between the five pronouns. The following issues are of importance here:

- Determining the meanings of these pronouns.
- Determining which pronouns everybody prefers to use on which occasion.
- Determining how the Leary dimensions relate to the use of the different pronouns.
- Determine also what assumptions underlie the use of each pronoun.
- Determining what use of the different pronouns is typical for the present culture.
- Discussing what use of the different pronouns is preferred for the 'new' culture.

Comments

- Preferences for the use of certain personal pronouns give clues about the perspectives and positions you take and how you present yourself.
- When people in the context of a dialogue session, coaching session, workshop or training program show a striking preference for a certain pronoun, you can spotlight that pronoun in the way described above, to get to a better understanding of its meanings and implications.
- The same, of course, applies to the present and the preferred 'new' culture.
- As the exercise generally is experienced as absurd and funny, it helps to improve the atmosphere.

Analoguous Exercises

The same format as used in 'You-we-it' can be applied in other exercises to examine the meanings, impact, personal preferences, occurrence in the culture and underlying assumptions of other words, phrases and forms of speech. The following words, phrases and forms of speech are especially interesting to examine:

- why
- (yes) but

- all-inclusive words such as everybody, everyone, all, always, everywhere
- all-exclusive words such as nobody, no one, nothing, none, never, nowhere, anywhere
- open, closed and suggestive questions

In the last case the goals of the exercise are somewhat different. Here the goals are learning what open, closed and suggestive questions are, what their advantages and disadvantages are, and how each of them can be best used.

In Addendum 2 some meanings and implication of the words, phrases and form of speech are discussed.

I MUST – CANNOT – AM AFRAID TO – HATE TO (Based on Stevens, 1973)

In championing the ideal organization or in dialogue you inevitably run into your own fears and weak spots. It is better to have inspected these fears and weak spots beforehand and not to be needlessly limited by them. The same goes for being effective as a leader or change agent.

Goals

- To make you aware of how you talk to yourself and hypnotize yourself into being condemned to voluntary confinement in a needlessly small 'comfort zone'.
- In addition, to experiment with other forms of self-talk, which leave you more room to move.

Procedure

This exercise can be done in small groups or pairs. Doing it on your own is possible as well, provided again that you use some audio-recording device. Take 15 minutes to make the following four lists of everything that:

- You *must* do (are obliged to do, feel it is necessary to do) to make the cultural change project a success.
- You think you *cannot do* in this project (are unable to do, is impossible for you).
- You *do not dare to do* (are afraid to do, avoid doing) in this project.
- You *hate to do* (annoys you, you detest doing) in this project.

Step 1

Be seated in pairs (or if on your own, in front of a mirror). As part of a pair, you each read your list to the other, so that you take turns to read a sentence that begins with 'I must . . .', 'I am obliged to . . .', 'It is necessary that I . . .' and so on. On your own, in front of a mirror, just read your sentences but take pauses to feel the impact of your mirror image speaking to you.

When the lists of all participants have been read you read the sentences again, in the same manner but with one big difference: this time you start the sentence each time with 'I choose to...'

Then tell each other what you experienced, how it felt. Did you perhaps feel that you were waking from a kind of self-hypnosis? What are the underlying assumptions on which this must be founded? And where do these come from in their turn? Make notes.

Step 2

Now the same with list 2. Start each sentence with 'I cannot...', 'I can only...', 'It is impossible for me to...', 'I am not able to...' and so on.

When you have read your list(s) in the same way as the previous one(s), read the same sentences once again in the same way, but now each time beginning with 'I do not want that...'

Discuss this in the same way as described in Step 1.

Step 3

The same with list 3: 'I fear to...', 'I am afraid to...', 'I avoid...' Now the second time start each sentence with: 'I dare to...', 'I have the courage to...', 'I take up the challenge to...'

Step 4

The same with list 4: the second time begin each sentence with: 'I like to...', 'I find it pleasant to...', 'I love to...'

Comments

- Of course, this exercise only works when you do it in a serious manner. Then the exercise can give you a clear understanding of how you paralyze yourself and how you can get yourself out of the paralysis. The next thing is choosing what you want and how you want to continue in this project.

MICRO-TEACHING: THE GENERAL FORMAT

Micro-teaching is a general format for teaching social skills. As such it can be used to improve the social skills of leaders and change agents, while it can also be useful for all participants in a dialogue.

Goal

- To learn social skills step by step by separately practicing the constituent skills.

Procedure

To illustrate micro-teaching in general, practicing interviewing techniques here serves as an example. In this example, each training group consists of four people:

- one interviewer
- one respondent
- one observer who pays special attention to how the interviewer applies the techniques to be practiced, takes notes and monitors the time
- one observer who pays special attention to the non-verbal behavior of the interviewer, the overall progress of the interview, the own emotional and bodily responses to that, and takes notes on this

By videotaping the interviewing it is possible to reduce the number of participants to two, provided that they play the observer roles as well when looking back to five-minute episodes of the recorded interview. You can also do the exercise on your own, but then you transform it into a reflection exercise. This transformation, however, asks for a great deal of concentration and a lot of going back on your steps when you lose track. Video-taping can be a great help here too.

In the case of foursomes, one of the observers introduces the exercise. After five minutes, he interrupts the interview. The two observers and the respondent then give their feedback together in a maximum of five minutes. Think of using the feedback rules appropriately (see Chapter 6). Subsequently, the interview again goes on for five minutes, to be discussed again for a maximum of five minutes, after which a third episode follows. At the end of a full round, the interviewer gets all the notes together.

When this sequence has been completed, a change of roles takes place and everything begins again. Subsequently there is a 15-minute break, after which the last two rounds take place. Apart from the reporting, the whole exercise takes about two hours and fifteen minutes

In the report, the experiences, learning points and difficulties in all four roles are addressed.

Comments

- This is a typical experience-oriented and extremely effective exercise format to improve social skills, which can be applied whenever needed.
- Though the exercises to follow are mainly focused on interviewing and questioning skills, the same principle can also be applied in an advocacy training program.
- The exercise can be so effective because it shows you the skill in question from different perspectives, including that of the coach or trainer when you lead the exercise.

MICRO-TEACHING: LISTENING

Listening obviously is a crucial skill in inquiry and therefore in dialogue.

Goal

- To explore your blind spots, particularities and distortions in the way you process spoken, verbal information, as well as the underlying assumptions and mechanisms from which these blind spots, particularities and distortions stem.
- To improve your listening skills.

Procedure

This is an initial variant of the micro-teaching format described in this book. There are, however, some deviations from the general format. The listening exercise is a straightforward but at the same time difficult exercise, which demands much concentration and may evoke some frustration.

In principle, the exercise is intended for foursomes: one narrator, one listener and two observers (who also keep an eye on the time). Though somewhat cumbersome, you can also do this exercise on your own. In that case you need two recording devices, one to play back a spoken text, and one to record your own reproductions of the text fragments. With the help of some running back and forth, you then can play all the roles.

In the case of four participants, the exercise takes 20 minutes plus 10 minutes of discussion for each speaker, whereupon there is an exchange of roles. In total therefore the exercise takes four rounds of half an hour, with a 15-minute break. Each participant plays all the roles.

- The narrator says why they are participating in the exercise.
- One of the observers each time says 'Stop' after three or four sentences. Don't make this too long a period.
- The listener reproduces fully, but in his own words, what he has heard. The observers and the narrator together determine whether this is a correct and full representation of what the narrator has said, and whether this has been done in his own words. They also say what went wrong.
- The observers make notes of this, also about the type of errors.
- If anything goes wrong, the listener then repeats his attempt to come up with a correct representation in his own words.
- The observers determine again whether this is a correct and full representation in his own words and, if needed, make notes again of what went wrong.
- The narrator now goes on with his story, even if the listener still makes errors. After three or four sentences, an observer says 'Stop' again, and so on.

After 20 minutes, all participants occupy themselves for 10 minutes with categorizing the errors made. The narrator makes notes of this and gets all notes of the observers for his report.

Categorize your errors in your report and take stock of the underlying factors. Describe also how you coped with the frustrations and annoyances generated by this exercise.

First Categorization

- What do you leave out?
- Is there any system in it? For example:
  - each time a first or last sentence
  - certain kinds of information
  - issues you consider to be unimportant
  - issues you find annoying
  - certain feelings
  - all feelings
- What meanings have been distorted?
- Do you change the emotional value?
- To what degree do these distortions and changes go in a certain direction?
- To what degree do you make interpretations that go beyond the information given?
- Are these interpretations going into a certain direction?

Second Categorization

- What is apparently important and interesting to you?
- What is apparently unimportant and uninteresting to you?
- Do you have a preference for certain feelings?
- Do you avoid (certain) feelings?

Third Categorization

- What is the effect of your way of dealing with spoken text on the other person?
- Are there family members (parents, brothers, sisters) who act in the same way?
- To what degree is your way of dealing with spoken text related with dominance and situational control?
- On what is your way of dealing with spoken text founded? This question can be answered by asking yourself questions such as:
  - What do I avoid when I . . .?
  - With what do I not need to occupy myself when I . . .?
  - What do I prevent when I . . .?
  - What does it bring me when I . . .?

Another point is how you match with and differ from the other three participants. What did you learn from this about yourself and the others?

Comments

- The exercise can give you an unsuspected insight into how you process spoken information and on what underlying thought that processing is founded. Though this is very useful, it is not always pleasant.
- The applicability of this exercise is limited, as it costs a great deal of effort and patience.

- For change agents and leaders, however, the exercise is indispensable, as it enables them to get to know their peculiarities in listening so that they are able to bring about some improvements.
- The exercise also helps you to recognize the peculiarities in listening in your interaction partners.
- Recognizing both your own and others' particularities in listening may help you to be more productive in dialogue.
- The exercise helps to improve mutual relationships and rapport.
- The exercise can also be applied to one person as a demonstration within another exercise, when certain 'noise factors' in that person become too interfering. However, this use of the exercise is very confronting, a bit of a last resort.

INTERVIEW TECHNIQUES

The different interview techniques are all central to questioning, and by that to dialogue, leadership and being a change agent. The subjects of the different interviews are so chosen that they are all important for dialogue, as well as for properly acting as a leader or change agent.

Interview techniques are practiced in a series of micro-teaching exercises. The procedure each time is more or less the same. The main differences are:

- The subject of the interview: the subject is different in each of the consecutive exercises.
- The specific interview techniques used: in the first exercise a limited number of the techniques described in Chapter 6 is used, in the second exercise the number of techniques is considerably extended, and in the third exercise and the ones after that all the techniques described in Chapter 6 are to be used.
- The assignments of the observer roles are extended in the fourth and following exercise.

Goal

- To practice the different interview techniques.
- To learn about the subjects you are interviewed about.

Procedure

Read the relevant section in Chapter 6 about the interview techniques, and the relevant texts about the specific subject of each exercise (mentioned each time after the subject of the exercise).

The Role of the Interviewer

Interview Exercise 1

- Begin with an open question.
- Keep on asking further questions to study the subject in more depth.

- Pay attention properly.
- Ask as few 'new' questions as possible.
- Don't ask suggestive or double-barreled questions.
- Don't build in unneccessary presuppositions.

Interview Exercise 2

The same as in Interview Exercise I, but in addition this time practice with the following techniques:

- mirroring
- summarizing
- asking about feelings
- naming feelings
- asking for examples to make things more concrete

Interview Exercises 3 to 10

Use all the interview techniques described in Chapter 6; that is, the same techniques as in Interview Exercise 2 plus:

- detecting and exploring assumptions
- confronting

Subject

Interview Exercise 1

- Why do you want to be a change agent?
- What is pleasurable about that?
- What does it do for you?
- What makes you suitable for it?

Interview Exercise 2 (see Chapter 7)

What is your most annoying characteristic? Examine this with questions such as:

- What do the people who are closest to you find your most annoying characteristic (that is, your personal pitfall)?
- When especially do you show this characteristic?
- How would you rephrase this annoying characteristic as a surplus, or 'too much', of an essentially good characteristic?
- To which degree do you recognize this characteristic as one of your core characteristics or basic motives?

Interview Exercise 3 (see Chapter 7)

- What kind of characteristic of other people do you find the most annoying and irritating characteristic (that is, your personal allergy)?
- To what degree is this annoying characteristic the opposite of one of your core characteristics or basic motives?
- How can you rephrase this annoying characteristic as a positive and essentially good characteristic?
- To what degree do you recognize this positively rephrased characteristic also as the positively rephrased opposite of your personal pitfall?
- To what degree are you willing to accept this positively rephrased characteristic as an important direction of growth for you; that is, as your developmental task?

Interview Exercise 4

- Who are your heroes? If you cannot think of a hero: who do you admire most? If you do not admire any people: what personal qualities in others do you appreciate most?
- What makes them into your heroes? Or what do you admire in them? Or what is it that you appreciate in these qualities?

This is about detecting underlying values. Values are here taken to be your actual or admired ethical as well as practical guidelines.

Interview Exercise 5

- What is the most important issue in your life?
- What is so important about that?
- How does that most important issue relate to being a change agent?

Interview Exercise 6 (see Chapter 7)

Suppose that it is almost time: your life has come to its end and you are looking back. A deep quiet has taken possession of you. Your life just has unrolled for you like a razor-sharp film and you feel a deep need for a definitive summing up. You are aware of a cool objectivity: you know everything, but there are no more interests. The only thing that still counts is the summing-up of all you have done and all that has happened to you.

- What have you done too much of in your life up to now?
- What would you have preferred to do instead?
- What have you done too little of up to now?
- How did that come about?
- How have you let that happen?
- What has it brought you?
- What did it cost you?
- What underlying values and assumptions have you followed as a guideline in this respect?
- What can you do to change that?

Interview Exercise 7 (see Chapter 7)

The subject of the interview is the influence of your societal and cultural background – and that of your parents and the wider family you come from – on your ideas, assumptions and goals. Successively it is concerned with the influence of:

- your parents' convictions and religious background
- your parents' socio-economic position
- their work and profession
- the place(s) of residence where you grew up
- their political background
- the schools you attended

A next question is then:

- Who else has been a determining factor in your ideas, assumptions and goals, and in what way?

Interview Exercise 8 (see Chapter 7)

- What assignments did you get from your parents?
- To what degree are these assignments functional?
- To what degree do you prefer to get rid of them?
- To what degree do these assignments still play a role?

Here too, this is essentially concerned with detecting underlying assumptions and values.

Interview Exercise 9 (see Chapter 7)

- What are the most radical transitions you have gone through?
- Can you describe the different stages in a transition such as they presented themselves to you?
- What influence did the transition have on your assumptions and goals?
- What has – or would have – helped you to move in a good way through this transition?
- What else would have helped you?

Interview Exercise 10 (see Chapter 7)

- When would you be completely satisfied and happy?
- To what degree do you admit to yourself that certain things in your life could be better?
- How are things with your good-enough solutions?
- How are things with your comfort zone?
- What do you avoid?
- What are you able and willing to do, but don't do?

Instructions for Observers

Interview Exercises 1 to 3

Observer 1 monitors the proper use of the different interview techniques. They also monitor which techniques are not used by the interviewer. Observer 2 monitors the non-verbal behavior of the interviewer and the respondent.

Interviews 4 to 10

Observer 1 gets the same assignment as in Interviews 1 to 3. Observer 2 also gets the same assignment, but to add a new dimension to this, Observer 2 also imitates the posture and movements of the interviewer for half the time, and those of the respondent for the other half.

- What feelings does that evoke?
- What information does it give you?

Comments

- Repeated micro-teaching of interview techniques may seem boring, but it remains the best way to quickly build up skills in this respect. This is especially important as good interviewing is crucial in organizational advice and coaching.

Interview Exercise I

- Concerning its content, this is part of advocacy: being able to articulate why you do something.

Interview Exercise VII

- We carry the opinions and views of our societal and cultural background with us during our whole life. Therefore, it is good to critically consider them for once. To what degree do you still subscribe to them? What influence do they still have? What influences would you like to make less determining? How can you go about that? In a dialogue context, it is especially important to have some knowledge of the origins of your underlying ideas and so on. This knowledge makes them somewhat less absolute and makes it easier to see them for what they are: ideas you entertain, but which, in the last instance, are not (wholly) your own.

Interview Exercise VIII

- Assignments often play the role of goals and values. The importance here lies in recognizing and acknowledging these assignments, especially also in a dialogue context. To what degree have they become a part of you? To what degree do you go along with them?

Do you want to adjust them? Here too, it is important to look at these assignments as ideas you entertain, but which, in the last instance, are not (wholly) your own.

- In addition, I recommend that you do the exercise 'Talking like your parents' (see below).

Interview Exercise IX

- Changes in organizations almost always imply individual transitions. Because these transitions can bring along a great deal of individual misery and lead to much resistance to change, it is important to examine well what transitions imply, especially also at the emotional level. That is why in every organizational change attention should be paid to the guidance of these transitions. This exercise helps you to recognize transition phenomena among the people involved in the change, and gives some pointers of what you can do. As a successful dialogue involves a transition too, all the experience you can get in this area is important.

Interview Exercise X

- For many people it is difficult to indicate when they would be completely satisfied and happy.
- By making this issue the object of an interview exercise, you get a broader view of forms of resistance, resistance in stereo as it were, and also as it is perceived by others.

TALKING LIKE YOUR PARENTS (Adapted From Stevens, 1973)

Goal

- To close off the interview about the assignments your parents gave to you (see Chapter 7) and to deepen your insight into these assignments.

Instructions

Have a discussion for five minutes in pairs as if you both were your own parent. Choose a parent and talk with each other about the following subjects:

- What has your child done with their life until now?
- How has your child met your expectations?
- How is he or she compared with other children?
- What assignments have you given your child?

Write your answers down. Discuss them with the other person.

You can also do this exercise on your own, for example in front of a mirror. You can then make it into a dialogue between your parents.

Comment

- The change of perspective can give new views or shed some new light on familiar views.

SOLUTION-FOCUSED COACHING I AND II

Goal

- To get acquainted with solution-focused coaching.
- To gain a first impression of how the organization you are working for ideally would look (Exercise I).
- To gain a first impression of how you can achieve that (Exercise II).

Procedure

Generally speaking, solution-focused coaching makes use of the same interview techniques as were discussed in the previous interview exercises. The solution-focused coaching exercises also follow the format of micro-teaching; that is, one interviewer (here called the 'change agent'), one respondent, two observers (one for the technical part, and one mirroring the change agent and the respondent for the non-verbal behavior) and four sessions per question.

The main difference is that the current two exercises start with a guided fantasy, induced by the interviewer or 'change agent', intended for the respondent only. The interviewer talks slowly and inserts sufficient silences, which need to be long enough as well.

Subject (see Chapter 6)

Solution-Focused Coaching Exercise I

- How would the organization you are working for ideally look?

Solution-Focused Coaching Exercise II

- How can your ideal organization be brought about?
- What do you need for that?
- Whom do you need for that?
- What are the principal difficulties along the way?
- How do you cope with these?

Instructions

Exercise I

Exercise I starts with a guided fantasy, which is introduced with the following instructions:

> 'Have a good stretch, like a cat. Sit in a relaxed though upright way, in a chair with your arms on the armrests. Close your eyes ... Take a deep breath and exhale slowly and

> fully ... Imagine that three years have passed and everything is going much better ... The organization in which you are working has changed considerably and has become much more effective and pleasurable, and you have a very good time there ... Have a look around you. How does it look? ... What are you doing? ... What is going differently now? ... Of what does the effectiveness consist? ... What exactly is pleasant about it? ... How does it feel? ... What do you hear? ... And what are you doing? Today for example? ... What are you looking forward to the most? ... And tomorrow? ... What are your plans for next week? ...
>
> 'So far ... And now quietly back again. Take another deep breath. Open your eyes. Stretch again.'

After the guided fantasy, the change agent then asks how the experience has been and what it has consisted of. He also asks whether the fantasy went well and what might have gone better. The change agent spends the remainder of the session clarifying what exactly about it was so effective and pleasant. To this end, the change agent uses all available interview techniques. This exercise explicitly is not yet about *how* you can realize all of this.

Sometimes it happens that a respondent can't get any pictures of the future organization. That is no problem. The change agent then holds a 'normal' interview about how an improved organization would look.

Exercise II

Exercise II also starts with a guided fantasy, which is introduced with the following instruction.

> 'Have a good stretch. Sit in a relaxed though upright way, in a chair with your arms on the armrests. Close your eyes ... Take a deep breath and exhale slowly and fully ... Imagine that again three years have passed and everything is going much better ... You are again in your own organization that has become much more effective and pleasurable ... Have a look around you ... Is everything still the same? ... How does it look now? ... How does it go now? ... Does it still feel the same? ... Now look back from this situation and examine what actions everybody has taken to bring this about ... How did it come about? ... How did it start? ... What did they do first? ... And what then? ... And what afterwards? ... What were in hindsight the principal difficulties? ... And how were they overcome? ... What means have been employed? ... And what other means? ... Who has been of help? ... And who else? ... Who has opposed the progress? ... What has been done about that?
>
> 'So far ... And now quietly back again. Take another deep breath. Open your eyes. Stretch again.'

The change agent then asks how the fantasy went, what it delivered and what could have been better. The change agent spends the remainder of the session clarifying:

- what was and was not done and what else could have been done
- what difficulties were encountered and how these were overcome
- what means were employed and what might have been used
- who helped

The change agent can apply all available interview techniques here.

Now too, it may happen that a respondent can imagine or picture only little or nothing at all about this future state. Then the same applies here as in Exercise I.

Comments

- The same exercises can also be done with more than one respondent at a time, for example in teams and small groups as the start of a change process. The content of the different fantasies then has to be integrated into a shared vision.

Sequels

The sequel of Exercise I consists of reflecting more about the question: 'How would the organization you are working would ideally look?' The sequel of Exercise II consists of reflecting more on questions about how this ideal future could be brought about.

This can be done from time to time during the week, for instance:

- during walks
- on your bicycle
- on public transport
- during waiting periods
- in the shower
- while brushing your teeth
- in front of the mirror
- with the help of focusing

It is important to spend sufficient time on the sequels as well. In the long run, the sequels can result in a way of living in which reflection plays a more important role.

TWO CHAIRS (Adapted From Perls, Hefferline & Goodman, 1951)

Goals

- To explore an internal dialogue in order to surface underlying goals and motives, and to reach a win–win solution (comparable with the 'left-right' exercise and 'delegating alternatives', see Chapter 6).
- To strengthen goal setting.

Procedure

Here too, the ideal organization, or one of its elements or aspects, is the subject to be discussed. Essentially, the procedure follows the micro-teaching format. In the present context it involves each time a discussion between yourself (A) and the biggest critic within you (B), led by your change agent and watched by two observers who do their usual micro-teaching job. A and B have their own chairs. You take part as A on one of the two chairs. The other chair is for B. The coach places his chair in such a way that he can see both chairs well.

The change agent starts and asks respondent A to describe his ideal organization, or the element of it that is being discussed. Then he invites the respondent to be seated, as B, in the other chair and to comment on A's story. B comments, and then the change agent invites A to respond to this from the other chair, and so on. The change agent can ask A as well as B questions, subject them to all the interview techniques, and should see to it that both A and B can sufficiently make their points.

The change agent's objective is to really see in both A and B the good intentions and the distortions or surpluses of these good intentions (see Chapters 5, 6 and 7). His next objective is to surface the underlying assumptions and goals, in order to finally integrate these assumptions and goals into a win–win solution.

The discussions afterwards in foursomes are intended to help realize the assignment of the change agent (that is, to surface the good intentions, distortions of the good intentions and underlying assumptions, and to achieve a win–win solution).

When some clarity has been reached – or if the change agent's assignment does not succeed at all – roles are changed until everybody has played all the parts once. That implies that you should keep an eye on the time.

When a respondent does not succeed, he can try later to finish the exercise on his own. A good format for that is the exercise 'Left hand/right hand', described in Chapter 6 in the section 'Helping creativity'.

Comments

- The exercise stems from Fritz Perls' Gestalt therapy.
- The exercise can have a strong emotional effect, especially when a breakthrough or solution is actually attained. Of course, this depends also on the nature of the dilemma or problem in question.
- A frequently occurring division of roles between A and B is that between a hypercritical 'parental' party and a criticized 'child' one.
- The exercise can be used in a dialogue-like setting to achieve fusion between two suppositions that are contradictory at first sight.

STRONG ANIMAL, WEAK ANIMAL

Goal

- To demonstrate the difference between how you are when you are strong and when you are weak.
- To learn about the gains and costs of both forms of existence.
- To know the connection between both forms of existence, and how you can go from the one form to the other when you want to do that.

Procedure

First answer the questions in writing. The rest of this exercise follows the usual micro-teaching format of an interview exercise. The following questions are asked:

- As what kind of animal would you characterize yourself when you are at your weakest?
- What is characteristic of that animal?

- When are you weak?
- What does the weak side cost you?
- What does the weak side gain you?
- Give three examples of things you have done well when you were strong, things you are really proud of.
- Why was that?
- As what kind of animal would you characterize yourself when you are at your strongest?
- What is characteristic of that animal?
- When are you strong?
- What do your strong sides cost you?
- What do these strong sides give you?
- How are your strong and weak sides related to each other? There is always some connection!

Comments

- It is important to know that you have both sides, as well as that both sides have their advantages and disadvantages. This also applies to people in change projects and dialogue sessions. Sometimes you meet people who have lost sight of their strong side. Then it is important to evoke some memories of the strong side and to seduce the person in question to look at the matter at hand as if their strong side were in charge now. If that does not succeed, you subsequently can ask what stops the other person from doing that.

WALKS

The goals and procedure are the same every time, unless stated otherwise.

Goal

- To think about the subject at hand and to find more appropriate and productive ways of thinking about that issue. The subjects are so chosen that they are all relevant for change agents, leaders and in dialogue.
- To practice reflection, which is a crucial skill in dialogue as well for leaders and change agents.

Procedure

Read the relevant texts.

Go for a walk, preferably somewhere in the country, in the woods, on the beach or through a quiet neighborhood, and bring along the list of questions you want to answer, as well as a writing pad or a small recording device. Ask yourself the questions about the issue at hand and record the answers.

Though walks are especially suited to reflect on a series of questions, there are other options as well. Looking in the mirror, waiting, swimming, running, traveling by public transport, standing under the shower and shaving – provided that you do not cut yourself – are excellent opportunities as well.

Walk 1: To Take Stock of Your Received Opinions (see Chapter 6)

This walk is concerned with your list of ideas about:

- good and evil
- coping with emotions
- coping with power
- work
- relationships and love
- education
- men and women
- money

Ask yourself for each of these areas what opinions you have received from your parents. To what degree do you still subscribe to these ideas and to what degree don't you? On what issues have you really changed your opinions and views?

Try to come to a short overview of your most important views and opinions on each issue. Describe these in your report.

Walk 2: To Question Your Own Unproductive Assumptions

This walk is intended to take stock of your own unproductive assumptions, to find out how you can cope with them in a more productive way.

Read Chapter 6 and Addendum 3, which gives a list of common unproductive assumptions.

Ask yourself what your most unproductive assumptions are and what their effects are.

- What assumption hinders you most at the moment?
- How does this assumption relate to your professional role?

Start a discussion with this assumption, an internal dialogue. Ask the assumption what it wants to accomplish:

- What are your objectives?
- Why are you there for me?

As it is, such assumptions essentially always have a positive intention: they want you to accomplish something or want to prevent you getting into trouble. The assumptions tend to behave as good sports and will give you answers. It is up to you to learn more about the assumption's intention by applying the interview techniques you have acquired:

- How do you mean that?
- Can you give an example? And so on.

When you have clarified the good intentions of your unproductive assumption, you clarify your own intentions: what you want and what you want from your assumption.

The next question then is:

- How can your assumption and yourself come to a solution with each other that is optimal for both parties?

This solution is not a compromise, but enables both parties to realize their underlying intentions as well as possible. This asks for some brainstorming and creativity (see Chapter 6).

- How can your assumption realize itself in a way that you profit from it without being troubled by it?
- When would your assumption have to assert itself clearly?
- And when certainly not?

Come to an agreement, that 'both parties' are able and willing to stick to. Make sure that the agreements are realistic. Monitor during the first weeks whether and how this works out, as well as how things can be improved.

Repeat the internal monologue once more when you have returned home and look in the mirror.

Comments

- Though this is an exercise with an internal dialogue, the general approach is the same as in a 'normal' dialogue. A normal dialogue also involves tracking down your own and others' underlying assumptions and goals, wording the difference of opinion as sharply as possible and trying to find a solution at the behavioral level, in which the intention and assumptions of both parties are done justice as fully as possible.
- Dialogue is always useful in organizations where a tough and seemingly unsolvable difference of opinion becomes manifest.
- Everyone has unproductive assumptions and it is very useful to learn about your own unproductive assumptions.
- Unproductive assumptions usually are only unproductive in certain contexts. For instance, living as if you are prepared for the worst can be useful indeed in an extremely unsafe situation, but sometimes it is not. The same applies to needing support from other people to accomplish something.
- Of course, you can do the same exercise with other unproductive assumptions.

Walks 3a and 3b: To Conclude Unfinished Business

These walks are intended to clean up matters from the past that cost you energy and can result in alienation.

Walk 3a is concerned with things that were done to you and still bother you. Read the first section of Chapter 7 and answer for yourself the following (written down) questions.

- What happened?
- What were the consequences?
- How bad was it?
- How did you respond?

- What did you feel?
- To what degree was what happened to you directed against you personally?
- How could this have happened?
- Would it have happened to any other person in your place as well?
- What did you do, and failed to do, which made this possible?
- Did the other person think that you gave reason for it?
- What can be learned from this?
- What are you going to do differently from now on?
- What has happened that would not have happened if this event had not taken place?
- What did you gain from that?
- If this had not happened, how would it then have gone on and what have you probably spared yourself by this?
- Did the person who did this to you have any alternative line of action?
- Does the answer to the previous question make the other person into somebody with whom you would like change positions?
- Would not it be better to have some compassion with such a person?
- Is it possible for you to forgive the other person, in order to go on and not to look back?

Walk 3b is concerned with things that you have done to others and that still bother you. Read the first section of Chapter 7 and answer for yourself the following (written down) questions.

- What exactly did or didn't you do?
- Could you have done otherwise?
- How?
- Why haven't you done that?
- How does that feel?
- How would you do that differently now?
- If the other person is still alive, what do you want to say to them about this?
- Do you want to apologize?
- What more can you do to make it up?

Comments

- To be able to work effectively, you must have most of your energy at your disposal. As unfinished business traps energy (see Chapter 7), you should get rid of that unfinished business.
- An approach focused on concluding unfinished business in groups, for example with people from one team or department, can be very useful too. You can think of one or two times during the annual retreat to clean up anything that has remained unfinished, especially in the interpersonal domain. Besides that, such an approach is often indispensable before starting a dialogue, but also as a prelude to implementing major reorganizations and cultural changes. Of course it does demand good supervision, with also an option for further individual or group coaching to solve more radical problems or conflicts.

Walk 4: To Examine Resistance to Change

This walk is intended to teach you to recognize resistance to change and to understand where it comes from. The walk is primarily concerned with examining your own resistance to change. Read the section on resistance to change in Chapter 7 and answer for yourself the following (written down) questions:

- To what degree do you admit to yourself that some things in your life could be improved?
- Are you completely honest in this respect?
- When you realized that you could do better on one of those points, what did you think?
- What did you tell yourself then?
- Are you really living authentically?
- Are you really satisfied and happy?
- To what degree are you settling for good-enough solutions?
- How strictly do you confine yourself to your comfort zone?
- What do you systematically avoid?
- What are you able and willing to do that you do not do?

Comments

As a change agent, you meet many people who have to change or do something else, but do not *want* to change or do something else. Sometimes this is completely justified from all available perspectives, except that of the ones in power. Often, however, it is not. The latter also is a normal and everyday phenomenon. The problem is that dealing with resistance to change in the wrong way makes the implementation of change unpleasant, lengthy and sometimes downright impossible. This exercise is about recognizing this kind of resistance and its background.

FANTASY ROOM

This exercise is adapted from Stevens (1973), but goes back on an old tradition of Buddhist meditation.

Goal

- To give you a method to make your thoughts less compelling and to counteract stress.
- To give you a method to make letting go easier.
- To stimulate you to think about who and what you are.

Procedure

Do this exercise on your own. Read the instructions and test it on yourself, for as long as you are comfortable with it.

'Have a good stretch. Sit in a relaxed though upright way, in a chair with your arms on the armrests. Close your eyes . . . Take a deep breath and exhale slowly and fully . . .

'You find yourself in a pleasant, spacious, oblong room. You are sitting in a chair, your back to one of the long walls, about a meter from the wall. In the short wall on your left is a door, in the short wall on your right too. Along the sides there is furniture, such as you would like to have in your dream house. Look around, and feel how pleasant it is here.

'Then there is a knock at the door on the left. You call 'Come in' and the door opens. A thought enters. It greets you politely and comes to a standstill a few meters in front of you, so that you can observe it well. You are the boss. That is clear. You watch the thought and when you want it to, the thought turns around in front of you so that you can watch it from all sides. You can also ask the thought questions, whatever you want, and the thought will answer you honestly. For example, you can ask where it is about, what it intends, where it comes from, why it walked in just now – exactly what you want to know.

'After a while you are finished with the thought. Then the thought says goodbye and leaves the room through the door on the right. If you wish, you can still think for a while about the thought. Then there is again a knock on the left door, after which the scene repeats itself. You can meet as many thoughts as you wish. And when you do not want to go on, you just stop.

'You can also play a little with locking the doors. You can lock the left door. Then no thought enters any more and everything becomes silent. You can lock the right door and then the thoughts cannot leave. Chances are then that it will become a little crowded. You can also lock both doors and catch a thought for as long as you wish.

'When you want to leave the room, that is perfectly OK too. You only need to open your eyes, have a nice stretch, and that is it.'

How did that feel? How did that put your thoughts in their proper place? Realize that you can always do this.

Comments

- You can apply this exercise each time you notice that you are worrying too much about something. Of course, you can apply it to other people as well.
- The exercise does evoke some questions about who you are: the thinker, the thought, the room, all of them or something else again. The exercise gives also you a good occasion for pondering a little about the nature of thoughts, assumptions and goals. How personal are they? As such, this exercise is an excellent interlude for a dialogue session.

PART III

Addenda

Some Meanings of the Non-Verbal Behavioral Elements in Chapter 8

The meanings mentioned here are written down from a western European perspective and do not claim any universal validity. Many of the meanings, however, can be corroborated by the literature references I came across when I studied this field (see Schabracq, 1987, Vrugt & Schabracq, 1991). Nevertheless, the exact meaning of all the elements is dependent on the context in which they occur. This context consists of the configuration of the rest of the behavioral elements, the kind of interaction, the kind of relationship with the interaction partner, the wider situation and the background culture.

The meanings are given in the same sequence as the elements are described in Chapter 8. Up, down, with, and against refer to dimensions of the Leary rose (see Chapter 6).

I

Raising Your Head

Dominance, up, more against than with, arrogance, as a movement: 'no' in Greek.

Holding Your Head Backwards, as if You Are Examining the Ceiling

Being out of the situation, often down–against, display of boredom or fatigue, daydreaming, trying to come up with an idea.

Holding Your Head to One Side

Part of female flirting, making yourself shorter, cute (with–down). Also while looking at a baby or a small cute animal (with–up). Looking at a piece of art (with–up). Evaluating, estimating, sizing up something or someone (up–with).

Shaking Your Head When Talking

Saying no, to the other person or to your own spoken text; slowly: disbelief; quicker: oh no; more energetically: denial (against).

Nodding

Agreement, yes, understanding, appreciation, recognition, approval (with). Frequent: more down. Infrequent: more up, selective rewarding of certain behavior of the other person. Disbelief: oh yes? (against).

Letting Your Head Hang Down

Tiredness, shame, depression, desperation (down).

II

Laughing, Smiling and Smirking

Laughing: merry, joy (with). Smiling: yes, acknowledgment, gratitude, ingratiation, recognition, politeness, selective rewarding of certain behavior of the other person (with; frequently: more down; infrequently: more up). A smile is 'real', i.e. attached to the emotion of joy, when the eye corners wrinkle. A smile becomes a smirk when it is not with but against: mocking, derision, malicious joy.

Baring Your Teeth

Big effort (against). Anxious smile or grin (down–with).

Pressing Your Lips Together

Effort (against). Being nice and silent, showing that you do your best (kindergarten: down–with).

Pursing and Pouting Your Lips

Tasting, evaluating, deliberating (up). Female icon of being sexually available (with). As a movement: a kissing gesture, greeting, appreciation, thankfulness (with).

Running Your Tongue Over Your Lips

Quickly: nervousness, dry mouth or lips, used as a sign of lying (down). Slowly: nice (of food; with), sexual invitation (with–up).

Drawing Mouth Corners Down and Up

Down: sad, depressed, serious (against). Up: glad, sunny, smiling (with).

Swallowing a Number of Times

About to cry, but suppressing that, sadness, working through a loss (down). Suppressing any emotional reaction, swallowing your pride or anger (down–against).

III

Gaze Direction in General

The object at which somebody is looking teaches you something about what occupies that person: a pickpocket always tries to visually locate a purse or wallet. A detective or plain-clothes police officer tries to spot perpetrators, a salesperson tries to detect interest in and preference for certain products.

Gazing Upwards

Out of the immediate situation, thinking. Briefly: eyes to heaven: my God help me (under), or disapproval (against); rolling your eyes (against–up).

Gazing Downwards

Shy, depressed, sad, ashamed, embarrassed, demure, monk behavior, part of female flirting (down).

Shifting Your Gaze Quickly and Frequently

Nervous, suspicious, paranoid, unrest, no stable attitude (down, more against than with).

Shutting Your Eyes

Out of the immediate situation, sleepy, escaping from something nasty, going into yourself, meditating, praying, thinking deeply, trying to remember (under).

Looking with Screwed-Up Eyes

Effort, focusing, serious, dealing with possible danger, male element (up–against).

IV

Shutting and Opening Your Eyes Slowly, While Looking at Somebody

Greeting, acknowledging, granting (up–against).

Blinking Frequently

Nervous, jumping from one (fragment of a) thought to another (under).

Not Blinking at All

Dominant, unmoved, staring down (up–against).

Raising Your Eyebrows

Surprise, wonder (down). Reproach, disdain, contempt (against–up).

Raising One Eyebrow

Disapproval, disdain, contempt (against–up; up–against).

Quickly Raising Your Eyebrows Just for a Moment ('Eyebrow Flash')

Yes to contact, greeting, flirting, a universal gesture (with).

V

Hunching Your Shoulders

Both shoulders: tense, anxious, as if awaiting a blow, fearful (down, more against than with). One shoulder: shutting somebody out, giving someone the cold shoulder, tense (against, more down than up).

Drawing Your Shoulders Back

Male: dominant, present, active (up). Female: showing off your breasts (with–up).

Direct Shoulder Orientation

Full involvement, contact and exposure, aggression or sex (up).

Orienting Your Trunk Away From the Other at Different Degrees

Little to no involvement and contact (down).

Turning Your Trunk Back and Forth

An element of female flirting (with). In males more a sign of uncertainty, nervousness, not knowing what attitude to assume (down).

VI

Holding Your Upper Arms Away From Your Body While Standing

Macho dominance, enlarging your body contour (John Wayne; up–against).

Clenching Your Elbows to Your Trunk

Submissive, more female than male, diminishing your body contour (down–with).

Putting Your Hand(s) on Your Hip(s)

Dominance, extending your body contour (up–against).

Putting Both Hands Behind Your Head, Your Elbows Sticking Out

Dominance, extending your body contour, 'look no hands' (up–against), often affected. The posture people have to assume at gunpoint (down–against).

Putting One Hand Behind Your Head or Your Neck, Your Elbow Not Sticking Out

Uncertain, defensive (down–against).

Folding Your Arms

As a movement: closing up, getting defensive, becoming inactive (against). When sitting and resting on a table: just at ease. As a posture: the same but less explicitly so, rest attitude.

Unfolding Your Arms

Opening up, becoming less defensive, becoming more active (with).

Making Your Hands Invisible

Behind your back, standing: supervising, inactive (up–against). Under the table, sitting: submissive, embarrassed (down–with). In your pockets, standing: inactive, sullen, defying (against–under).

VII

Running Your Forefinger or the Side of Your Hand Under Your Nose

Itching, runny nose, inner dividedness, doubt, no to self or other's behavior, lying (against–down).

Keeping Your Forefinger Alongside Your Nose

Thinking, waiting to take the floor (up–with).

Holding Your Nose with Your Thumb and Forefinger

Insecurity, uneasiness, comforting yourself (down).

Sniffing

Contempt, reproach, disapproval (against–up).

Wrinkling Your Nose

Smelling something bad, disapproval (against–up).

VIII

Touching, Holding, Rubbing and Caressing Your Face or Body

Insecurity, nervousness (down). Comforting and supporting yourself if you are insecure or nervous, trying to concentrate (down–with). Sometimes with a sexual overtone, depending on the body part. Arranging your hair as a female: flirting element (with–down). Sometimes when entering or leaving a social interaction, or when going through a transition within an interaction.

Wiping Your Face

Cleaning yourself, getting rid of an image or thought, trying to concentrate, nervous (down–against).

Scratching

Itching, irritation (against–down).

Touching with the Left or Right Hand

The non-writing hand (for most people the left hand): more unaware and unconscious in nature, more against (shadow side).

IX

Speech-Supporting Gestures

In general: dominant, emphasizing, clarifying (up).

Gestures that Illustrate or Imitate a Meaning or Content

In general: dominant (up).

Putting the Palm of Your Hand Next to Your Head

Female flirting element, inviting, part of a greeting, at the beginning and end of an interaction (with–up).

Holding Up Your Hand or Forefinger

Asking for attention, claiming the floor and a speaking turn (the one who holds his hands the highest usual gets the speaking turn), dominance (up).

Clenching Your Fist(s)

Tension, anger (against).

Pointing with Your Forefinger

Indicating, 'you', aggressive, reproachful (against–up).

Starting a Gesture Strongly and Then Letting Your Hand Flop Down

Tired, agitated, depressive (against–down).

X

Holding Your Breath

Undivided attention, tense, watchful, unsafe (against).

Sighing

Letting go, relief (with-down). Frequently: depressive, sad, bereaved (down).

Panting

Exertion, great effort, great arousal, great fear.

Inhaling Deeply

Preparation (up). frustration (against).

Breathing Quickly

Nervousness, anxiety (down).

XI

Sitting Inclined Forward

With head up: involved, attentive (with–up). Somewhat tense. With head down: sad, depressed, ashamed (down).

Sprawling in Your Chair

Out of the immediate situation, watching television, rebellious teenager element (under–against). Totally at ease (with).

Sitting with Your Legs Folded Under You

Cozy, at ease, female (with–under).

Sitting on Your Hands

Child element, tense, submissive, full of expectation (with–down).

Sitting Very Straight

Stern, rigid, authoritarian, dignified (up–against).

Sitting on the Edge of Your Chair

Restless, full of expectation, ready to jump up.

Fidgeting in Your Chair

Nervous, not knowing what attitude to assume, restless (under–against).

XII

Sitting Reclining with Your Feet on a Desk or Table

Relaxed, authority, enlarged body contour, male (up–with), sometimes affected.

Sitting with Your Legs Crossed, so that the Ankle of One Leg Rests on the Knee or Upper Leg of the Other One

Relaxed, dominant, enlarged body contour, male (up).

Sitting with Your Legs Wide Apart

Relaxed, dominant, enlarged body contour, male (up).

Sitting with Your Legs Pressed Against Each Other

Female, prim and proper (ankle behind heel), submissive, tense (down).

Making Kicking Movements While Seated

Teenager rebellious element, aggressive, wanting to leave (down–against).

Fidgeting with Your Feet While Seated

Tense, anxious, wanting to leave (down–against).

Flexing Your Foot Upwards

Tense, suppressing emotion (down–against).

Some Connotations of the Words in the You-We-It Exercise in Chapter 8

The meanings are given in the same sequence as the elements are described in Chapter 8.

YOU

- Used instead of I of we: impersonal, anonymous, 'flat', hiding in the collective, taking no responsibility, uncommitted, suggesting general validity.
- Used to indicate the other(s): pointing, accusing, stressing differences.

WE AND US

- We instead of I: suggesting communality and solidarity, hiding in the collective, taking no responsibility, trying to circumvent resistance.
- Also making yourself bigger than life: 'We, Queen Victoria.'
- Used instead of you: suggesting equality, glossing over differences with the other most of the time from a position of authority.
- Being together, being with, solidarity.
- Emphasizing the differences with another group: we against you or they.

IT

- Instead of 'I find': suggesting being factual, objective, true, legally appropriate, decisive, certain.

ONE

- Impersonal, general, indirect, no individuality, often instead of I, you, he or she.

I AND ME

- Personal, individual, responsible, committed, suggesting honesty, egocentric, subjective, stressing the difference with you, him or her.

ANALOGOUS EXERCISES

Why

Open question. Being competent with 'why' is essential for inquiry and advocacy, the crucial skills in a dialogue, because it questions goals as well as underlying motives and assumptions. In other words, 'why' can yield causal as well as final reasons and explanations.

'Why' often leads to questions that are difficult to answer, which can be experienced as rude, impertinent and aggressive, certainly when you ask 'why' each time anew.

(Yes) But

'Yes but' and 'But' at the beginning of a sentence signify more or less the same as a plain 'No'. Being sensitive to 'Yes but' and 'But' helps to detect differences of opinion, rejections and disqualifications. Differences of opinion are important in dialogue, because they are often its *raison d'être*. Disqualifications lastly do not belong in a good dialogue and should be treated as such.

Absolute Words

All-inclusive words such as everybody, everyone, all, always and everywhere, as well as all-exclusive words such as nobody, no one, nothing, none, never and nowhere, are 'strong' words that advocate an absolute and inevitable truth, order, regularity or pattern. The frequent use of such words often implies that some truth has to be defended at any cost. As such, these words often pop up in standard explanations, when assumptions are questioned, and in the defense of unthinkables and undoables.

Examples of Unproductive Assumptions (Chapter 8, Walk 2)

- Things happen to me, without me being able to influence them in any particular way.
- I can and must fully determine my own fate.
- To feel good, everybody must value me.
- I always have to take into account that the very worst can happen to me.
- I cannot enjoy myself as long as there are other people who do not feel good.
- For every problem there is only one best solution.
- When I do something wrong, it becomes obvious that I really am not good enough.
- I have to earn others' love by doing all kinds of things for them.
- Without applause, life is not worthwhile.
- A solution must always be original and creative.
- Feelings and emotions always have a negative influence on my powers of judgment.
- As long as it is not proved otherwise, it is good to assume that the other person cannot be trusted.
- Pursuing one project for a long time is boring.
- People are either good or bad.
- Keeping the peace wins over everything.
- My past has an all-determining influence on me.
- To succeed, I always need somebody to support me.
- It is very bad when things go differently than I want them to.
- I have to change people.
- Enjoying yourself is a sin.
- To be really happy, I need other people around me.

Obviously, this list can be extended ad infinitum. What assumptions that are relevant to you can you add to the list?

Bibliography

Allen, V.L. & Vliert, E. van der (eds) (1984) *Role Transitions*. New York: Plenum Press.

Antonovsky, A. (1987) *Unraveling the Mystery of Health: How People Manage Stress and Stay Well*. San Francisco, CA: Jossey-Bass.

Argyris, C. (1983) *Strategy, Change and Defensive Routines*. Boston, MA: Pitman.

Argyris, C. (1990) *Overcoming Organizational Defenses: Facilitating Organizational Learning*, Boston, MA: Allyn and Bacon.

Argyris, C. & Schon, D.A. (1978) *Organizational Learning*. Reading, MA: Addison-Wesley.

Aristotle (1941) Metaphysics, in *The Basic Works of Aristotle*. New York: Random House, pp. 689–926.

Asch, S.E. (1971) The doctrine of suggestion, in L.L. Barker & R.J. Kibler (eds), *Speech Communication Behavior*. Englewood Cliffs, NJ: Prentice Hall, pp. 255–266.

Ashcraft, N. & Scheflen, A.E. (1976) *People Space*. Garden City, NY: Anchor Press/Doubleday.

Bandura, A. (1977) Social Learning Theory. Englewood Cliffs: NJ, Prentice Hall.

Baudouin, C. (1924) *Psychologie de la suggestion et de l'autosuggestion* (Psychology of suggestion and autosuggestion) (4th edn) Neuchâtel/Paris: Editions Delachaux & Niestlé.

Bellow, S. (1971) *Mr Sammler's Planet*. Harmondsworth: Penguin.

Bellow, S. (1982) *The Dean's December*. New York: Pocket Books.

Bennis, W.G. & Thomas, R.J. (2002) *Geeks and Geezers: How Era, Values and Defining Moments Shape Leaders*. Boston, MA: Harvard Business School Press.

Benson, H. (2001) *The Relaxation Response* (revd edn). New York: Quill.

Berlin, I. (1998) *The First and the Last*. London: Granta.

Berlin, I. (2000) *Three Critics of the Enlightenment: Vico, Hamann, Herder*. Princeton/Oxford: Princeton University Press.

Berlyne, D.E. (1960) *Conflict, Arousal and Curiosity*. New York: McGraw-Hill.

Berne, E. (1966) *Transactional Analysis in Psychotherapy*. New York: Grove Press.

Berne, E. (1972) *What Do You Say After You Say Hello?* New York: Grove Press.

Bernstein, A.J. & Craft Rozen, S. (1989) *Dinosaur Brains*. New York: Ballantine Books.

Blake, A.G.E. (1996) *The Intelligent Enneagram*. Boston, MA/London: Shambhala.

Boerlijst, J.G., Heyden, B.I.J.M. van der & Assen, A. van (1993) *Veertig-plussers in de onderneming* (People over 40 in the corporation). Assen: Van Gorcum.

Bohm, D. (2004) *On Dialogue*. London/New York: Routledge Classics.

Bolen, J.S. (1989) *Gods in Everyman*. San Francisco, CA: Harper and Row.

Branden, N. (1987) *How to Raise Your Self-Esteem*. New York: Bantam Books.

Breznitz, S. (1983) The seven kinds of denial, in S. Breznitz (ed.), *The Denial of Stress*. New York: International Universities Press, pp. 257–280.

Bruyn, M. de, Bruyn, R. de & Gier, G. de (2000) *Brood voor iedereen, feestwijn voor iedereen, creatief denken voor iedereen* (Bread for everybody, festive wine for everybody, creative thinking for everybody). Rumst: Creatief Atelier Windekind.

Buber, M. (1957) *De vraag naar de mens* (The question about man). Utrecht: Erven J. Bijleveld.

Buber, M. (1966) *Sluitsteen* (Keystone). Rotterdam: Lemniscaat.

Buber, M. (1978) *Ik en Gij* (I and thou) Utrecht: Erven J. Bijleveld.

Calvin, W.H. (1989) *The Cerebral Symphony*. New York: Bantam.

Campbell, J. (1988) *The Power of Myth*. New York: Doubleday.

Chance, M.R.A. & Larsen, R.R. (eds) (1976) *The Social Structure of Attention*. Chichester: John Wiley & Sons Ltd.

Cherniss, C. (1995) *Beyond Burnout*. New York: Routledge.

Cicero, M.T. (1909–14) *On Old Age*. Cambridge MA: Harvard Classics, http://www.bartleby. com/9/2/1.html.

Claxton, G. (1997) *Hare Brain Tortoise Mind*. London: Fourth Estate.

Cohen, S. (2006) Management ethics, accountability and responsibility, in S.R. Clegg & C. Rhodes (eds) *Management Ethics: Contemporary Contexts*. London/New York: Routledge, pp. 113–134.

Confucius (1979) *The Analectics* (trans. and intro. D.C. Lau). Harmondsworth: Penguin.

Damasio, A. (2003) *Looking for Spinoza: Joy, Sorrow, and the Feeling Brain*. New York/San Diego, CA: Harcourt.

Davis, M. (ed.) (1982) *Interaction Rhythms*. New York: Human Sciences Press.

Dawkin, R. (1976) *The Selfish Gene*. Oxford: Oxford University Press.

De Bono, E. (1990) *I Am Right, You Are Wrong*. London: Mica Management Resources.

Deese, J. (1952) *The Psychology of Learning*. New York: McGraw-Hill.

Dixon, N.M. (1998) *Dialogue at Work*. London: Lemos and Crane.

Doeglas, J.D.A. & Schabracq, M.J. (1992). Transitiemanagement (Transition management). *Gedrag and Organisatie* (Behavior and organization), 5: 448–466.

Dorpat, T.L. (1985) *Denial and Defense in the Therapeutic Situation*. New York: Aronson.

Erickson, M.H., Rossi, E.J. & Rossi, S.I. (1976) *Hypnotic Realities*. Chichester: John Wiley & Sons Ltd.

Erikson, E.H. (1968) *Identity: Youth and Crisis*. London: Faber and Faber.

Esser, A.H. (ed.) (1971) *Behavior and Environment*. New York: Plenum Press.

Exline, R. (1971) Visual interaction: the glances of power and preference, in J.K. Cole (ed.), *Nebraska Symposium on Motivation*. Lincoln, NE: University of Nebraska Press, pp. 163–206.

Faragher, E.B., Cooper, C.L. & Cartwright, S. (2004) A Shortened Stress Evaluation Tool (ASSET). *Stress and Health*, 20: 189–201.

Foucault, M. (1975) *Surveiller et punir: Naissance de la prison* (Surveying and punishing: Birth of the prison). Paris: Gallimard.

Frankl, V.E. (1978) *De zin van het bestaan* (Man's search for meaning). Rotterdam: A. Donker.

Freire, P. (1970) *Pedagogy of the Oppressed*. New York: Seabury Press.

Freud, A. (1971) *Das Ich und die Abwehrmechanismen* (The I and the resistance mechanisms) München: Taschenbücher Kindler.

Frijda, N.H. (1986) *The Emotions*. Cambridge: Cambridge University Press.

Gadamer, G. (1960) *Wahrheit und Methode* (Truth and method) Tübingen: Mohr.

Garfinkel, H. (1967) *Studies in Ethnomethodology*. Englewood Cliffs, NJ: Prentice-Hall.

Gendlin, E. (1981) *Focusing*. New York: Bantam.

Gendlin, E. (1986) *Let Your Body Interpret Your Dreams*. Wilmette, IL: Chiron.

Gibson, J.J. (1979) *The Ecological Approach to Visual Perception*. Boston, MA: Houghton Mifflin.

Glouberman, D. (1989) *Life Choices and Life Changes through Image Work*. London: Grafton.

Goffman, E. (1963) *Behavior in Public Places*. Glencoe, IL: Free Press.

Goffman, E. (1968) *Asylums*. Harmondsworth: Penguin.

Goffman, E. (1971) *Relations in Public*. New York: Harper and Row.

Goffman, E. (1972a) *Encounters*. Harmondsworth: Penguin.

Goffman, E. (1972b) *Interaction Ritual*. Harmondsworth: Penguin.

Goffman, E. (1974) *Frame Analysis*. New York: Harper and Row.

Goldratt, E. (1990) *What Is This Thing Called Theory of Constraints and How Should It Be Implemented?* Croton on Hudson, NY: North River Press.

Gopnik, A. & Meltzoff, A.N. (1997) *Words, Thoughts, and Theories*. Cambridge, MA: MIT Press.

Groot, W. & Maassen van den Brink, H. (1997) *Bedrijfsgerelateerde scholing en arbeidsmarktflexibiliteit van oudere medewerkers* (Corporation-related education and labour market flexibility of senior employees). Den Haag: Welboom.

Grube, M. (2006) Towards an empirically based validation of intuitive diagnostic: Rumke's 'praecox feeling' across the schizophrenia spectrum: Preliminary results *Psychopathology*. 39: 209–217.

Gudykunst, W.B. & Kim, Y.Y. (1992) *Communicating with Strangers: An Approach to Intercultural Communication*. New York: McGraw-Hill.

Hackman, J.R. & Oldham, G.R. (1980) *Work Redesign*. Reading, MA: Addison-Wesley.

Hall, E.T. (1969) *The Hidden Dimension*. Garden City, NY: Doubleday.

Hammer, M. (2001) *The Agenda*. New York: Crown Business.

Hampden-Turner, C. (1994) *Corporate Culture*. London: Piatkus.

Handy, C. (1987) *Gods of Management*. London: Arrow Books.

Handy, C. (1994) *The Age of Paradox*. Boston, MA: Harvard Business School Press.

Hare, R.D. (1993) *Without Conscience*. New York/London: The Guilford Press.

Harré, R. (1979) *Social Being*. Oxford: Blackwell.

Hatfield, E., Cacioppo, J.T. & Rapson, R.L. (1994) *Emotional Contagion*. Paris: Cambridge University Press.

Heidegger, M. (1962) *Being and Time* (trans. J. Macquarrie & E. Robinson). New York: Harper and Row.

Heidegger, M. (1991) *Over denken, bouwen, wonen: Vier essays* (About thinking, building, dwelling: Four essays). Nijmegen: Sun.

Hendricks, G. (1998) *The Ten-Second Miracle*. San Francisco, CA: Harper.

Henkens, K. & Solinge, H. van (2003) *Het eindspel* (The endgame). Assen/Den Haag: Van Gorcum/ SMS.

James, W. (1890/1950) *The Principles of Psychology, Vol. II*. New York: Dover.

James, W. (1978) The sentiment of rationality, in W. James, *Essays in Philosophy: The Works of William James*. Cambridge, MA: Harvard University Press, pp. 32–64.

Jung, C.G. (1970) *Civilization in Transition*. Princeton, NJ: Princeton University Press.

Kanner, A.D., Coyne, J.C., Schaefer, C. & Lazarus, R.S. (1981) Comparison of two modes of stress management: Daily hassles and uplifts versus major life events. *Journal of Behavioral Medicine*, 4: 1–39.

Kaplan, S. & Kaplan, R. (1982) *Cognition and Environment*. New York: Praeger.

Karasek, R.A. & Theorell, T. (1990) *Healthy Work: Stress, Productivity and the Reconstruction of Working Life*. New York: Basic Books.

Kendon, A. (1970) Movement coordination in social interaction in some examples described. *Acta Psychologica*, 32: 101–125.

Kessels, J. (1997) *Socrates op de markt: Filosofie in bedrijf* (Socrates on the market: Philosophy in action). Amsterdam/Meppel: Boom.

Kets de Vries, M.F.R. & Balazs, K. (1997) The downside of downsizing. *Human Relations*, 50: 11–50.

Kiritz, S. & Moos, R.H. (1981) Physiological effects of social environments, in A. Furnham & M. Argyle (eds), *The Psychology of Social Situations*. Oxford: Pergamon Press, pp. 136–158.

Kleber, R.J. & Velde, P.G. van der (2003) Acute stress at work, in M.J. Schabracq, J.A.M. Winnubst & C.L. Cooper (eds). *Handbook of Work and Health Psychology* (2nd revd edn). Chichester: John Wiley & Sons Ltd, pp. 367–382.

Klein, G. (2003) *Intuition at Work*. New York: Currency Doubleday/Random House.

Knope, M. (1998) *De creatiespiraal* (The creation spiral). Nijmegen: KIC.

Kotter, J. (1996) *Leading Change*. Boston, MA: Harvard Business School Press.

Krieken, R. van (2006) The ethics of corporate legal personality, in S.R. Clegg & C. Rhodes (eds), *Management Ethics*. London/New York: Routledge, pp. 77–96.

Krijnen, M.A. (1993) *Onderzoek WAO-Instroom 1991, AH-Operations* (Study Influx Disablement Insurance Act 1991, AH-Operations). Amsterdam: UvA.

Laborde, G. (1987) *Influencing with Integrity*. Palo Alto, CA: Syntony Press.

Lakoff, G. & Johnson, M. (1999) *Philosophy in the Flesh: The Embodied Mind and Its Challenge to Western Thought*. New York: Basic Books.

Lencioni, P. (1998) *The Five Temptations of a CEO: A Leadership Fable*. San Francisco, CA: Jossey-Bass.

Lewin, K. (1952) Field theory in social science, in K. Lewin, *Selected Theoretical Papers*. London: Tavistock.

Long, R.J. (2005) Aquinas and Franciscan nature: Mysticism. *Logos*, 8: 56–64.

Lynn, R. (1966) *Attention, Arousal and the Orientation Reaction*. Oxford: Pergamon Press.

Maslach, C. & Leiter, M.P. (1997) *The Truth about Burnout*. San Francisco, CA: Jossey-Bass.

Maturana, H.R. & Varela, F.J. (1980) *Autopoiesis and Cognition*. Dordrecht: D. Reidel.

May, R. (1969) *Love and Will*. New York: Norton.

McGraw, P. (1999) *Life Strategies*. New York: Hyperion.

McNeilly, M. (2001) *Sun Tzu and the Art of Modern Warfare*. Oxford: Oxford University Press.

Meerloo, J.A.M. (1972) *De taal van het zwijgen* (The language of silence). Wassenaar: Servire.

Meertens, R.W. (1980) *Groepspolarisatie* (Group polarization). Deventer: Van Loghum Slaterus.

Merleau-Ponty, M. (1945) *Phénoménologie de la perception* (Phenomenology of perception). Paris: Gallimard.

Montaigne, M. (1580/1981) *Essays*. Harmondsworth: Penguin.

Moscovici, S. (1984) The phenomenon of social representation, in R.M. Farr & S. Moscovici (eds), *Social Representations*. Cambridge: Cambridge University Press, pp. 3–69.

Nair, K. (1998) *Waarde[n]vol leiderschap* (Valuable leadership). Schiedam: Scriptum.

Naranjo, C. (1994) *Character and Neurosis*. Nevada City, CA: Gateways.

Nietzsche, F. (1909) Also sprach Zarathustra (Thus spoke Zarathustra), in *Friedrich Nietzsche's Werke, Vol. 7*. Leipzig: Alfred Kröner Verlag.

Nisbett, R.E. & Ross, L. (1980) *Human Inference*. Englewood Cliffs N.J.: Prentice-Hall.

von Oech, R. (1983) *A Whack on the Side of the Head*. Menlo, CA: Creative Think.

Ofman, D.D. (1995) *Bezieling en kwaliteit in organisaties* (Inspiration and quality in organizations). Cothen: Servire.

Ollman, B. (1971) *Alienation: Marx's Conception of Man in Capitalist Society*. London: Cambridge University Press.

Palmer, H. (1991) *The Enneagram*. San Francisco, CA: HarperSanFrancisco.

Parsons, T. (1960) *Structure and Process in Modern Societies*. Glencoe, IL: Free Press.

Perls, F., Hefferline, R.F. & Goodman, P. (1951) *Gestalt Therapy*. New York: Delta Books.

Postman, N. (1999) *Building a Bridge to the Eighteenth Century: How the Past Can Influence the Future*. New York: Vintage.

Prahalad, C.K. & Hamel, G. (1990) The competence of the organization. *Harvard Business Review*, 68(3): 79–91.

Pranger, B. (2002) *De zonde der traagheid* (The sin of sloth). Lecture at the Studium Generale of the University of Amsterdam, 23 April.

Razran, G. (1961) The observable unconscious and the inferable conscious in current Soviet psychophysiology: Interoceptive conditioning, semantic conditioning and the orienting reflex. *Psychological Review*, 68: 109–119.

Reichheld, F.F. (1996) *The Loyalty Effect*. Boston, MA: Harvard Business School Press.

Revans, R. (1998) *ABC of Action Learning*. London: Lemos & Crane.

Rizzolatti, G. & Craighero, L. (2004) The mirror-neuron system. *Annual Review of Neuroscience*, 27: 169–192.

Ryan, K.D. & Oestreich, D.K. (1988) *Driving Fear out of the Workplace*. San Francisco, CA: Jossey-Bass.

Sartre, J.P. (1943) *L'être et le néant* (Being and not being). Paris: Gallimard.

Schabracq, M.J. (1987) *Betrokkenheid en onderlinge gelijkheid in sociale interacties* (Involvement and mutual similarity in social interaction). Dissertation. Amsterdam: UvA.

Schabracq, M.J. (1991) *De inrichting van de werkelijkheid* (The design of reality). Amsterdam/Assen: Boom.

Schabracq, M.J. (2003a) Everyday well-being and stress in work and organisations. In M.J. Schabracq, J.A.M. Winnubst & C.L. Cooper (eds), *Handbook of Work and Health Psychology* (2nd revd edn). Chichester: John Wiley & Sons Ltd, pp. 9–36.

Schabracq, M.J. (2003b) Issues of the second career half, in M.J. Schabracq, J.A.M. Winnubst & C.L. Cooper (eds), *Handbook of Work and Health Psychology* (2nd revd edn). John Wiley & Sons Ltd, pp. 333–348.

Schabracq, M.J. (2003c) What an organisation can do about its employees' well-being and health: An overview, in M.J. Schabracq, J.A.M. Winnubst & C.L. Cooper (eds), *Handbook of Work and Health Psychology* (2nd revd edn). Chichester: John Wiley & Sons Ltd, pp. 585–600.

Schabracq, M.J. (2005a) Well-being and health: What HRM can do about it, in R.J. Burke & C.L. Cooper (eds), *Reinventing HRM: Challenges and New Directions*. London/New York: Routledge, pp. 187–206.

Schabracq, M.J. (2005b) Stress, alienation and shared leadership, in A.-S.G. Antoniou & C.L. Cooper (eds), *Research Companion to Organizational Health Psychology*. Cheltenham/Northhampton, MA: Edward Elgar, pp. 122–131.

Schabracq, M.J. (2006) Leadership and organizational culture, in R.J. Burke & C.L. Cooper (eds), *Inspiring Leaders*. London/New York: Routledge, pp. 212–233.

Schabracq, M.J. & Cooper, C.L. (2000) The changing nature of work and stress. *Journal of Management Psychology*, 15: 227–241.

Schabracq, M.J. & Cooper, C.L. (2001) *Stress als keuze* (Stress as a choice). Schiedam: Scriptum.

Schabracq, M.J. & Cooper, C.L. (2003) To be me or not to be me: About alienation. *Counselling Psychology Quarterly*, 16: 53–79.

Schabracq, M.J., Cooper, C.L., Travers, C. & Maanen, D. van (2001) *Occupational Health Psychology: The Challenge of Workplace Stress*. Leicester: British Psychological Association.

Schabracq, M.J., Cooper, C.L. & Winnubst, J.A.M. (2003) Epilogue, in M.J. Schabracq, J.A.M. Winnubst & C.L. Cooper (eds), *Handbook of Work and Health Psychology* (2nd revd edn). Chichester: John Wiley & Sons Ltd.

Schabracq, M.J., Maassen Van den Brink, H., Groot, W., Janssen, P. & Houkes, I. (2000). *De prijs van stress* (The price of stress). Maarsen: Elsevier.

Schabracq, M.J., Winnubst, J.A.M. & Cooper, C.L. (eds) (2003) *Handbook of Work and Health Psychology* (2nd revd edn). Chichester: John Wiley & Sons Ltd.

Schaufeli, W.B. & Buunk, A.P. (2003) Burnout, in M.J. Schabracq, J.A.M. Winnubst & C.L. Cooper (eds), *Handbook of Work and Health Psychology* (2nd revd edn). Chichester: John Wiley & Sons Ltd.

Scheflen, A.T. (1964) The significance of posture in communication systems. *Psychiatry*, 27: 316–321.

Scheflen, A.E. (1982) Comments on the significance of interaction rhythms, in M. Davis (ed.), *Interaction Rhythms*. New York: Human Sciences Press, pp. 13–22.

Schein, E.H. (1985) *Organizational Culture and Leadership*. San Francisco, CA: Jossey-Bass.

Schelling, T.C. (1960) *The Strategy of Conflict*. Cambridge, MA: Harvard University Press.

Schneider, B. (1987) The people make the place. *Personnel Psychology*, 40: 437–453.

Schon, D. (1983) *The Reflective Practitioner*. New York: Basic Books.

Schutz, A. (1970) *On Phenomenology and Social Relations*. Chicago: Chicago University Press.

Scott Fitzgerald, F. (1945) *The Crack-Up* (ed.E. Wilson). New York: New Directions.

Seligman, M.E.P. (1990) *Learned Optimism*. New York: Pocket Books.

Senge, P.M. (1990) *The Fifth Discipline*. New York: Doubleday.

Senge, P.M., Kleiner, A., Roberts, C., Ross, R.B. & Smith, B.J. (1994) *The Fifth Discipline Fieldbook*. London: Nicholas Brealey.

Seymour, J. & O'Connor, J. (1994) *Training with NLP*. London/San Francisco, CA: Thorsons.

Shadish, W.R., Cook, T.D. & Campbell, D. (2001) *Experimental and Quasi-Experimental Designs for Generalized Causal Inference*. Boston, MA: Houghton Mifflin.

Siebert, A. (1996) *The Survivor Personality*. New York: Perigee.

Sjah, I. (1969) *The Sufis*. London: Jonathan Cape.

Smit, I. (1997) *Patterns of coping*. Dissertation. Utrecht: Universiteit van Utrecht.

Sokolov, Y.N. (1963) *Perception and the Conditioned Reflex*. New York: Pergamon.

Spence, J. (2000) *Mao*. Amsterdam: Balans.

Sprangers, M. & Hoogstraten, J. (1989) Pretesting effects in retrospective pretest-posttest designs. *Journal of Applied Psychology*, 74: 265–272.

Stevens, J.O. (1973) *Awareness: Exploring, Experimenting, Experiencing*. New York: Bantam Books.

Stokvis, B.B. (1947) *Psychologie der suggestie en autosuggestie* (Psychology of suggestion and autosuggestion). Lochem: De Tijdstroom.

Stone, R. (1997) *Genezende vertelkunst* (The healing art of story art). Amsterdam: Bres.

Storrs Hall, J. (2000) Ethics for machines. http://discuss.foresight.org/˜josh/ethics.html.

Stout, M. (2005) *The Sociopath Next Door*. New York: Broadway Books.

Störig, H.J. (1966) *Geschiedenis van de filosofie* (History of philosophy) (trans. P. Brommer) Utrecht/Antwerpen: Het Spectrum.

Strongman, K.T. (1970) Communicating with the eyes. *Science*, 6: 47–52.

Strongman, K.T. & Champness, B.G. (1968) Dominance hierarchies and conflict in eye contact. *Acta Psychologica*, 28: 376–386.

Sun Tzu (1993) *The Art of War*. Ware: Wordsworth Reference.

Surowiecki, J. (2005) *The Wisdom of Crowds: Why the Many Are Smarter than the Few*. London: Abacus.

Tarde, G. (1890) *Les lois de l'Imitation* (The laws of limitation). Paris: Ancienne Librairie Germer Baillière et Cie.

Taylor, S.E., Cousino Klein, L., Lewis, B.P., Gruenewald, T.L., Gurung, R.A.R. & Updegraff, J.A. (2000) Biobehavioral responses to stress in females: Tend-and-befriend, not fight-or-flight. *Psychological Review*, 107: 411–429.

Taylor, S.E. & Fiske, S.T. (1978) Salience, attention and attribution, in L. Berkowitz (ed.), *Advances in Experimental Social Psychology*, Vol 11. London/New York: Academic Press, pp. 250–288.

Thijssen, J.G.L. (1988) *Bedrijfsopleidingen als werkterrein* (In-company training as a field of work). Den Haag: Vuga.

Thorndike, E. (1911) *Animal Intelligence: Experimental Studies*. New York: Macmillan.

Trompenaars, F. & Hampden-Turner, C. (2002) *21 Leaders for the 21st Century*. New York: McGraw-Hill.

von Uexküll, J.J. (1909) *Umwelt und Innenwelt der Tiere*. Berlin: J. Springer.

Usher, R. (2006) Management ethics and organizational networks, in S.R. Clegg & C. Rhodes (eds), *Management Ethics: Contemporary Contexts*. London/New York: Routledge, pp. 135–154.

Varela, F., Thompson, E. & Rosch, E. (1991) *The Embodied Mind: Cognitive Science and Human Experience*. Cambridge, MA: MIT Press.

Verhoeven, C. (1967) *Inleiding tot de verwondering* (Introduction to wonder). Bilthoven: Ambo.

Vrugt, A. & Schabracq, M.J. (1991) *Vanzelfsprekend gedrag* (Behavior that speaks for itself). Amsterdam/Assen: Boom.

Watzlawick, P., Beavin, J.H. & Jackson, D.D. (1968) *Pragmatics of Human Communication*. London: Faber and Faber.

Weekley, E. (1921/1971) *An Etymological Dictionary of Modern English*. New York: Dover.

Williams, B. (1985) *Ethics and the Limits of Philosophy*. Cambridge, MA: Harvard University Press.

Winnubst, J.A.M. & Schabracq, M.J. (1995) Type A gedragsstijl en werkstress (Type A behavior style and work style), in M.J. Schabracq, J.A.M. Winnubst, A.C. Perreijn & J. Gerrichhauzen (eds), *Mentale belasting* (Mental load). Open University/Lemma: Heerlen/Utrecht.

Wittgenstein, L. (1961) *Tractatus Logico-Philosophicus*. London: Routledge and Kegan Paul.

Woodworth, R.S. & Schlosberg, H. (1954) *Experimental Psychology* (revd edn). New York: Holt.

Wright, R. (2001) *Nonzero. History, Evolution and Human Cooperation*. London: Abacus.

Index